Poverty in Scotland

2016

Tools for transformation

Edited by: John H McKendrick, Gerry Mooney, Gill Scott, John Dickie and Fiona McHardy

CPAG • 30 Micawber Street • London N1 7TB

CPAG promotes action for the prevention and relief of poverty among children and families with children. To achieve this, CPAG aims to raise awareness of the causes, extent, nature and impact of poverty, and strategies for its eradication and prevention; bring about positive policy changes for families with children in poverty; and enable those eligible for income maintenance to have access to their full entitlement. If you are not already supporting us, please consider making a donation, or ask for details of our membership schemes, training courses and publications.

Published by the Child Poverty Action Group, in association with The Open University in Scotland, Glasgow Caledonian University and the Poverty Alliance.

The views expressed are those of the authors and do not necessarily represent the views of the Child Poverty Action Group.

30 Micawber Street
London N1 7TB
Tel: 020 7837 7979
staff@cpag.org.uk
www.cpag.org.uk

© Child Poverty Action Group/The Open University in Scotland/Glasgow Caledonian University/the Poverty Alliance 2016

This book is sold subject to the condition that it shall not, by way of trade or otherwise, be lent, resold, hired out or otherwise circulated without the publisher's prior consent in any form of binding or cover other than that in which it is published and without a similar condition including this condition being imposed on the subsequent purchaser.

A CIP record for this book is available from the British Library
ISBN: 978 1 910715 18 5

Child Poverty Action Group is a charity registered in England and Wales (registration number 294841) and in Scotland (registration number SC039339), and is a company limited by guarantee, registered in England (registration number 1993854). VAT number: 690 808117

Cover design by Colorido Studios
Typeset by Devious Designs
Printed in the UK by CPI Group (UK) Ltd, Croydon CR40 4YY
Cover photos by Timm Sonnenschein/reportdigital

About the editors

John Dickie is the Director of CPAG in Scotland. He is responsible for promoting policies that will contribute to eradicating child poverty, as well as overseeing the strategic development of second-tier welfare rights services that ensure frontline agencies are able to support families to receive the financial support to which they are entitled. He previously worked at the Scottish Council for Single Homeless and before that directly with young people experiencing homelessness.
Visit: www.cpag. org.uk/scotland.

Fiona McHardy is Research and Information Manager at the Poverty Alliance. She has been involved in a diverse range of research projects, working at Scottish, UK and European levels, and has written on a number of subjects, including austerity impacts, welfare reform, homelessness, rural poverty and health inequalities. Her specialism is participatory research projects with people experiencing poverty. Prior to joining the Poverty Alliance, she worked as Research Assistant in the Scottish Poverty Information Unit at Glasgow Caledonian University.

John H McKendrick is based in the Glasgow School *for* Business and Society at Glasgow Caledonian University. His research is primarily concerned to inform the work of practitioners and campaigners beyond the academy who seek to tackle poverty in Scotland. In recent years, he has completed research for the Joseph Rowntree Foundation (redistribution of social and societal risk) and the STV Children's Appeal (attitudes towards child poverty in Scotland). He has published several guides and briefings for practitioners in Scotland, and delivers many presentations to seminars and conferences organised by third sector organisations in Scotland.
Visit: www.gcu. ac.uk/gsbs/staff/drjohnhollandmckendrick.

Gerry Mooney is Senior Lecturer in Social Policy and Criminology in the Faculty of Social Sciences at The Open University in Scotland. He has written widely on various aspects of social and welfare policies, devolution, nationalism, poverty and inequality, urban studies, class divisions and criminal justice. Among other publications, together with Gill Scott, he edited *Social Justice and Social Policy in Scotland* (Policy Press, 2012) and together with Hazel Croall and Mary Munro, he was editor of *Crime, Justice and Society in Scotland* (Routledge, 2016).

For further information about Gerry's publications, please visit his Open University webpage: www.open.ac.uk/socialsciences/staff/people-profile. php?name=gerry_mooney. Gerry's Open University online materials can be accessed at: www.open.edu/openlearn/profiles/gcm8

Gill Scott is Emeritus Professor of Social Inclusion and Equality at Glasgow Caledonian University. Gill was Founding Director of the Scottish Poverty Information Unit, which she led until she retired. She was external adviser to the Scottish government from 2003 to 2006 on poverty issues and Lead Expert for URBACT European Network Women, Employment and Enterprise from 2008 to 2011. She edited, with Gerry Mooney, *Social Justice and Social Policy in Scotland* (Policy Press, 2012).

About the contributors

Annabelle Armstrong-Walter is the Strategic Lead Officer for Tackling Poverty and Welfare Reform at Renfrewshire Council, where she manages Renfrewshire Council's £6 million Tackling Poverty Programme. She moved to Paisley in 2014 specifically to support Renfrewshire's Tackling Poverty Commission, having previously been the Equalities Manager at Bristol City Council.

Andrea Bradley is a former secondary school teacher of English, a life-long trade unionist and is now Assistant Secretary (Education and Equality) of the Educational Institute of Scotland, which is Scotland's largest teacher trade union and which has campaigned for many years on the impact of poverty in education. She is a member of the STUC (Scottish Trades Union Congress) Women's Committee.

Paul Bradley is Campaigns and Public Affairs Officer at Shelter Scotland, a national charity that works to alleviate the distress caused by homelessness and bad housing. Before taking on this role with the charity, Paul project managed the independent Commission on Housing and Wellbeing and previously worked in the UK government's international Trade Policy Unit.

David Eiser is a Research Fellow in Economics at the University of Stirling and the Centre on Constitutional Change. His research interests include labour markets and inequality, and the economics of devolution. He has given evidence to a number of Scottish Parliament Committees, including Finance, Devolution, Welfare and Economy.

Jackie Erdman is Head of Inequalities, Corporate Planning and Policy in NHS Greater Glasgow and Clyde. She was a community worker in Glasgow for 15 years and has worked in the NHS for 20 years. Her interests are child poverty, gender, socio-economic inequality, inequalities sensitive practice, the impact of prejudice and discrimination on health and the role of the NHS in tackling inequality.

Peter Kelly has been Director of the Poverty Alliance since 2004. He previously worked at the Scottish Low Pay Unit and is currently chair of the Scottish Living Wage Campaign.

Mary Anne MacLeod is a Research Officer with the Poverty Alliance and a PhD student in the Urban Studies Department at the University of Glasgow. Her research interests broadly focus on poverty, social welfare policy and the impacts of welfare state retrenchment. Her PhD research is a mixed-methods comparative study of the rise of emergency food aid within the welfare state in both Scotland and Finland.

Hanna McCulloch is Policy and Parliamentary Officer for Child Poverty Action Group (CPAG) in Scotland. Her role involves working with CPAG colleagues to run the Early Warning System, a framework used to gather case evidence from frontline workers about the impact changes to the social security system are having on children and families in Scotland.

Dr Pauline Nolan is the Routes to Inclusion Projects Manager at Inclusion Scotland, a national disabled people's organisation which takes a human rights approach to addressing the many barriers disabled people face to achieving equality with non-disabled people in Scotland. Before taking on her previous role at Inclusion Scotland in 2011, Pauline achieved a PhD in Social Anthropology (2008) in which she also focused on human rights and access to justice of marginalised farm workers in rural South Africa. She has also worked in the care sector and for Amnesty International in Scotland. She is a passionate advocate of human rights and social equality.

Martin Sime is the Chief Executive of the Scottish Council for Voluntary Organisations (SCVO), the national body representing the interests of charities, voluntary organisations and social enterprises. Prior to joining SCVO, Martin worked for 10 years in the mental health field, latterly as Director of the Scottish Association for Mental Health (SAMH).

About the organisations

CPAG in Scotland is part of the Child Poverty Action Group, a charity working for children and families. It believes no child should grow up in hardship or lose out through poverty – but right now, one in five children in Scotland are doing just that. Child poverty is not inevitable. CPAG exists to promote the action that will prevent and end child poverty in Scotland and across the UK by advocating evidence-based solutions to policy-makers. It also provides the expertise to help frontline advisers and support workers across Scotland help families who are struggling with difficult circumstances to access the financial support they are entitled to. It achieves this by providing authoritative information on social security entitlements through its publications, training and advice line. If you are not already supporting CPAG, please consider making a donation, or ask for details of membership schemes, training courses and publications. For further information, please visit www.cpag.org.uk/scotland.

With almost 200,000 students, **The Open University in Scotland** is one of the largest universities in Europe. More than 14,000 of those students are based in Scotland and The Open University in Scotland is the country's leading provider of part-time higher education. With a mission to be open to people, places, methods and ideas, The Open University seeks to contribute to social justice through access to learning and knowledge. Its open entry policy – most courses do not require any entrance qualifications – means that it is central to efforts to widen access to higher education in Scotland, and this is reflected in the fact that almost two-thirds of Open University students in Scotland have low incomes and therefore qualify for support with their fees. As part of its goal to make quality teaching and learning accessible, The Open University makes thousands of hours of learning and hundreds of courses freely available via its OpenLearn platform. To find out more about studying with The Open University in Scotland, please visit www.open.ac.uk/scotland.

Established in 1992, the **Poverty Alliance** is the national anti-poverty network in Scotland. It works with a range of community, voluntary and statutory organisations to find better solutions to the problems of poverty in Scotland. The Alliance seeks to influence anti-poverty policy by lobbying and campaigning, organising seminars and conferences, producing briefing papers and other information. A key goal for the Alliance is to have the voices of people experiencing poverty heard in policy processes. For further information, please visit: www. povertyalliance.org.

The Scottish Poverty Information Unit at **Glasgow Caledonian University** was the driving force behind the first edition of *Poverty in Scotland*. The study of poverty in Scotland remains a focus within Glasgow Caledonian University and Emeritus Professor Gill Scott and Professor John H McKendrick continue its long-standing association with this publication. As the University for the Common Good, Glasgow Caledonian University has a reputation for delivering social benefit and impact through education, research and social innovation with strategic goals to transform lives, enrich cities and communities, innovate for social and economic impact, engage globally and align with others in partnership and collaboration.

Acknowledgements

We are very grateful to all the people who contributed to this book. Their enthusiasm for tackling poverty and highlighting the major issues that must be addressed in Scotland at the current time was much appreciated.

Gerry Mooney is grateful to Michelle Hynd, Louise Davison and Kate Signorini at The Open University in Scotland, Edinburgh, for their support with this edition.

We very much appreciate the financial support from the Educational Institute of Scotland that has helped make publication of this book possible.

Finally, the editors would like to thank colleagues in Glasgow Caledonian University, the Poverty Alliance, Child Poverty Action Group and The Open University in Scotland for their support.

Contents

Section One
Introduction

One

Poverty in Scotland 2016: beyond 'austerity'?

Gerry Mooney

Summary

- Issues of poverty, inequality and social welfare are among the top policy-making priorities as identified by the present Scottish government and which are likely to remain at the top of the political agenda, irrespective of the outcome of the 2016 Scottish elections.
- Poverty, disadvantage and inequalities remain significant features of contemporary Scottish society, despite significant progress on reducing child and pensioner poverty since the mid-1990s.
- An increasing proportion of the population is being negatively affected by the ongoing programme of welfare 'reforms' and cuts in public services and provision.
- More and more people in Scotland are experiencing a range of social insecurities and increasing personal risks that affect many aspects of their lives.
- An increasing number of people are working in insecure and precarious forms of paid employment and this is contributing to an increase in the numbers who are 'working poor'.
- The stigmatisation, demonisation and misrepresentation of people experiencing poverty and disadvantage continues to feature prominently in public and political accounts of poverty.
- The future direction of social welfare in Scotland is likely to diverge from other parts of the UK.

Introduction: setting the scene

Two years have passed since the publication of our previous edition in the Poverty in Scotland series. Then, in *Poverty in Scotland 2014: the independence referendum and beyond*, our primary concern was to ensure that issues around poverty, disadvantage and inequalities contributed to the debates taking place around Scotland's constitutional future.[1] Our key objective was to argue that the struggle against poverty and disadvantage was both integral to the future shape of Scottish politics and policy making – and to Scotland as a society more generally. Further, and importantly, we wanted to highlight that issues and questions of poverty would be relevant whatever the constitutional settlement and to consider how competing settlements, for instance, the status quo, further devolution or full independence, would generate different ways of addressing poverty. Many of the questions and issues with which we were concerned in 2014 still shape this particular volume. Following internationally and historically unprecedented falls in child and pensioner poverty between the mid-1990s and 2010, the deepening levels of poverty (it is becoming more severe for those who experience it) and the increasingly widespread range of social insecurities of various forms affect more and more of the population.

As with the 2002, 2007 and 2011 editions, *Poverty in Scotland 2016* marks a return to using the book to foreground the discussion of poverty and inequality in the period before and during Scottish Parliament elections. Our primary concern is with policy making – that is, with the effectiveness or otherwise of policies in place or with prospects to tackle the different dimensions of poverty and disadvantage in Scotland.

It has almost become a standard refrain for these introductions to highlight that we are living in a period of rapid economic, social and, perhaps especially, political change. In our 2002 and 2007 editions, the introduction of and early years of devolution were rightly the focus of concern, but from the vantage point of 2015/16, it all seems a very long time ago. Likewise, the independence referendum held in September 2014 is now quickly passing as history, even if it is a history that has important enduring legacies for the dominant discussions around politics and policy making today. Despite the oft-quoted claim from the then First Minister and SNP leader, Alex Salmond, that the 2014 independence referendum would settle the constitutional question for 'a generation',[2] arguably, the referendum and the May 2015 UK general election have propelled the constitutional future of the entire UK to a new level.

As with our 2014 edition, the editors and contributors to this volume have a diverse range of political and constitutional visions. Some are in favour of Scottish independence, others for much greater devolution, or some for a limited range of additional devolved powers, often referred to as 'devo-plus'. Overall, the book remains agnostic on the question of Scotland's constitutional future. We are not agnostic when it comes to our shared perspective that much can be done now, however, – whatever the constitutional context – to progress the development of more effective approaches to combatting poverty and disadvantage.

A changing Scotland and a changing UK: beyond the 2014 independence referendum

Politicians from both sides of the independence debate staked claims to pursuing a social justice agenda, arguing that this should be central to the future shape and direction of Scottish society. Labour MP and former Prime Minister Gordon Brown, who was to play a key part in the 'Better Together' campaign in the week before the referendum, argued that social justice lies at the heart of Scottish political values, but commended the UK union as 'a union of social justice'. The Scottish government's vision for independence, as outlined in *Scotland's Future: your guide to an independent Scotland*, also made claims to the centrality of social justice, but within the context of a fully independent Scottish nation state.[3]

Of course, social justice and 'a fairer' approach to social welfare have long been presented as key components of Scottish political rhetoric, often seen as both integral to and reflecting long-standing arguments and debates around the existence of what are assumed to be distinctive 'Scottish values' and about the supposedly egalitarian and collectivist hue of Scottish society more generally[4] that mark Scotland as a very different place from the rest of the UK. Leading SNP politicians have since 2011 made repeated claims[5] that they would develop policies that are not only in tune with Scottish attitudes and values, but which would stand against the UK government's austerity programme and welfare reforms.

In recent years then, issues of social justice and social welfare in Scotland have been linked both with questions of constitutional futures and the policy directions of successive UK governments. We are reminded through this that social welfare was central to discussions in the post-Second World War period of Britishness. Institutions such as the NHS and the social security system – and the welfare state more generally – have long been held up as crucially important elements in cementing the UK union, a union which in key respects was for long periods a 'welfare union'. The welfare state in the post-1945 UK played a significant part in binding the UK together, supporting nation-building objectives.

Ironically, many of the 45 per cent of Scottish voters who supported withdrawal from the UK believed that in a fully independent Scotland the welfare system would continue to reflect one of the principal institutional signifiers of post-1945 Britishness, the UK welfare state. The institutional embodiment of post-war Britishness has been heavily diluted, if not almost entirely eroded in recent decades. A declining sense of a unified UK welfare state has been viewed as contributing to an erosion of a sense of Britishness.

This might help to explain the political geography of voting in the 2014 independence referendum. It was evident that, in many of the country's most deprived areas, people were favouring independence. The four local authority districts that registered a majority 'Yes' vote – Dundee, Glasgow City, West Dunbartonshire and North Lanarkshire – between them account for the majority of the most deprived areas in Scotland. In those areas with a marginal 'No' vote (of between less than 1 per cent and 3 per cent) – Inverclyde, North Ayrshire, East Ayrshire and Renfrewshire – patterns also aligned with the prevailing geographical distribution of poverty and affluence. There was a clear split between areas of poverty and affluence. The outcomes of the 2014 referendum, and the key themes that shaped that result, remain matters of political controversy and debate. However, an important factor was the future of the National Health Service amidst concerns that the NHS in Scotland would follow the NHS in England, where the outsourcing of key services has increased. Concerns around the future of public health provision was also related to separate concerns about the future of local authority service provision, an issue which is likely to become even more prominent following the December 2015 Scottish government budget settlement.[6] The 2014 Scottish Social Attitudes Survey has provided additional insights into the issues that were prevalent in the independence referendum.[7] Questions around the Scottish economy and how it would fare under independence were important factors that shaped attitudes. Relatedly, issues related to social inequality in general also appeared to have influenced the voting preferences of a significant number of voters, with the great majority of those thinking that inequalities of income and wealth would be markedly lower in an independent Scotland supporting independence.

Again, as we highlighted in *Poverty in Scotland 2014*, some of the groups that emerged through the independence debates, most notably perhaps, Common Weal, also offered visions of a Scottish approach to welfare that went beyond defending existing provision. Here, proposals for a Nordic-type Scottish welfare state founded on a radically different economic order were argued. In turn, claims were made that better funding and a greatly enhanced provision of public services would be a feature of an independent Scotland built upon principles of social justice.

More powers to tackle poverty in Scotland? The Smith Commission and beyond

A key outcome from the 2014 referendum, and this was supported by all the main political parties, was that more devolved policy-making powers should be accorded to the Scottish Parliament, beyond those due to be implemented in 2016 under the Scotland Act 2012.[8] While the extent of further devolution remains hugely contentious, nonetheless this is important for our understanding of the greater opportunity and potential that may emerge for a devolved Scottish government with more powers to tackle poverty and advance equalities.

In the final days of the 2014 referendum campaign, the leaders of the three main pro-union parties vowed to give Scotland a range of additional powers if voters returned a 'No' vote. Evidence that many voted 'No' in the belief that such powers would be forthcoming emerged in the days that followed.[9] The question of additional powers – and the range of powers – came to occupy centre stage in the period following the referendum. The Smith Commission was tasked by the UK coalition government with investigating and offering recommendations on additional devolved powers for Scotland.[10]

The key legislative outcome of the Smith Commission is the 2015 Scotland Bill, presented to the UK Parliament in May 2015 and before the House of Lords at the time of writing. Claimed by the new Conservative UK government as making 'the Scottish Parliament one of the world's most powerful devolved parliaments', the Bill will, when legislated, increase the financial responsibility and accountability of the Scottish Parliament. Scotland will receive significant additional financial powers, including over income tax and VAT, the devolution of key aspects of the social security system and a range of other powers.[11]

While political disagreements accompanied the publication of the Bill, nonetheless it is clear that it represents a marked shift in the constitutional landscape – not only of Scotland, but of the entire UK. For the purposes of this discussion, the focus is rightly on the proposed further devolution of social security powers. Understandably, this has been one of the most contentious aspects of the new devolution proposals. In this respect, the continuing controversy follows from where the 2014 independence referendum left off – in the centrality of social welfare and how it should be resourced.

CPAG in Scotland highlighted concerns, echoed elsewhere, that any further devolution of welfare provisions to the Scottish Parliament should be matched with adequate economic and fiscal powers. This point reflects wider claims that Scotland may end up with all the responsibilities – but inadequate income-generating powers to meet such responsibilities. However, while this is frequently interpreted as referring to the fiscal ability of any Scottish government to meet apparently widespread aspirations in Scotland for a much more 'generous', less punitive and residualised welfare system, we should not neglect that it is also about the ability of the Scottish government to maintain current minimum entitlements.[12]

While CPAG Scotland, the Poverty Alliance and many other organisations claim that further devolution has the capacity to lead to new ways of addressing different dimensions of poverty and disadvantage across Scotland, it is important that devolution of social security is administered in ways that do not penalise benefit recipients. Further, the provision to make new discretionary payments or to develop new forms of devolved benefits needs to be implemented in ways which do not lead to hardship through cuts in other benefits. However, it is also recognised that the bulk of social security measures will remain reserved to Westminster, together with the national minimum wage, as well as other tax and revenue generating measures. And there is no provision for a Scottish government to directly mitigate the negative impact of sanctions on claimants in Scotland who are deemed to have been 'non-compliant'.

In late 2015 the political debate over the provision of additional welfare powers to Scotland and how they might be used reached a new level, following increasing concern around the impact on working families of new cuts to tax credits. Announced by the UK government in its summer Budget, although these cuts were suspended (or postponed) later that year, the debate around their impact and how a Scottish government should respond remains high on the political agenda. A commitment by Scottish Labour leader Kezia Dugdale to, if elected, use new tax and benefit powers, specifically the power to 'top up' reserved benefits, to fully mitigate the impact of these cuts in Scotland led to Scottish government ministers also committing to use new powers to make up for specific UK tax credit cuts.[13] While the cuts in question were abandoned (or more accurately, postponed, as similar cuts remain in the new universal credit set to replace tax credits),[14] the debate drew into the open the real choices politicians, and the electorate, in Scotland will face on whether, and how, to use new tax and benefit powers to invest in social security and reduce inequalities.

The capacity of a Scottish government of any political colour to ameliorate the worst impacts of UK social security cuts has now come to the fore in these debates. Such questions go to the heart of long-held beliefs about the apparent progressiveness of Scottish values – and will test such values in ways unseen before.

The government in Scotland is already mitigating the impact of the 'bedroom tax' and introduced, in 2013, the Scottish Welfare Fund (allocating an additional £9 million a year to the resources transferred from the UK government on the abolition of DWP crisis loans and community care grants). While tax credits look set to remain reserved, the ability of the Scottish government to top-up reserved benefits and tax credits, and to set rates and bands of income tax will be enacted. 'Mitigating the impacts of UK government welfare reforms' has become a prominent part of Scottish government political narrative over the past five years. It looks likely to further become part of the political landscape in Scotland over the years to come, irrespective of the outcome of the May 2016 Scottish elections.

Poverty in Scotland: policy controversies

It is not surprising, though somewhat depressing, to note once again that Scotland remains a society characterised by widespread and deepening levels of poverty and disadvantage (Section Three).

In Section Two John H McKendrick explores the ongoing controversies around the definition and measurement of poverty in the UK. While needing little in the way of added fuel to keep it burning away, long-term controversies and disputes around the definition of poverty were heightened as a result of the decision in mid-2015 by Iain Duncan Smith, the minister responsible for work and pensions in the UK government, to announce that the 2020 target for child poverty reduction put on statute with cross-party support in 2010 was to be scrapped. The long-established method for measuring household poverty (below 60 per cent of median household income) is set to be abolished by the UK government as its key measure of child poverty. This will be replaced by a new 'life chances' measure under new legislation which will abolish the 2010 Child Poverty Act. This new measure will focus on: the proportion of children living in workless households as well as long-term workless households; the educational attainment of all pupils and the most disadvantaged pupils at age 16; and on a range of other measures and indicators of root causes of poverty, including family breakdown, debt and addiction, all of which impact on a child's life chances.[15]

Such proposals were met by strong opposition from the Scottish government, demanding that Scotland be excluded from any new legislation and withdrawing from the UK government's Social Mobility and Child Poverty Commission.[16] Scottish Social Justice Secretary Alex Neil has claimed that the UK government is effectively 'sweeping the issue of child poverty under the carpet'. The effect of such changes in measurement and definition, he argues, will be to 'characterise poverty as a lifestyle choice', marginalising more structural causes of poverty.

Amidst other widespread claims that the welfare cuts announced by the UK government in its Budget in summer 2015 will see a further 700,000 UK households, both in and out of work, in poverty by 2020,[17] with four million households predicted to be in poverty by this time, it is evident that policy has a huge impact on poverty levels. It is now widely recognised that during the period of New Labour governments between 1997 and 2010, there were significant reductions in particular dimensions of poverty, not least child poverty. Government policies directly affect the levels and extent of poverty and related problems. This recognition helps to counter claims that little can be done to tackle poverty; that poverty will always be with us and that, in some way, poverty is almost natural and inevitable.

The impact of welfare reform across the UK and Scotland is increasingly being made evident. A series of studies by Christina Beatty and Steve Fothergill highlight that the impact of pre-2015 welfare changes is highly uneven geographically.[18] While the costs of housing and the Scottish government's compensation for the effects of the 'bedroom tax' mean that, on certain indicators, Scotland fairs relatively well in comparison with England and Wales, Beatty and Fothergill demonstrate that it is the poorest local authority areas that are suffering the greatest financial loss as a result of welfare reforms between 2010 and 2014. Glasgow, Inverclyde, Dundee and North Ayrshire fare the worst, while Shetland,

Aberdeenshire, Aberdeen and East Dunbartonshire are the least affected. The ward most affected in Scotland is Calton in the inner east end of Glasgow. It is hit five times harder by welfare reforms than the least impacted district, St Andrews. It is estimated that £880 a year per adult of working age will be removed from the local economy in Calton, compared with £180 in St Andrews.[19] Overall, this amounts to some £1.6 billion per annum to be lost from Scotland, £260 million per year in Glasgow alone. Glasgow emerges as the second most affected city in the UK, second only to Birmingham in the scale of overall loss, but Birmingham has a population considerably higher than that of Glasgow.

A strategy of inequality? The deepening impact of 'austerity' and insecurity in Scotland

Space prevents a much fuller discussion at this point of the extent of poverty in Scotland – for that please read on to Section Three, in particular Chapter 5 (Is poverty falling?). Here though it is important to recognise that predictions of rising levels of poverty by 2020 have not strengthened arguments that the main causes of this lie in a combination of structural factors, for instance, low pay, irregular and poorly paid employment and social security cuts, or that patterns of poverty in the UK, including Scotland, are shaped by social divisions and social inequalities of class, gender and race. The predominant approach to poverty too often presents and understands poverty as largely the consequence of individual and family lifestyle, behavioural patterns and a range of other assorted deficits. While in Scotland the language of 'troubled families' is less prevalent than in England,[20] nonetheless this way of thinking about poverty – poverty as caused by recalcitrant or feckless individuals – also exists in Scotland to diminish the appreciation that poverty is a widespread and prevalent aspect of modern Scotland.

 The overriding focus of UK government policy is on paid work as the solution to poverty – and it must also be noted that Scottish government statements also tend to fall into a 'work first' approach. However, there are many dimensions of poverty and its impact extends well beyond 'economic' aspects to encompass physical and psychological health, levels of morbidity and mortality.

 The relationship between poverty and inequality has long been a matter of huge debate and dispute. However, today, the question of inequality and its causes is becoming more and more prevalent in political and public debates. Over recent years there has been no shortage of media stories highlighting different aspects of inequality. 'Sunday Times rich list: number of billionaires in Britain doubles in five years' was a head-line in *The Independent* on 26 April 2015.[21] The collective wealth of the thousand richest people in the UK increased from £98 billion in 1997, to £336 billion in 2010 and by 2014 had reached £519 billion. Elsewhere, again in *The Independent*, on 15 May 2015, a lead story highlighted Britain as 'a deeply divided nation', with the estimated £9 trillion of wealth unequally distributed between rich and poor, the richest 20 per cent of the population owning 105 times more wealth than the poorest fifth.[22] It is truly astonishing to appreciate the extent of income and wealth inequality in the UK today.

The widespread publicity that has accompanied the publication in 2014 of Thomas Piketty's book on the rich, *Capital in the Twenty-first Century*, has helped to put the question of inequality – of the unequal dis-tribution of economic and social resources – at centre stage in discussions about the nature of modern societies.[23]

As Piketty and others have highlighted, as we look back to the years of the post-1945 economic 'boom', for some the classic period of social democracy in the UK, during which large-scale state interventions worked to reshape the distribution of social goods in society, it now stands out as an exceptional period in UK history. Before and since the post-sec-ond world war boom time the picture has been one where the share of national income enjoyed by the richest was increasing.

In 2013/14, the wealth of the richest 1 per cent in the UK increased by 15 per cent alone – that is around £519 billion.[24] Such figures are hard to grasp and appear somewhat abstract – what do they really mean? If we look at UK public spending, we can begin to grasp the enormity of these sums.[25] This amount – £519 billion – would fund the entire UK education system for almost six years, or the state pension bill for four years, or the NHS for just over four years. It is also almost five times the size of the country's annual welfare bill – which is currently the target of government spending reductions, or 'cuts', amidst claims that 'the country' can no longer afford such expenditure.[26]

In Scotland, the ratio between the highest paid 10 per cent and the lowest paid 10 per cent is close to its highest level since the mid-1970s and the difference between the incomes of the top and bottom 1 per cent is now over twenty times. The Stirling-based economist David Bell notes that:[27]

... it is hard to avoid the conclusion that the major increases in inequality that have taken place over the last few decades were related to the industrial restructuring that took place during the 1980s.

Wealth inequality is even more unevenly distributed, with the top 20 per cent owning 44 per cent of all personal wealth. Also, in 2015, a report by Oxfam Scotland estimated that Scotland's four richest families are wealthier than the poorest 20 per cent of the population, with the richest 14 families sharing greater levels of income and wealth than the most deprived 30 per cent.[28]

There are numerous definitions and conceptualisations of inequality, reflecting the hugely contested and debated nature of the subject matter. How we make sense of the poverty-inequality relationship will reflect such contestations; it is a matter of how we view inequality itself. The following quote from Goran Therborn's *The Killing Fields of Inequality* represents both a powerful statement of the meaning of inequality and the extent and effects of profound inequalities in contemporary society:[29]

Inequality is a violation of human dignity; it is a denial of the possibility for everybody's human capabilities to develop. It takes many forms, and it has many effects: premature death, ill-health, humiliation, subjection, discrimination, exclusion from knowledge or from mainstream social life, poverty, powerlessness, stress, insecurity, anxiety, lack of self-confidence and of pride in oneself, and exclusion from opportunities and life-chances. Inequality, then, is not just about the size of wallets. It is a socio-cultural order, which (for most of us) reduces our capabilities to function as human beings, our health, our self-respect, our sense of self, as well as our resources to act and participate in this world.

There is then considerable and mounting evidence that there are growing economic inequalities in the UK. Wealth inequality is both widespread and deepening, increasingly concentrated in fewer and fewer hands. This has a major negative impact on levels of wellbeing in society. Income insecurity is also a growing problem for more and more people in the UK today and, in turn, this is linked to the growing use of food banks and other forms of emergency food aid. Between 2013 and 2014, the number of people given three days' emergency food by Trussell Trust food banks alone in Scotland was 117,689. Amidst growing concerns that more and more schoolchildren are going hungry or appear to be underfed, the main teachers' union, the Educational Institute of Scotland, issued guidelines to its members on how to identify malnourished children.[30] The wider issue of food poverty is one that is gaining much more recognition among researchers, some policy makers and some politicians (see Chapter 18). It reflects not only the growing number of people forced to utilise emergency food aid providers, of which the Trussell Trust is only one provider, but also that such provision is not a long-term, sustainable response to food poverty. Low pay, the impact of punitive sanctioning as a result of changes in social security benefits, insecure work and financial precarity are together the key root causes of food poverty and while meeting real needs, food banks and other forms of food aid cannot in the long term fill the gaps and increasing vulnerability created by government policy and low income.[31]

Inequalities are deeply entrenched in all areas of social life; there are different kinds of inequality, but they all have massively negative impacts on the social health of society and on wellbeing.[32] Many studies have been published over recent years that reflect the growing concerns about the impact of inequality on society.[33]

There are a number of factors that could explain this rising interest in inequality: the impact of cuts in social welfare spending, in benefits and in public services (Chapter 11); 'austerity' policies that are viewed as impacting unevenly and unequally on different sections of society; the growth of food banks (Chapter 18) and evidence of rising fuel poverty, the so-called 'heat or eat' dilemma;[34] continuing concerns about inequalities in health (Chapter 16) and in educational attainment (Chapter 14); and while this plays out differently in our towns and cities and across UK regions and nations, the growing sense that Britain is facing an acute housing crisis (Chapter 17). 'Financial distress' is a catch-all term that encompasses personal and household debt, fuel and food poverty, ability to pay bills, the ill health caused by stress as a result of low or no incomes and so on. This is now an issue affecting more and more people and households across the UK.[35]

The ability of local government to address and compensate for the impact of such insecurities and distress is increasingly limited, if not completely eroded, by long-term funding cuts (Chapter 20). One oft-overlooked consequence of this is that the poorest people living in the poorest communities are the ones being hardest hit by the withdrawal of local services and cuts in local provision. These are the very groups who not only bear the brunt of cuts, but are the least able to cope with this.[36]

The social harms created by economic inequalities reach almost every part of our society, and affect daily life in so many different ways, many of which we may never have considered. It is important to understand that the increasing social harms caused by rising inequalities are occurring at the same time as unprecedented cuts in public spending, welfare and in public sector employment.

However, we have yet to explore the vexed question of how we explain such inequalities. Do they matter? Why do they matter? And what should be done about them? These are not new questions and they reflect vast differences across the political spectrum. We have seen that the distribution of economic resources is hugely different – there are marked disparities within and across Scotland and the UK. But are they inequalities? Is there a relationship between the accumulation of vast income and wealth for the richest at the top of society and increasing impoverishment and disadvantage for those on the lowest incomes?

In the 1980s, changes in taxation and welfare benefits, the privatisation of key industries and utilities and the rise of mass unemployment was integral to what the social policy academic Alan Walker referred to as a 'strategy of inequality':[37]

> ...rather than seeing inequality as potentially damaging to the social fabric, the Thatcher governments saw it as an engine of enterprise, providing incentives for those at the bottom as well as those at the top.

The idea that there is a relationship between rich and poor – that there is a causal link between the growth of wealth, rising inequalities and increasing poverty – is a matter of huge and ongoing debate. The dominant perspective in our society is one that believes that we must have the rich; high income inequalities are necessary if investment, risk taking and economic competition and growth are to be achieved. Further, this is to the benefit of us all as the wealth and affluence of the most wealthy 'trickles down' through the rest of society – we all gain from this.

Arguably, there are huge parallels between the 'strategy of inequality' pursued from 1979 to the mid-1990s, and the 'austerity' approaches since 2010. 'Austerity' has been presented, strongly echoing claims in the 1970s and 1980s, as the only way to deal with the UK's economic and fiscal crisis. Such an approach has led to huge reductions in public funding, in public services and in welfare benefits, as well as across other areas of social provision.

The notion of 'austerity' has become arguably the central political idea today, informing not only the approaches of the UK government, but also political debate across the UK and within Scotland. The idea has been the subject of considerable and ongoing debate, but too often it is portrayed as little more than a politically neutral, a socially neutral, approach to overcoming the UK's fiscal problems. However, if we analyse austerity from a more critical position, it might be argued that cuts to welfare, public spending and public services are not only a strategy to address financial deficit, but a deliberate programme of reducing state provision – with the most disadvantaged bearing the brunt of the costs of the fiscal crisis.

The Scottish dimensions of the 'austerity' debate reflect the ongoing and Scotland-specific political environment. It has already been highlighted that before, during and since the 2014 independence referendum, there have been widespread and continual claims from the Scottish government that it is anti-'austerity'. There is no doubt that this has been an important element of the Scottish government's political rhetoric – if not always its practice.[38] The myth of Scottish society as progressive, as social democrat-inspired and pro-welfare, positions it against some of the most punitive anti-welfare narratives that circulate elsewhere in the UK. The Scottish government's council tax reduction scheme, discretionary housing payments to mitigate the 'bedroom tax' and investment in income maximisation advice have all been political and budget decisions that are pro-welfare/anti-austerity, albeit perhaps limited and in the context of political reluctance to use tax powers to lessen cuts to wider services. In 2011 the new SNP Scottish government's inequality agenda called on the work of the 2010 Christie Commission on the delivery of public services in Scotland. In its findings, the Commission noted that:[39]

> ... on most key measures social and economic inequalities have remained unchanged or become more pronounced... This country is a paradoxical tapestry of rich resources, inventive humanity, gross inequalities, and persistent levels of poor health and deprivation... In education, the gap between the bottom 20 per cent and the average in learning outcomes has not changed at all since devolution. At the same time, the gap in healthy life expectancy between the 20 per cent most deprived and the 20 per cent least deprived areas has increased from 8 to 13.5 years and the percentage of life lived with poor health has increased from 12 to 15 per cent since devolution. The link between deprivation and the likelihood of being a victim of crime has also become stronger.

In 2015/16, acknowledging that it is only five years since this claim was made, it would be difficult to dispute that such a picture is as relevant today as it was then in 2011. Ongoing political controversies around the thrust of Scottish government's policies, their effectiveness and their impacts, not least in the field of educational attainment, focus on the persistence of widespread inequalities.

Here, the interplay of Scottish and UK policy making, of devolved and of reserved powers, continues to shape the landscape around which poverty and inequality are fought over and contested issues. There is little doubt that austerity impacts in Scotland as it does in other parts of the UK. While the Scottish government has moved to mitigate the impact of some aspects of UK government welfare changes, it has to date arguably lacked the resources and control of the key income-generating systems to make a serious dent. Risk, social insecurity and precariousness across different dimensions of everyday life are a deepening problem for a greater number of Scots, as they are for many people across the UK.

However, it is also important to appreciate that for some communities and some groups within Scotland, much of this is hardly new – even if the negative impact and intensity of public spending cuts and welfare changes are reaching new levels. Historic problems of economic decline, deindustrialisation and disinvestment in already impoverished localities remind us that, for many Scots, what is now termed 'austerity' has been part and parcel of daily life across successive generations.

Taken together, this serves as a timely reminder that the problem of an unequal Scotland is not a new one: inequalities are not a new development. What has changed are the patterns, extent, depth and intensity of poverty and inequality – with more and more of the population being pulled towards a precarious life in which the daily struggle to make ends meet is becoming ever more difficult.

Scottish policy interventions: taking anti-poverty policy further

From the discussion thus far we can see that, in relation to questions of social welfare, social security and inequality, the Scottish and UK governments appear to be moving in different directions. While the extent of this is often greatly overplayed, nonetheless it is clear that greater tensions surround the question of tax and welfare than, probably, most other policy-making areas. Space has opened up for discussions and debates around poverty, inequality and welfare that have been needed for generations. In the process, alternative strategies and new ways of thinking have emerged. Again, while not wishing to overstate the impact of these, nonetheless there is room now for those who are concerned with poverty and disadvantage in Scotland to have a voice in challenging existing policy failures, the lack of political will and also to advance different perspectives.

There is evidence in a range of Scottish government policy announcements over the past year that this debate is being reflected in policy narrative. The 2015/16 programme for government, *A Stronger Scotland*, reflects an increased emphasis on tackling poverty and deploys a language that focuses more on questions of social justice.[40] It talks of a commitment to a much 'fairer and prosperous nation' and promises to greatly reduce inequalities in educational attainment levels. In the Foreword, First Minister Nicola Sturgeon claims that the Scottish government:

> … will create a fairer country. We will promote a proper living wage, fair work and use new powers to improve the welfare system, mitigating some of the worst impacts of the UK government's cuts… We will take the first steps to delivery of a new social security system and abolish the bedroom tax as soon as we have the power to do so…

> Overall, this Programme for Government demonstrates how enduring values – a belief in enterprise, a faith in the importance of education, a commitment to fairness, equality and solidarity, and a passion for democratic engagement – are being applied to make Scotland a fairer and more prosperous country.

While few of us who are concerned with poverty would be at serious odds with what is outlined here, the rhetoric is strong but does not, in itself, necessarily lead to the kinds of policies that will have the most impact on reducing levels of poverty and is also largely silent on tackling the fundamental drivers of poverty – that is, the unequal nature of Scottish society.

However, Sturgeon's statement here – and the vision she outlines – reflects again the increasing separation of the political debate and policy narratives that surround the discussion of disadvantage and inequality in Scotland and at a UK level. How we approach the question of poverty and explain its causes is key to how it is understood and the policies that emerge from this. There is already a different space in Scotland to begin to take this much further.

To mention one aspect of this, the idea that work is the only real route out of poverty is increasingly viewed in highly critical ways, reflecting the increasing precariousness of the labour market and the enormous growth in poor work in recent times.[41] From this there is now a greater understanding that only an anti-poverty strategy that empowers the poorest to gain greater income and provides more bargaining power to workers can adequately address poverty. Work can be a route out of poverty, but only if employees have the power to bargain for decent wages and conditions.

Reviewing the extent of poverty in the UK since the 1970s and UK government policies since that time, investing in child benefit and tax credits from the mid-1990s did lead to significant reductions in the level of child poverty, and similar investment also saw a large fall in the extent of pensioner poverty. However, alongside these it is evident that successive social policy changes reduced the levels and provision of social security for working-age adults as well as repeatedly undermining entitlement to benefits.

One of the most significant shifts in the patterns of poverty and inequality across the last ten years is the transition from poverty being a result of 'worklessness' to one in which 'in-work' poverty is now the dominant characteristic of those experiencing poverty today. There are different ways in which the available data for this need to be interpreted. There is a difference here between composition and risk. Risk is much lower among those in work but as there are more of them, they comprise more of the total number of people experiencing poverty. The extent to which in-work poverty is the dominant feature of poor households indicates the limitations of the 'work as a route out of poverty'/'work first' approach by successive governments. In Scotland, the latest figures show that the majority of working-age adults and children in poverty live in working households.[42]

The explanation for why this matters is that these high levels of poverty and inequality are a testament to the limitations of anti-poverty strategies adopted by successive UK and devolved governments and local authorities which continue to administer them. Within the realms of social policy, despite the language of tackling poverty, the reality has too often been the opposite: an extension of means testing and the withdrawal of social security benefits has been the picture since the mid-1970s. The increasingly draconian nature of repeated rounds of welfare 'reforms', for which read 'cuts', are a feature of the increasingly punitive nature of the current social security system. The capping of benefits, increased conditionality and sanctioning and cuts in disability benefits mark a major shift in political attitudes to poverty and to those experiencing poverty. Underpinning this is an ideology in which a distinction between the 'deserving' and 'undeserving' has been utilised to abandon the use of taxation as a means to deliver sufficiently redistributive outcomes.

This understanding brings forth important questions that should be asked of the Scottish government. While more attention should be devoted to the promotion of 'fair' work and 'fair' wages, this must not in any way detract from a concern to protect those who cannot work. There are signs of some movement on the former with the appointment of a Cabinet Secretary for Fair Work and the establishment of a Fair Work Convention which, among other issues, will focus on: progressive work-place policies that improve productivity and innovation; the potential extension of collective and sectoral bargaining; increased levels of gender equality and workplace democracy across the private, public and third sectors; and the living wage.[43] While (anti-) trade union legislation and employment law more generally remain reserved areas of legislation, there are still ample devolved areas where labour could be empowered in Scotland. Scottish government procurement policy already permits the removal of contracts from anti-union firms, such as blacklisting construc-tion companies.[44]

In conclusion, we should recognise that inequalities in the work-place are central to understanding the inequalities in society more gener-ally. The solutions we should be seeking are the ones which recognise these links and aim to ensure the maximum solidarity between those in work and those out of work. We should be seeking a return to a notion of a social security system for all and a move away from the increasingly dra-conian social security system currently on offer.

The structure of *Poverty in Scotland 2016*

Reflecting on previous editions of *Poverty in Scotland* – of which, including this issue, there have now been five in the current format – we can see that particular 'traditions' have emerged. An important aim is to provide as up-to-date an account of poverty in Scotland as is possible. That is also accompanied by the inclusion of a range of, while relatively short, more in-depth chapters, which focus on particular dimensions of poverty, disad-vantage and policy making. In this edition, we focus on the tools and levers that can be used to prevent and tackle poverty, and the extent to which those tools have been used over the last five years, and should be used in the coming five years. At the same time, we encourage readers of this volume to also revisit the 2014 edition, *Poverty in Scotland 2014: the independence referendum and beyond*, where in Sections Four, Five and

Six, in particular, much of the discussion and exploration of the different dimensions and policies remain relevant today.

The structure of *Poverty in Scotland 2016: tools for transformation* follows in the now traditional way. Here in **Section One**, this chapter provides the wider political and policy-making context which sets the scene for the detailed exploration of the nature of poverty in Scotland in **Section Two**. Comprising three chapters, **Section Two** discusses some of the main definitions of poverty, the different ways of measuring poverty and some of the primary arguments as to the underlying causes of poverty.

As in previous editions, it is the task of **Section Three** to outline the extent of poverty in Scotland. Calling on a range of sources of evidence, the discussion here unfolds over four chapters, addressing the key questions: Is poverty falling? Is inequality falling? Who lives in poverty? And what is life like for people experiencing poverty?

Reflecting the subtitle of this edition, **Section Four** contains 12 chapters that offer a range of different accounts of specific aspects of poverty and how it should be addressed, and an introductory chapter that summarises recent writing on poverty in Scotland. In previous editions we have structured this particular section around broad themes, groups or principles. In this edition, we are structuring the contributed chapters around the 'tools' for tackling poverty in Scotland. The central aim of each short chapter in Section Four is, in considering the past five years or so, to appraise what that specific tool has contributed – and could contribute – to ameliorating, avoiding or ending poverty in Scotland. These chapters work across both devolved and reserved policy arenas and take account of the changing balance and nature of powers between Scottish and UK governments. The tools disscussed are organised by domain or provider – ie, tax, social security, human rights frameworks, work, education, childcare and early years provision, health, housing, food security, third sector and local government. This is preceded by a review of recent writing on poverty in Scotland (knowledge as a tool to tackle poverty).

Section Five comprises the concluding chapter. Here, the focus is on revisting some of the central themes of the book as a whole, drawing out links, connections and presenting priorities for the next Scottish government.

Notes

1 Available at www.open.edu/openlearn/people-politics-law/poverty-scotland-2014-the-independence-referendum-and-beyond

2 See G Mooney, 'Independence referendum one year on: nothing is settled in Scotland', The Conversation, 17 September 2015, available at: http://the conversation.com/independence-referendum-one-year-on-nothing-is-settled-in-scotland-47712

3 Scottish Government, *Scotland's Future: your guide to an independent Scotland*, 2013, available at www.gov.scot/publications/2013/11/9348/downloads

4 See G Mooney and G Scott (eds), *Social Justice and Social Policy in Scotland*, Policy Press, 2012 and G Mooney and G Scott, 'The 2014 Scottish Independence Debate: questions of social welfare and social justice', *Journal of Poverty and Social Justice*, 23, 1, 2015, pp5–16

5 See, for example, A Salmond, Hugo Young Speech, London, January 2012, available at www.theguardian.co.uk/politics/2012/jan/25/alex-salmond-hugo-young-lecture; N Sturgeon, 'Bringing the powers home to build a better nation', speech delivered at Strathclyde University, Glasgow, December 2012, available at www.scotland.gov.uk/News/Speeches/betternation-031212 and A Salmond, Jimmy Reid Memorial Lecture, Glasgow, January 2013, available at www.gov.scot/news/speeches/jimmy-reid-lecture-29012013

6 Scottish Government, 16 December 2015, available at http://news.scotland.gov.uk/news/budget-local-government-funding-2084.aspx; see also G Braiden, 'Scottish Budget: £500m council cuts will cost 15,000 jobs or 50 Tata Steelworks, local government leaders warn', *The Herald*, 16 December 2015, available at www.heraldscotland.com/politics/14149469.scottish_budget_500million_cut_to_councils_will_cost_15_000_jobs_or_50_tata_steelworks

7 ScotCen Social Research, *Has the Referendum Campaign Made a Difference?*, 2014; see also J Eichhorn and GH Frommholz, 'How Political Mobilization Can Still Work on Substantive Issues: insights from the Scottish referendum', Europa Bottom-Up/European Civil Society Working Papers 10, 2014

8 Scottish Parliament, *The Scotland Act 2012*

9 Ashcroft, 'Post-referendum Scotland poll 18–19 September 2014', accessed at http://lordashcroftpolls.com/wp-content/uploads/2014/09/Lord-Ashcroft-Polls-Referendum-day-poll-summary-1409191.pdf

10 The Smith Commission, *Report of the Smith Commission for Further Devolution of Powers to the Scottish Parliament*, 2014; see also P Spicker, 'The Devolution of Social Security Benefits in Scotland: the Smith Commission', *Journal of Poverty and Social Justice*, 23, 1, 2015, pp17–28

11 UK government, *2015 Scotland Bill: legislation and explanatory notes*, May 2015, accessed at www.gov.uk/government/publications/scotland-bill-2015-

legislation-and-explanatory-notes; see also J Gallagher, *All Aboard the Constitution Express? Where is the Scotland Bill taking the UK?* A Gwilym Gibbon Centre for Public Policy Working Paper, Nuffield College, 2015, accessed at www.nuffield.ox.ac.uk/research/politics%20group/working%20papers/documents/all%20aboard%20the%20constitutional%20express.pdf

12 See CPAG in Scotland at www.cpag.org.uk/sites/default/files/CPAGScot-briefing-ScotlandBill%28June15%29_0.pdf

13 www.bbc.co.uk/news/uk-scotland-scotland-politics-34720846

14 http://thirdforcenews.org.uk/tfn-news/autumn-statement-third-sector-reaction

15 See 'Government to strengthen child poverty measure', Department for Work and Pensions press release, 1 July 2015, available at www.gov.uk/government/news/government-to-strengthen-child-poverty-measure

16 See S Carrell, 'Scotland prepares to rebel over DWP's child poverty changes', *The Observer,* 12 September 2015, available at www.theguardian.com/uk-news/2015/sep/12/scotland-distinct-strategy-eliminating-child-poverty

17 Resolution Foundation, *A Poverty of Information: assessing the government's new child poverty focus and future trends*, 7 October 2015, available at www.resolutionfoundation.org/publications/a-poverty-of-information-assessing-the governments-new-child-poverty-focus-and-future-trends

18 See for instance, C Beatty and S Fothergill, *Hitting the Poorest Places Hardest: the local and regional impact of welfare reform*, Centre for Regional Economic and Social Research, Sheffield Hallam University, 2013; *The Impact of Welfare Reform on the Scottish Labour Market: an exploratory analysis*, report for the Scottish Parliament, Centre for Regional Economic and Social Research, Sheffield Hallam University, 2015; both available from www.shu.ac.uk/cresr

19 Scottish Parliament Welfare Reform Committee press release, 23 June 2014, available at www.scottish.parliament.uk/newsandmediacentre/78669.aspx

20 For a critical account of the troubled families programme, see Stephen Crossley's blog, 'A kind of trouble', available at https://akindoftrouble.wordpress.com/author/akindoftrouble

21 Available at www.independent.co.uk/news/uk/home-news/sunday-times-rich-list-number-of-billionaires-in-britain-doubles-in-five-years-10205138.html

22 Available at www.independent.co.uk/news/uk/analysis-of-britains-9-trillion-of-wealth-reveals-a-deeply-divided-nation-10251573.html

23 T Piketty, *Capital in the Twenty-first Century*, Belknap Press, 2014

24 D Dorling, *Inequality and the 1%*, Verso, 2014; T Piketty, *Capital in the Twenty-first Century*, Belknap Press, 2014

25 See www.ukpublicspending.co.uk/central_spending_2013UKbs

26 A Sayer, *Why We Can't Afford the Rich*, Policy Press, 2015

27 D Bell and D Eiser, 'Inequality in Scotland: trends, drivers and implications for

the independence debate', University of Stirling Management School Working Paper, 2013, p8 and Figure 9

28 See www.oxfam.org.uk/scotland/blog/2015/09/glasgow-to-get-on-board-oxfams-global-campaign-against-inequality and a BBC news report at www.bbc.co.uk/news/uk-scotland-34474162

29 G Therborn, *The Killing Fields of Inequality*, Polity Press, 2013, p1

30 See C Green, 'Scotland's child poverty levels so severe teachers are sent advice on spotting malnourished students', *The Independent*, 10 September 2015

31 See MA MacLeod, *Making Connections: a study of emergency food aid in Scotland*, Poverty Alliance, 2015

32 R Wilkinson and K Pickett, *The Spirit Level*, Penguin, 2010

33 See for example, AB Atkinson, *Inequality: what can be done?* Harvard University Press, 2015; D Dorling, *Inequality and the 1%*, Verso, 2014; J Hills, *Good Times, Bad Times: the welfare myth of them and us*, Policy Press, 2014; S Lansley and J Mack, *Breadline Britain: the rise of mass poverty*, Oneworld Books, 2015; M O'Hara, *Austerity Bites*, Policy Press, 2014; T Piketty, *Capital in the Twenty-first Century*, Belknap Press, 2014; A Sayer, *Why We Can't Afford the Rich*, Policy Press, 2015; J Stiglitz, *The Price of Inequality*, Penguin, 2013

34 See J Duffy, 'The 'heat or eat' dilemma: fuel poverty figures soar by 130 per cent in five years', *Sunday Herald*, 25 October 2015, available at www.heraldscotland.com/news/13894440.the_heat_or_eat_dilemma_fuel_poverty_soars_by_130_as_tory_cuts_hit_poorest

35 See J Hills, *Good Times, Bad Times: the welfare myth of them and us*, Policy Press, 2015; L McKenzie, *Getting By: estates, class and culture in austerity Britain*, Policy Press, 2014; M O'Hara, *Austerity Bites*, Policy Press, 2014

36 See A Hastings, N Bailey, G Bramley, M Gannon and D Watkins, *The Cost of Cuts: the impact on local government and poor communities*, Joseph Rowntree Foundation, 2015

37 A Walker, 'The Strategy of Inequality: poverty and income distribution in Britain 1979–1989', in I Taylor, *The Social Effects of Free Market Policies*, Harvester Wheatsheaf, 1990

38 See G Mooney, 'Anti-austerity backlash is moving up a gear – even in 'progressive' Scotland', The Conversation, 1 June 2015, available at https://theconversation.com/anti-austerity-backlash-is-moving-up-a-gear-even-in-progressive-scotland-42454; C Morelli and G Mooney, 'Class, Austerity and Inequality', *Scottish Left Review*, 89, 2015, available at www.scottishleftreview.org/article/class-austerity-and-inequality

39 *Report of the Commission on the Future Delivery of Public Services*, 2011, available at www.gov.scot/Resource/Doc/352649/0118638.pdf

40 Available at www.gov.scot/resource/0048/00484439.pdf

41 See for example, Scottish Government/Poverty Truth Commission, *Poverty in Scotland*, June 2015, p8, available from www.gov.scot/resource/0048/0048 0340.pdf

42 JH McKendrick, G Mooney, J Dickie, G Scott and P Kelly, *Poverty in Scotland 2014: the independence referendum and beyond*, CPAG, 2014, p19. After housing costs, 300,000 working-age adults in poverty were in working households in Scotland and 120,000 children in poor households were in working households in Scotland in 2013/14.

43 See Scottish Government press release, 17 April 2015, available at http://news. scotland.gov.uk/news/scotland-a-fair-work-nation-1851.aspx

44 In late September 2015, the Convention of Scottish Local Authorities, representing 28 of Scotland's 32 councils, announced that it would not implement the Trade Union Bill being proposed by the Conservative UK government. The Scottish government has called for opt-outs for all public bodies in Scotland, falling short of calls for Scotland to be exempt from the legislation.

Section Two

The nature of poverty in Scotland

Two

What is poverty?

John H McKendrick

Summary

- Poverty is about not having enough. Typically, 'poverty' is understood to be a lack of resources. It can also mean inadequate outcomes or a lack of opportunities.
- Poverty is not the same as income inequality or multiple deprivation. However, poverty is closely related to both these issues.
- Poverty is multi-dimensional, and a wide range of resources may be lacked, including housing, fuel, education, health and income.
- Income is the primary resource that is lacking for people living in poverty. Insufficient personal or household income has a central role to play in creating or sustaining poverty in many areas of life.
- For almost twenty years, 'income poverty' has also been of central importance in anti-poverty activity, debate and policy in Scotland. Thus, for practical purposes in Scotland, 'not having enough' is understood to be a point below which people have insufficient disposable income to purchase what it is reasonable to expect that the majority of the UK population should be able to afford.
- In Scotland (and the UK), income poverty tends to be understood in one of three main ways: 'absolute poverty'; 'relative poverty'; and 'persistent poverty'. The interpretation that is used most is relative poverty.
- In 2015, the Scottish government introduced the idea that some of those living in relative income poverty in Scotland should be considered to be experiencing either 'severe poverty' or 'extreme poverty'.
- Also in 2015, the UK government, when announcing that it would replace the Child Poverty Act 2010, suggested that the primary focus of poverty should be tackling inadequate outcomes and inadequate opportunities relating to worklessness and educational attainment, rather than directly addressing inadequate resources.
- Attitude surveys suggest that the wider Scottish public is not, as yet, fully supportive of the understanding of poverty that underpins anti-poverty activity in Scotland. On the other hand, people in Scotland

appear more supportive than the British population as a whole of this understanding of poverty.

Poverty: a deceptively simple idea

The heart of the matter is that poverty is about 'not having enough'. However, this straightforward idea is quickly complicated as attempts to define and measure poverty become overly technical and theoretical, written by academics and statisticians for 'people like them'. This can be off-putting. However, the way in which we understand and define poverty has far-reaching implications on anti-poverty activity, debate and policy. It determines the number of people who are counted as living in poverty and it can have a major influence on the policy solutions that are developed to address 'the problem'.

There is little doubt that ideas about poverty are complex, occasionally contradictory, and influenced by factors such as personal experiences, value judgements and belief systems. Consequently, definitions of poverty are also contested. Although there is no single, universally accepted, definition or measure of poverty, there is broad agreement among social policy experts, anti-poverty campaigners and government in Scotland (and until recently in the UK) about what poverty means. In this chapter, we explain what we mean by poverty, and we describe how poverty is related to ideas that are widely used in Scotland, such as income inequality. We note new ideas promoted by the Scottish government in 2015 and end by considering the extent to which the wider Scottish public agrees with three different ways of defining poverty.

Poverty as not having enough

It is not sufficient to state that poverty is about 'not having enough'. It begs the question: 'enough of what?' Broadly speaking, poverty might be understood as either inadequate outcomes (such as not being adequately clothed), inadequate opportunities (such as not having access to an adequate education) or inadequate resources (such as not having enough disposable income to purchase what is necessary to maintain an adequate standard of living).

Furthermore, in each case, it is possible to consider poverty *as a whole*, or to consider one particular dimension of poverty. For example, rather than define poverty as a bundle of poor outcomes in aggregate (using a multi-dimensional measure such as material deprivation), it is possible to measure particular dimensions of poverty. Campaigning organisations often adopt a focus on a particular dimension of poverty – for example, the Trussell Trust is concerned with 'food poverty', and Energy Action Scotland is concerned with 'fuel poverty'.

The idea of poverty as having inadequate opportunities focuses on the root cause of the problem. One example of this is the 'capability approach' that is most closely associated with the work of Amartya Sen.[1] Sen uses this idea to promote the understanding that development is about more than economic output (our equivalent would be that poverty is about more than income deprivation). However, in our consumer society, we must acknowledge that living life on a low income might be one of the reasons why people are deprived of 'capabilities' (opportunities to achieve an adequate life). For example, 'bodily health' is one capability that is associated with Sen's theory. It is widely accepted that income poverty, at least in part, has a negative impact on people's health – for example, having insufficient income to adequately heat a home may lead to dampness going unchecked, which in turn might exacerbate respiratory conditions.[2]

It is also pertinent to note that achieving fulfilment might be viewed as a worthier outcome than possessing an adequate income. Indeed, the UK government now generates national estimates of life satisfaction, sense of worth in life, happiness and anxiousness, and mental wellbeing.[3] Similarly, Oxfam UK has developed a Humankind Index to provide intelligence on the things that 'really matter to the people of Scotland'.[4] At present, progressive social policy finds it easier to focus on 'lack of resources' than 'lack of personal fulfilment'. However, further development of this work may open up the possibility for a policy-driven approach to improve national wellbeing, happiness or 'the good life' in the future. Measuring poverty or measuring fulfilment should not, however, be viewed as two options over which a choice must be made. In the same way that a focus on 'capabilities' need not mean ignoring income deprivation, poverty should not be ignored when we focus on 'fulfilment'. Although they are different ideas, inadequate income and fulfilment are inextricably linked. On the one hand, living life on a low income is argued by many to be a contributory factor towards not achieving happiness.[5] On the other hand, there is undoubtedly the need to accord more importance to psychological wellbeing in understanding poverty.[6]

Thus, lack of resources (and lack of income, in particular) has a role to play in directly producing inadequate outcomes (material and immaterial) and in making it more difficult to achieve adequate outcomes (by compromising the 'capabilities' that are needed to achieve them). Pragmatically, measures of income poverty are also easier to digest and utilise than measures of capability deprivation or fulfilment. However, there is a more significant reason for an income poverty focus in *Poverty in Scotland 2016*. It is also a fundamental right that people should have adequate resources to enable them to participate in society. In a consumer economy, adequate resources means adequate income. It must also be acknowledged that 'income poverty' has been the pre-eminent focus of anti-poverty activity, debate and policy in Scotland and the UK. Hence, in the first two sections of this book, 'income poverty' is the point of entry to this wider poverty debate.

Understanding income poverty

Absolute poverty

Absolute poverty refers to the level of resources needed to sustain physical survival. People are poor if they cannot feed, clothe or house themselves and their dependants. This is a definition of poverty that is only about subsistence; the amount needed to keep body and soul together. As Ruth Lister points out, absolute definitions of poverty are closely linked to nutrition, whereby a person or family can be considered to be poor if they do not have sufficient resources to feed themselves.[7] This conception of poverty is one that tends not to be associated with contemporary Scotland, based on attitudes such as 'there is real poverty in Malawi, but not here', or 'we used to have poverty in Scotland, but not any more'. However, as Mary Anne MacLeod discusses later in this book, the proliferation of food banks in Scotland in recent years may lead us to question whether Scotland has truly rid itself of absolute poverty.

In this absolute definition of poverty, income is central to the way we conceptualise poverty, as poverty is not having enough income to buy life's necessities. However, the definition of 'necessity' must be based on some assessment of need, and our understanding of what is an essential need varies over time and across place. For this reason few serious analysts, and none of the major political parties, would use an absolute measure alone to understand poverty in Scotland in the twenty-first century. One additional source of confusion is that one of the indicators in the Child Poverty Act 2010 is described as a measure of 'absolute low income poverty' (Table 3.1). Strictly speaking, this is not a measure of absolute poverty as understood above, as it compares contemporary household income against typical levels in 2010/11.

Relative poverty

Relative poverty is defined in relation to the standards of living in a society at a particular time. People live in poverty when they are denied an income sufficient for their material needs, and when these circumstances exclude them from taking part in activities that are an accepted part of daily life in that society. However, there are issues with this approach. In times of economic growth, people may be reclassified as being poor, even when their material standard of living is improving (the decade following the mid-1990s in Scotland). On the other hand, it is possible that, in times of recession, people may be considered to have stopped being poor when their material standard of living is falling or has not changed. Perhaps ironically, this apparent paradox was used, arguably disingenuously, by the UK government minister Iain Duncan Smith in July 2015 to justify the replacement of the Child Poverty Act 2010:[8]

> The current child poverty measure – defined as 60 per cent of median income – is considered to be deeply flawed and a poor test of whether children's lives are genuinely improving… This was shown when the number of children in poverty went down significantly as the economy shrank during the recent recession, when in reality there was little change to those children's lives.

These apparent 'anomalies' arise because people are considered to be poor relative to the norm, and are not only based on what their personal circumstances happen to be. In any case, as the following chapter explores, the Child Poverty Act 2010 in fact contains four measures, including an 'absolute' measure and a combined relative poverty and material deprivation measure.

Despite the perceived shortcomings, in this book we primarily use the relative measure of poverty, believing that poverty should be defined by the standards of society as it is today. By using a relative measure, we arrive at an understanding of poverty that is fit for purpose in the twenty-first century:[9]

> … an understanding based on a measure that has the lack of income at its heart, but which acknowledges that poverty is about what that lack of income implies – the inability to obtain the types of diet, participate in the activities and have the living conditions and amenities which are customary… in the societies to which they [the poor] belong.

As is discussed in Chapter 3, it is important to take account of the wider economic context when interpreting data on relative poverty.

Persistent poverty

There are also limitations to only using moment-in-time measures of poverty, as the population experiencing poverty is not static. Poverty dynamics research has shown that poverty can be transient (a condition experienced only for a short period of time) or recurrent (a condition into which households repeatedly enter and leave at different points in time).[10] Persistent poverty is defined over time. Where attempts have been made to measure persistent poverty in the UK, the approach that has been used is to define persistent poverty as that which occurs when relative income poverty is experienced by a household in three of the preceding four years.

Scotland: severe and extreme poverty?

In 2011, Save the Children Scotland published a policy briefing that introduced the idea of severe child poverty.[11] Four years on, the Scottish government released a report to estimate the number of children, working-age adults and pensioners who are living in 'severe poverty' and 'extreme poverty'.[12] The motivation for these new ways of thinking about poverty is that the 'depth of poverty' that is experienced varies in important ways among those who are defined as living in relative income poverty. As will be discussed in the following chapter, these new ideas set different thresholds for defining the point at which a household is judged to be 'severely' or 'extremely' poor, as opposed to living in 'relative low income' poverty. Although a more nuanced understanding of poverty should be welcomed, a risk is created: the poverty that is not considered to be 'severe' or 'extreme' will, through time, come to be considered less important, more marginal and even less 'authentic' in anti-poverty activity. The challenge must be to take all poverty equally seriously, while at the same time addressing the particular issues faced by those who experience the severest and most extreme disadvantage.

Poverty and related ideas

There are many ideas, such as wellbeing, social exclusion, social justice and material deprivation, which are closely related to poverty.[13] In contemporary Scotland, two concepts are widely used, which differ to poverty, but are closely related to it.

Poverty and income inequality

The SNP Scottish government has set itself apart from earlier Scottish governments and the current UK government by asserting its intention to tackle income inequality, while retaining a focus on reducing income poverty. Through the Solidarity Purpose Target, the Scottish government aims to 'increase overall income and the proportion of income earned by the three lowest income deciles as a group by 2017'. More generally, growing interest in income inequality in the UK has followed the publication of *The Spirit Level* by Kate Pickett and Richard Wilkinson, in which international evidence is used to demonstrate that societies with higher levels of income inequality have excessively high negative social outcomes – ie, inequality *per se* contributes directly to social problems.[14] These shifts in political and academic thinking also reflect concerns in wider society with growing levels of discontent at what are deemed to be excessive levels of, for example, executive pay.

There is a close relationship between income inequality and income poverty, and all too often they appear to be used interchangeably, in particular when relative poverty is discussed. The confusion is understandable, although it should be avoided. Income inequality is not a direct measure of income inadequacy; rather, it is a measure of the way in which income is distributed across a population. In contrast, income poverty specifies a level below which income is deemed to be inadequate. Of course, it is highly likely that where there is high income inequality, there will be income poverty and that the eradication of poverty will require action to tackle income inequality.[15] However, income inequality does not provide us with an estimate of how many people exist on an inadequate income. Although we consider the question of income inequality in Chapter 6, in this book we are primarily focused on the character and experiences of those who do not have sufficient income (income poverty).

Poverty and multiple deprivation

As the name suggests, multiple deprivation is used to describe the situation when individuals, households or collections of people in small geographical areas are deprived of a range of conditions at the same time – for example, they are deprived of adequate housing, education *and* employment. In Scotland, multiple deprivation is most closely associated with small geographical areas through the Scottish Index of Multiple Deprivation. Areas of multiple deprivation in Scotland are currently identified using 38 indicators spread across seven domains (see Chapter 3). Multiply deprived areas are defined relatively; most typically, 15 per cent or 20 per cent is used as the threshold for defining a multiply deprived area – ie, of the 6,505 data zones in Scotland, those whose deprivation score is ranked 1 to 975 (the bottom 15 per cent) or 1 to 1,301 (the bottom 20 per cent) are described as 'multiply deprived' areas.

Intuitively we would expect that people living with income poverty would be more likely to live in the most deprived areas. However, in reality, not all people residing in multiply deprived areas are living in poverty. Similarly, many people living in poverty do not reside in multiply deprived areas.

Poverty, fairness and social justice

Although there would appear to be a natural affinity between both poverty and social justice (poverty is unjust) and poverty and fairness (poverty is unfair), this cannot be taken for granted. However, terms such as 'social justice' are interpreted and related to poverty in very different ways. For example, the Centre for Social Justice is a right of centre think tank that aims to 'put social justice at the heart of British politics', but identifies 'family breakdown', 'educational failure' 'worklessness', 'addiction' and 'debt', rather than lack of income, as the 'pathways to poverty' that amount to social breakdown. On the other, and as Annabelle Armstrong-Walter discusses in Chapter 20, ideas of fairness that are more closely aligned to poverty as understood by this book are gaining currency in Scotland, as both local government and the Scottish government seek to re-evaluate their social mission. So, although our understanding of poverty is robust, we must take care not to uncritically and blindly align this to fairness and social justice, as these ideas can mean very different things to different groups.

How people in Scotland define poverty

To this point, we have considered what professional experts working in the anti-poverty field (from academia, the third sector and government) mean when they talk about poverty. It cannot be assumed that the wider public agree with these definitions of poverty. Indeed, social attitudes research tends to suggest that there is a gap between public and professional thinking (Figure 2.1).

Figure 2.1 shows public support, in Scotland and in the rest of Great Britain, for three different definitions of poverty. Members of the public were asked whether they agreed or not with each definition of poverty. Least support is given for a definition whereby 'someone in Britain is in poverty if they had enough to buy the things they really needed, but not enough to buy the things most people take for granted'. A small majority support a conception of poverty as 'someone having enough to eat and live, but not enough to buy other things they needed'. On the other hand, there is almost universal support for the idea that 'someone in Britain is in poverty if they had not got enough to eat and live without getting into debt'.

What is particularly interesting about these recent results is that there now seems to be more support in Scotland than in the rest of Great Britain as a whole for each definition of poverty, particularly for the definition that might be seen by some as closest to the one used most often to measure income poverty in the UK (the first in Figure 2.1 perhaps resonates with the thinking that underpins how relative poverty is measured). On the other hand, although there would appear to be attitudinal divergence between Scotland and the rest of Great Britain as a whole in recent years and although the direction of travel in Scotland is such that more Scots are reporting agreement with how income poverty is understood by anti-poverty campaigners in Scotland, it remains a minority opinion held by only one in three Scots. Work remains to be done in Scotland by anti-poverty activists in academia, government and the third sector to further increase public support for an understanding that poverty is about more than the basic requirements for existence and survival.

Figure 2.1:

Public support for different definitions of poverty, Scotland and the rest of Great Britain, 2013

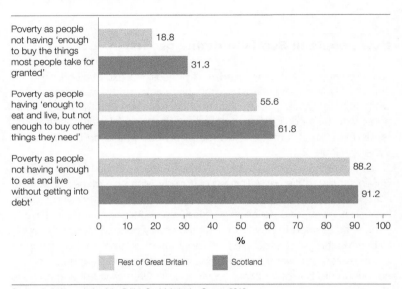

Source: Author's analysis of the British Social Attitudes Survey, 2013

Notes:
1. Great Britain totals exclude Scotland.
2. See text for explanations of definitions.

Conclusion

We would argue that poverty in Scotland can perhaps best be understood in terms of Peter Townsend's definition that:[16]

> Individuals, fami. ~s and groups in the population can be said to be in poverty when they ~k t ~ resources to obtain the types of diet, participate in the activities and have the living conditions and amenities which are customary, or are at least widely encouraged and approved, in the societies in which they belong.

Several key issues should be drawn from Townsend's ideas. First, resources can accrue through both incomes and services. However, the marketised nature of Scottish society means that income must be central to discussions about poverty. Second, poverty is relative to the needs and wants of the wider society. This means that poverty in Scotland is qualitatively different to that experienced in the global South (or in earlier historical periods in Scotland). Third, poverty in the twenty-first century is not only about survival and minimum subsistence to avoid starvation; it is about a standard of living that allows adequate participation within society. Finally, work remains to be done to convince the wider public in Scotland that this is a definition of the problem of poverty that befits contemporary Scotland.

We must also recognise that focusing on 'severe' poverty risks promoting a much narrower understanding of poverty than the consensus that has prevailed for the last twenty years. Of even greater concern is the UK government's notice of intention to shift its focus away from income poverty altogether. Convincing government and political opposition of the need to maintain a focus on relative income poverty must now become more central to campaigning and political work in the years ahead.

Notes

1 A Sen, *Commodities and Capabilities*, Oxford University Press, 1985

2 C McCormack, *The Wee Yellow Butterfly*, Argyll Publishing, 2009

3 See www.ons.gov.uk/ons/guide-method/user-guidance/well-being/index.html

4 See http://policy-practice.oxfam.org.uk/publications/oxfam-humankind-index-the-new-measure-of-scotlands-prosperity-second-results-293743

5 D Walsh, M Taulbut and P Hanlon, *The Aftershock of Deindustrialisation: trends in mortality in Scotland and other parts of post-industrial Europe*, Glasgow Centre for Population Health, 2008

6 C Craig, 'Ringing the Bell', in *Tears That Made the Clyde: well-being in Glasgow*, Argyll Publishing, 2010, pp356–78

7 R Lister, *Poverty*, Polity Press, 2004

8 'Government to strengthen child poverty measure', Department for Work and Pensions and Iain Duncan Smith press release, 1 July 2015, available at www.gov.uk/government/news/government-to-strengthen-child-poverty-measure

9 P Townsend, *Poverty in the United Kingdom*, Penguin, 1979

10 N Smith and S Middleton, *Poverty Dynamics Research in the UK*, Joseph Rowntree Foundation, 2007

11 C Telfer, *Severe Child Poverty in Scotland*, 2011, Save the Children Scotland, available at www.savethechildren.org.uk/sites/default/files/docs/Severe_Child_Poverty_In_Scotland_February2011.pdf

12 Scottish Government, *Severe Poverty in Scotland*, 2015, available at www.gov.scot/publications/2015/03/4673/0

13 JH McKendrick, 'What is Poverty?', in JH McKendrick, G Mooney, J Dickie, G Scott and P Kelly (eds), *Poverty in Scotland 2014: the independence referendum and beyond*, CPAG, 2014, pp31–43

14 R Wilkinson and K Pickett, *The Spirit Level: why more equal societies almost always do better*, Penguin, 2009

15 Those who ascribe to 'trickle down' theory would disagree that income inequality and income poverty are mutually reinforcing. In contrast, they would contend that income poverty will fall in a growing economy when capital accumulation and the pursuit of profit (drivers of income and wealth inequality) lead to growing demand for services and products, the provision of which being the means through which others can prosper.

16 See note 9, p31

Three

How do we measure poverty?

John H McKendrick

Summary

- In Scotland, the UK and across Europe, household income is used to estimate poverty – those with low household income are considered to be living in poverty.
- Over the last twenty years, a consensus has emerged – poverty is considered to be present when a household's income is below 60 per cent of the median national income.
- Four indicators of child poverty were specified in the Child Poverty Act 2010, which were to be used to monitor progress toward eradicating child poverty in the UK by 2020.
- In the UK, the government's official targets in the Child Poverty Act 2010 are based on household income *before* housing costs are deducted. This is common in Europe and allows international comparisons to be made. CPAG and many poverty experts argue that poverty should be estimated based on household income *after* housing costs have been deducted, as this gives a better indication of disposable income, which is a clearer indication of the lived experience of poverty.
- Measuring poverty is far from straightforward. Challenges are faced in getting accurate income data in the first instance and then there are a series of technical issues that must be addressed by experts before poverty can be estimated from household income data.
- In 2015, the UK government brought forward legislation repealing most of the Child Poverty Act 2010, abandoning poverty-reduction targets and proposing new measures that do not include income. Proposed new reporting requirements on worklessness, educational attainment, apprenticeships, troubled families and social mobility are useful, but are not measures of poverty.
- Scotland is well served with sources of information on poverty and household income. With due care and caveat, these data can be used to understand the risk of poverty for a wide range of population groups and geographical areas.

- In recent years, alternative ways of estimating poverty have been developed. Each of these alternatives can make a useful contribution to understanding poverty in Scotland.
- Income-based measures of poverty should remain central to how poverty in Scotland is estimated in the future.

Introduction

This chapter's review of how poverty is measured in Scotland first considers what might be described as the 'expert measurement consensus' and recent challenges to it. Issues in using household income to estimate poverty are appraised, before a summary is provided of the range of data that are available to estimate poverty in Scotland.

The expert measurement consensus

What is the measurement consensus?

Notwithstanding the position adopted by the UK government in 2015, there remains a broad consensus among many politicians, devolved government, anti-poverty campaigners and expert analysts that household income can be used to estimate poverty (when poverty is defined as a lack of resources). Having a very low income indicates poverty. Typically, this approach involves asking people for information about household income and composition, and then using this data to find out if that household's income is below a threshold income value that defines the point below which that particular household should be considered to be living in poverty. The threshold value that is most commonly used is 60 per cent of the median income for similar households. In monetary terms, in 2013/14 this was equivalent to a weekly income, after housing costs were deducted, of less than £355 for a couple with two children aged five and 14.[1] The use of a 60 per cent threshold value is the main way in which poverty is measured in Scotland (the UK and Europe).

It is important to note that this is not an annual count (or census) of household income. Rather, the number of people living in poverty in Scotland is estimated from annual survey data. First published in 1988,

Households Below Average Income (HBAI) is an annual review of the UK income distribution compiled by the Department for Work and Pensions (DWP) using data collected in the Family Resources Survey.[2] It is a major source of information on people living on low incomes and provides '… an explicitly relative measure which looks at how people at the bottom of the income distribution have fared in relation to the average'.[3] HBAI provides official figures on low income. Currently, it is based on data provided by just over 20,000 households in the UK (including almost 3,500 households in Scotland). It is sufficiently well-designed to allow robust national estimates to be made from these data, with the Scottish sample being boosted (doubled, relative to its proportionate share) in order to improve the quality of estimates for Scotland.

In the same year that HBAI was introduced, the Statistical Programme Committee of the European Union decided that 60 per cent of median income (before housing costs are deducted) should be used as the measure of income poverty when making international comparisons.[4]

From consensus to legal obligation

In 1999, the UK government committed itself to eradicating child poverty within a generation, a vision that is shared by the Scottish government and which was re-affirmed in 2010 with the passing of the Child Poverty Act.[5]

Following a user consultation between 2002 and 2003, the DWP, in conjunction with HM Treasury, initially devised a three-tier measure of child poverty, which consisted of measures of absolute low income, relative low income, and material deprivation and low income combined (Table 3.1).[6] A fourth tier – persistent low income – was added as part of the Child Poverty Act 2010. Where poverty is to be measured by low income alone, the threshold of 60 per cent median income is used. The baseline year for absolute low income was redefined in the Child Poverty Act 2010 from 1998/99 to 2010/11.

Table 3.1:

UK government's four-tier measure of child poverty[7]

Tier 1: Absolute low income

Number and proportion of children in households whose equivalised income before housing costs is below 60 per cent of inflation-adjusted UK median income in 2010/11. This is a measure of whether the poorest families are seeing their incomes rise in real terms. Success is defined as when less than 5 per cent of children live in households with absolute low income.

Tier 2: Relative low income

Number and proportion of children in households whose equivalised income before housing costs is below 60 per cent of UK median income in the same year. This is a measure of whether the poorest families are keeping pace with the growth of incomes in the economy as a whole. Success is defined as when less than 10 per cent of children live in households with relative low income.

Tier 3: Material deprivation and low income combined

Number and proportion of children that are both materially deprived and are in households whose equivalised income before housing costs is less than 70 per cent of the UK median in the current year. This is to provide a wider measure of children's living standards. Success is defined as when less than 5 per cent of children live in households with material deprivation and low income combined.

Tier 4: Persistent low income

Number and proportion of children in households whose equivalised income before housing costs is below 60 per cent of UK median income in the same year for three of the previous four years. This is a measure of how many children live in relative poverty for long periods of time. Success has been defined for this indicator as when 7 per cent or less of children live in households with relative low income in three of the previous four years.

The Child Poverty Act 2010 formalised targets to reduce child poverty by 2020 using these measures. Although child poverty has been the driver of the measurement consensus in the UK, in Scotland annual updates on 'income poverty' are also presented for adults of working age and pensioners. Data on 'income poverty' in Scotland are routinely published as part of the HBAI annual report (Scotland can be compared to other UK nations and regions in England in all tables comparing Government Office regions).[8] Furthermore, the Scottish government publishes a shorter annual report on income inequality and income poverty that focuses exclusively on Scotland as a whole.[9]

A consensus lost?

On the first day of July in 2015, Iain Duncan Smith and the Department for Work and Pensions gave notice that they would cast aside the consensus position on measuring poverty that had held sway in the UK for almost twenty years. Under the headline of 'Government to strengthen child poverty measure', news was relayed that unspecified new measures were to be introduced that would primarily focus on levels of work within a family and improvements in educational attainment, with a wider range of measures and indicators concerning issues such as family breakdown, debt and addiction, which collectively were described as being 'the real causes of poverty'. The argument underlying the desire to introduce a more broadly based 'measure of child poverty' would have been familiar to those who were aware of the last coalition government's consultation on measuring child poverty in 2012[10] and the Social Mobility and Child Poverty Commission's response in 2013 to it.[11] What may have been more surprising was the U-turn and marginalisation in less than three years on the contribution of income poverty to this more 'broadly based' approach to measuring poverty:

> Central to any measure of child poverty will be the inclusion of household income... The government is not playing a zero-sum game with child poverty measurement. There can be no doubt that *income is a key part of our understanding of child poverty and who it affects.*[12]

> The current child poverty measure – defined as 60 per cent of median income – is considered to be deeply flawed and a poor test of whether children's lives are genuinely improving.[13]

On closer analysis, the UK government makes no new proposal on how poverty should be measured. Rather, what is proposed is a shift of focus away from measuring the incidence of poverty, towards measuring what the UK government understands to be the causes of poverty. Although arguing that the current child poverty measure [*sic*][14] is flawed, no alternative measure of child poverty is proposed. Furthermore, there is no proposal to stop publishing estimates of income poverty using existing indicators. In short, the measurement consensus remains, but the UK government has withdrawn from it.

Using household income to estimate poverty

There is no single monetary value that defines the level below which all households in Scotland would be deemed to be living in poverty; a whole range of monetary values must be used as threshold levels of 'income poverty' in order to compare fairly household income across different household types. After all, a couple with four children will require a higher level of income to maintain the same standard of living as one adult living alone and therefore the 'poverty threshold' must be higher for the larger household.

Table 3.2 describes the key poverty threshold values for 2013/14 for four common household types. In addition to describing the median weekly household income for each household type for Scotland and the UK as a whole, the final two columns of this table specify the 'income poverty thresholds', set against the UK median.

Table 3.2:

Weekly income (after housing costs) and income-based poverty lines (before and after housing costs), including the self-employed, for different family household types, UK, 2013/14

Family household type	Weekly income (after housing costs)		Weekly income-based poverty lines (60% median)	
	£	£	£	£
	Scottish median	UK median	Before housing costs	After housing costs
Single with no children	275	259	182	155
Couple with no children	411	386	272	232
Single with two children (aged 5 and 14)	493	464	326	278
Couple with two children (aged 5 and 14)	628	591	416	355

Source: Scottish Government, *Poverty and Income Inequality in Scotland: 2013/14*, 2015, Tables 1 and 2

Note: Poverty would be defined at an income below the figures listed in columns 4 and 5 of this table.

This adjustment of household income to account for household composition is known as equivalisation. From 2005/06, the HBAI series has used the modified OECD equivalisation scale. The Scottish government has published online guidance to aid understanding of how equivalisation works.[15]

Second, a much more controversial issue among poverty analysts is whether poverty should be measured *before* housing costs or *after* housing costs have been deducted (Box 3.1). Although this seems a mundane and technical issue, its impact is significant. The number of people considered to be living in poverty in Scotland is much higher using an *after* housing costs measure – 940,000 in Scotland in 2013/14, compared with 730,000 using a *before* housing costs measure.[16]

Box 3.1:

Measuring poverty *before* housing costs or *after* housing costs?

Many poverty analysts argue that it is more accurate to determine whether a household is living in poverty *after* housing costs have been deduced from total household income, as this better reflects the actual disposable incomes of low-income households (housing being a fixed cost over which people living in poverty have little control). In contrast, the UK government targets for tackling child poverty use a *before* housing costs estimate. The difference this makes is explained in this chapter. For clarification, the *after* housing costs approach is used throughout this book, unless specific reference is made to the UK government's targets.

Furthermore, the risk rate of poverty changes dramatically for different groups. Poverty rates are lower for those groups whose direct housing costs are lower (such as those owning their homes outright, but living on a low income) if an after housing costs measure is used. The impact this difference makes is most marked by comparing children and pensioners. Using a *before* housing costs measure suggests that the number of children living in poverty in Scotland is lower (140,000, compared with 210,000 with an *after* housing costs measure), whereas the level of poverty among pensioners is higher with a *before* housing costs measure (160,000, compared with 120,000 with an *after* housing costs measure).[17]

Many poverty analysts would argue that the after housing costs measure should be used, as housing costs represent a fixed budget item over which low-income families have little choice. This is particularly important when comparing across Government Office regions and national regions, as it also smoothes out the distorting effect of the marked variations in housing costs across the UK. It is argued that deducting housing costs from calculations of low income ensures that we are better able to compare what low-income families across different regions have at their disposal to spend. However, in line with practice in Europe, official government measures for tracking progress on poverty tend to be based on measuring poverty before housing costs, as do the definitions used for the targets set by the Child Poverty Act 2010. HBAI and the annual Scottish report on poverty and income inequality provide poverty estimates using both the before housing costs and after housing costs approaches. For the reasons outlined in Box 3.1, this book tends to present data using an after housing costs measure. This avoids the risk of underestimating the number of children living in poverty in Scotland that comes with using a before housing costs measure.

Third, far more consensus has been reached about the technical challenge of whether household income should be calculated using the mean or median. Mean and median refer to different ways of measuring the average. Although the mean is most commonly used as the way of measuring an average, the favoured way of measuring poverty and low income is to use the median. *Mean* income is found by adding all the incomes of households and dividing the total by the number of households. Mean income can be easily distorted by very low or very high income. The *median* refers to the mid-point of an ordered range of data. The median measure of average income is less susceptible to distortions, in particular from those on high incomes, and hence is a more appropriate measure of what constitutes a typical income.

A fourth and final technical challenge is whether 'income poverty' should be considered as *absolute* low income or *relative* low income. Until the Child Poverty Act 2010, 'absolute low income' in relation to the HBAI figures referred to those households with less than 60 per cent of 1998/99 UK median income before housing costs were deducted. This threshold was adjusted by inflation for each subsequent year. More recently, the base year against which absolute low income has been set has been changed from 1998/99 to 2010/11. According to the DWP, absolute low income '… is important to measure whether the poorest families are seeing their incomes rise in real terms'.[18] 'Relative low income' in relation to the HBAI figures refers to the number and proportion of households with below 60 per cent of UK median income before housing costs were deducted for each year. The threshold is, therefore, recalculated every year to account for increases in median incomes, rather than simply being fixed for the base year then adjusted to account for inflation. This measure allows us to consider whether those on low incomes are keeping up with the rest of society.

As the absolute and relative figures for low income are measured in different ways, it is necessary to be clear about what these figures may mean. Relative low income is a useful way of assessing whether government policies are specifically ensuring that those at the bottom of the income distribution are seeing their incomes improve. Absolute low income indicates whether overall conditions have improved or worsened through time. Most sense can be made of these data when the results are set against each other at the same point in time (see Chapter 5).

HBAI and the annual Scottish report on poverty and income inequality provide poverty estimates using both the absolute and relative measures. Something that neither measure is able to do is to tell us anything about the standard of living that anyone living below the threshold experiences.

Limitations of household analysis

Poverty based on household income is, by definition, a measure of poverty for private households. Thus, the main measure of poverty used in Scotland does not claim to measure whether those living in communal establishments are living in poverty. For example, almost 1,500 looked-after children in Scotland live in 'residential establishments'[19] and the prison population in custody in Scotland is just over 8,000 adults.[20] National poverty statistics do not relate to such groups.

Furthermore, a household income does not necessarily imply that all members of that household will have equal access to this income resource. Gender-sensitive analysis has demonstrated that women, in particular, in Scotland are prone to foregoing their household share for the benefit of other household members.[21] On the other hand, due to the dependency of their parents, children of substance abusers, for example, may not have access to the level of resource that household income suggests.[22]

A national estimate of *household* poverty is not designed to account for poverty in institutions (or intra-household inequities in terms of how this household income is utilised); a fuller understanding of poverty in the UK would require data or studies that are complementary to HBAI data.

Limitations of disposable household income as a measure of poverty

All things being equal, disposable household income – gross income, net of tax and national insurance and housing costs – should provide a measure of how much income households have available to meet their living needs. If that level of income falls below a benchmark, the household is considered to be living in poverty. However, disposable household income is not always an accurate indicator of the extent to which households are able to meet their daily living needs.

For example, disposable household income does not adequately reflect the income that is actually available to meet daily living needs for all households. Specifically, households with individuals who have a high level of debt to service may have less income to use (and therefore a lower standard of living) than others who earn less, but have no debts. These debt problems may be compounded for those on the lowest incomes by the greater likelihood that they will be using financial service providers who charge a relatively higher fee for their service.

Even if disposable net income adequately reflects the income that is available to meet daily living needs, it may not adequately reflect what some groups are able to purchase with it – ie, some groups face higher costs of living. For example, there has been longstanding concern that the additional social security payments that supplement the income of families with disabled people are insufficient to meet the additional costs of living with disability.[23] Similarly, costs of living vary across place. The Centre for Social Research at Loughborough University acknowledges this and has used research-based evidence to adapt its minimum income calculator to account for the higher cost of rural living in remote and rural Scotland, which it estimates at between 10 per cent and 40 per cent more than in other parts of the UK.[24]

Sources of information on income poverty in Scotland

As might be expected, household income data that is available to measure poverty is more readily available for Scotland as a whole than for local areas or sub-populations within Scotland. There are four regular sources of household income data that can be used to estimate income poverty for Scotland as a whole: HBAI data; Scottish Household Survey; Growing Up in Scotland; and Understanding Society, the UK household longitudinal study,[25] some of which are also able to provide estimates for sub-populations or local areas. As a rule, wherever possible, the HBAI sources should be used to provide an estimate of poverty in Scotland. However, the only groups for which regular annual updates of income poverty in Scotland are provided using HBAI data are the broad age groups of children, working-aged adults and pensioners. Although the Scottish government publishes occasional estimates for other groupings (see column 2, Table 3.3), many interest groups are poorly served by the routine publication of poverty rates. Table 3.3 suggests some alternative sources, which could be used to estimate poverty in Scotland for a wide range of interest groups. It is important to acknowledge that these alternatives are not direct substitutes, and considerable caution is required when utilising, for example, summary household income data as a proxy for poverty. Nevertheless, used with due caution and caveat, there is a wealth of information that can be used to profile poverty and monitor change for a wide range of populations and interest groups.

Table 3.3:

Sources for estimating the incidence of poverty in Scotland

Sub-population	Scottish HBAI	Accessible alternative sources	Access
Age	Regular	Data for children, adults of working age and pensioners in annual report	Tables in annual report
Gender	Occasional	Occasional supplementary analysis of HBAI data by Scottish government	Tables in occasional report
Ethnicity	Occasional	Occasional supplementary analysis of HBAI data by Scottish government	Tables in occasional report
Disability	Occasional	Occasional supplementary analysis of HBAI data by Scottish government	Tables in occasional report
Tenure status	Occasional	Scottish Household Survey: household characteristics by tenure Occasional supplementary analysis of HBAI data by Scottish government	Tables in reports
Household size	Occasional	Occasional supplementary analysis of HBAI data by Scottish government	Tables in occasional report
Household composition	Occasional	Occasional supplementary analysis of HBAI data by Scottish government	Tables in occasional report
Work status	Occasional	Occasional supplementary analysis of HBAI data by Scottish government	Tables in occasional report
Educational qualifications	No	Scottish Household Survey: highest level of qualifications by net annual household income	Table in annual report
Car ownership	No	Scottish Household Survey: number of cars available to household for private use by net annual household income	Table in annual report
Internet usage	No	Scottish Household Survey: use of internet by net annual household income	Table in annual report
Perceived health	No	Scottish Household Survey: self-perception of health by net annual household income	Table in annual report

Sub-population	Scottish HBAI	Accessible alternative sources	Access
Volunteer status	No	Scottish Household Survey: whether provided unpaid help to organisations or groups in last 12 months by net annual household income	Table in annual report
Schools	No	Free school meal entitlement data	Annual School Meals Census
Streets	No	Problematic, although postcodes can identify the data zone to which an address belongs (there are often boundary problems in using data zones for street analysis)	Scottish Index of Multiple Deprivation data
Neighbourhoods	No	Problematic, although aggregation of data from data zones which comprise neighbourhood may provide an estimate (there are often boundary problems in aggregating data zones to neighbourhoods)	Scottish Index of Multiple Deprivation data
Electoral wards	No	End Child Poverty, Poverty in Your Area (child poverty)	Annual local area reports
Settlements	No	Problematic, although aggregation of data from data zones which comprise settlement may provide an estimate (there are often boundary problems in aggregating data zones to settlements)	Scottish Index of Multiple Deprivation data
Local authority/ community planning partnership	No	End Child Poverty, Poverty in Your Area (child poverty)	Annual local area reports
Urban/rural	Occasional	Rural Scotland Key Facts: fuel poverty by geographic area Rural Scotland Key Facts: annual net income of highest income householder by geographic area Rural Scotland Key Facts: income deprivation by geographic area	Tables in report

Measuring poverty without household income

Although poverty tends to be measured using household income and although (as discussed earlier) a range and reasonable quality of household income data sources for Scotland are available, it is acknowledged that household income alone (and even household income combined with material deprivation) cannot fully capture the ways in which poverty impacts on people's lives. For this reason, it is worth acknowledging some of the alternatives ways of understanding poverty in Scotland without household income.[26] Table 3.4 summarises the strengths, weaknesses and possible applications of alternative sources of measuring poverty in Scotland.

Conclusion

Every edition of *Poverty in Scotland* has reported on new developments and better data for measuring poverty in Scotland, suggesting that the immediate priority was to make better use of the array of resources that are now available to measure poverty, particularly at the sub-national scales of data zones, neighbourhoods and local authority areas. From 2015, it would appear that both opportunity and constraint lie ahead. The UK government's proposed new reporting requirements on worklessness, educational attainment, apprenticeships, troubled families and social mobility are welcome, but are not measures of poverty. On the other hand, the veracity of the UK government critique of the existing child poverty measure is a cause for concern. It is more fruitful to deliver a rounded interpretation of these income-based estimates of poverty, rather than to dismiss them off-hand on account of their limitations. Those concerned with how poverty is measured in Scotland (and in the rest of the UK) must be vigilant to any attempt to downscale or renege on our existing commitments to monitor change in income-based measures of poverty.

Table 3.4:

Alternatives to using household income to estimate poverty in Scotland

Approach	Strengths	Weaknesses	Application in Scotland
Benefits and administrative data	• Updated regularly • Available for small geographical areas • Local welfare benefits can be useful proxies for local poverty – eg, free school meals	• Benefit levels are often below the relative poverty threshold – in-work poverty can be missed • Counts may be based on claimants, rather than those entitled to claim	Useful for estimating the prevalence of poverty in schools (using free school meal data). Otherwise, only useful for profiling some of the people who are experiencing poverty (benefit claimants)
Material deprivation (whether people do not have items that are deemed indicative of necessities, which they want but cannot afford)	• Updated regularly • Based on a consensus – indicators may be deemed more credible • Accounts for the impact of resourcing from the wider family and community	• Data not available for small geographical areas • Data difficult to access • Major research effort to generate data independently	Useful for understanding the impact of poverty on people in Scotland, but requires research expertise and effort to be applied to local areas
Areas of multiple deprivation	• Income deprivation can be used as a proxy for poverty • Available for very small geographic areas • Accessible • Useful for tracking changes for very small areas through time	• The Scottish Index of Multiple Deprivation is only updated every four years • Ineffective in rural Scotland due to the dispersed nature of poverty • Not always possible to aggregate data into meaningful area units (such as neighbourhoods)	Income deprivation is useful for estimating the prevalence of poverty in very small areas in urban Scotland

Approach	Strengths	Weaknesses	Application in Scotland
Minimum income standard	• Updated annually by Joseph Rowntree Foundation • Factors in the additional cost of living in rural areas • Based on a consensus – indicators may be deemed more credible • Can be used as an alternative poverty threshold for existing income data	• Data not available for geographic areas • Data difficult to access • Major research effort to generate data independently • Might be argued that cost of living differences extend beyond urban versus rural	Provides Scotland-wide alternative household income threshold to determine existence of poverty
Multi-dimensional indices or basket of indicators	• More comprehensive analysis of poverty • Overcomes the specific limitations of household income data • Can be used in conjunction with household income data	• A single measure of poverty from a multi-dimensional index is an artificial construction that can be difficult to grasp • Data may not be available for geographic areas • No consensus over what should be included in the index	Not yet available, but currently of interest to the UK government and may be developed in the years ahead

Notes

1 Scottish Government, *Poverty and Income Inequality in Scotland: 2013/14*, 2015

2 See www.gov.uk/government/collections/households-below-average-income-hbai–2

3 C Oppenheim and L Harker, *Poverty: the facts*, CPAG, 1996

4 Eurostat Task Force, 'Recommendations on Social Exclusion and Poverty Statistics', Paper presented to the 26–27 November Meeting of the EU Statistical Programme Committee, 1998

5 *Child Poverty Act 2010*, The Stationery Office, 2010

6 Department for Work and Pensions, *Opportunity for All: eighth annual report*, 2006, available at www.bris.ac.uk/poverty/downloads/keyofficialdocuments/Opportunity%20 for%20All%202006.pdf

7 See http://legislation.data.gov.uk/ukdsi/2014/9780111121870/data.html

8 See note 1

9 See note 1

10 HM Government, *Measuring Child Poverty: a consultation on better measures of child poverty*, Cm 8483, 2012, available at www.official-documents.gov.uk/document/ cm84/8483/8483.pdf

11 Commission on Social Mobility and Child Poverty, *Measuring Child Poverty: consultation response*, 2013, available at www.gov.uk/government/publications/measuring-child-poverty-consultation-commission-response

12 See note 11, point 24, p14, original emphasis

13 'Government to strengthen child poverty measure', Department for Work and Pensions and Iain Duncan Smith press release, 1 July 2015, available at www.gov.uk/government/news/government-to-strengthen-child-poverty-measure

14 It is more accurate to acknowledge that there is a suite of four inter-related measures.

15 www.gov.scot/Topics/Statistics/Browse/Social-Welfare/IncomePoverty/Methodology

16 See note 1

17 See note 1

18 Department for Work and Pensions, *Measuring Child Poverty*, 2003

19 Scottish Government, *Children's Social Work Statistics Scotland 2013/14*, 2015, Table 1.1

20 Scottish Prison Service, 'Prisoner population', Scottish prison population as at Wednesday 23 September 2015, available at www.sps.gov.uk/Corporate/Information/SPSPopulation.aspx

21 JH McKendrick, S Cunningham-Burley and K Backett-Milburn, *Life in Low-income Families in Scotland*, Scottish Executive, 2003

22 M Barnard and N McKeganey, 'The Impact of Parental Problem Drug Use on Children: what is the problem and what can be done to help?', *Addiction*, Vol. 99.5, pp552–59, 2004

23 N Smith, S Middleton, K Ashton-Brooks, L Cox, B Dobson and L Reith, *Disabled People's Costs of Living*, Joseph Rowntree Foundation, 2004

24 D Hirsch, A Bryan, A Davis and N Smith, *A Minimum Income Standard for Remote and Rural Scotland*, Highlands and Islands Enterprise, 2013

25 JH McKendrick, 'Sources of information for household income', in JH McKendrick, G Mooney, J Dickie, G Scott and P Kelly (eds), *Poverty in Scotland 2014: the independence referendum and beyond*, CPAG, 2014, pp53–56

26 JH McKendrick, 'Measuring poverty without household income', in JH McKendrick, G Mooney, J Dickie, G Scott and P Kelly (eds), *Poverty in Scotland 2014: the independence referendum and beyond*, CPAG, 2014, pp56–60

Four

What causes poverty?

John H McKendrick

Summary

- Some policy interventions from local, Scottish and UK governments have helped reduce, but not yet eradicate, poverty in Scotland.
- The reasons for poverty are complex and multi-faceted. The primary poverty-generating mechanisms are social, economic and political. Tackling poverty requires a sustained and long-term comprehensive strategy, rather than a quick-fix, single-issue intervention.
- The way in which poverty-inducing factors take effect is complicated. It is overly simplistic both to reduce poverty to a single cause and to ignore the intervening factors that policy solutions need to take into account.
- Political will and policy action, alongside a growing economy, have contributed to reductions in the level of poverty in Scotland and elsewhere in the UK, particularly among pensioners and children. However, progress has now stalled, and independent forecasts suggest a reversal of that progress with significant increases in poverty anticipated as a result of current UK government tax and benefit policies.
- A much more ambitious and focused anti-poverty strategy is now needed if poverty in Scotland is to be reduced in the years ahead.
- The wider Scottish public are more likely to focus on individual factors when asked to explain why poverty exists.

Introduction

This chapter accounts for the causes of poverty in Scotland. This is by no means a straightforward task.

First, there are several possible reasons for why people experience poverty. Poverty is sometimes attributed to the **behaviour of individuals**. Here, consideration is given to how personal knowledge of the 'feckless poor', grounded in everyday social theorising based on stereotypes, is used to support the viewpoint that poverty results from the failings of individuals. Although such explanations have popular appeal, it is argued that this type of explanation is of limited value in accounting for poverty in Scotland. Poverty can be attributed to **social factors**, that is, characteristics that define groups of people and which place additional demands on their resources and/or make them more vulnerable to other poverty-inducing factors. Here, reference is made to the social factors that induce poverty among the groups identified as being vulnerable to poverty. Poverty in Scotland can also be attributed to **political factors**, that is, the extent to which government is prepared to intervene to tackle poverty and the effectiveness of these interventions. Of course, the core concern of *Poverty in Scotland 2016* is to reflect on the ways in which the next Scottish government could tackle poverty in Scotland. Finally, poverty can also be attributed to **economic factors** – for example, the strength of the macro-economy.

Second, the poverty experienced by individuals tends to result from more than one of these poverty-inducing factors. For example, the susceptibility to poverty of single adults without children, migrating to work in remote rural Scotland from Eastern Europe, might be attributed to: language barriers limiting their ability to move beyond the low-paid employment which brought them to Scotland to work in jobs that are populated with other migrants who share their cultural background (social factor); limited opportunity in the wider local labour market to earn a decent living wage (economic factor); and a lack of state intervention, as rural poverty is not deemed to be a pressing priority for policy intervention (political factor). Progress in one of these factors may not be sufficient to counteract the persistence of these other drivers of poverty for this group.

Third, the factors which cause people to experience poverty are inter-related. For example, the susceptibility to poverty of lone parents might be attributed to restricted labour market options given lone parents' need to combine work with parental responsibilities (social factor), resulting in difficulties in accessing employment that pays a decent living wage (economic and political factor). Here, the social situation influences the economic possibilities, both of which contribute to the poverty experienced by the individual.

Finally, the ways in which poverty-inducing factors influence individuals can be complex, hidden and indirect. For example, Scotland has a small domestic market and, like other small European nations, it is dependent on exports and inward investment. It is, therefore, vulnerable to changes in the global economy and UK national economy. However, the extent to which these macro-economic forces result in poverty is dependent on a host of intervening factors, such as the economic strategies of transnational corporations, inducements and support from inward investment agencies, national social protection and pay policies, and the ability of the local economy to absorb job losses or supply workers with the skills demanded in growth sectors.

Individual factors

Many of us have anecdotal knowledge of an individual who seems to do little to arrest the poverty that s/he experiences. Individuals are sometimes deemed to be the primary cause of their poverty and the large number of people who are described as being poor in official measures of poverty is perceived to be an overstatement of the problem. Such arguments carry some intuitive appeal and are reinforced by sensationalist or superficial media coverage.

There are five key points that critique the line of thinking that attributes poverty to the action or inaction of individuals. First, poverty experienced by children has little to do with children's own actions; the 210,000 children experiencing poverty in Scotland do so exclusively on account of chance, that is, the accident of birth, which determined the families into which they were born. Clearly, not all people experiencing poverty can be held responsible for this condition. Second, reducing explanations for poverty simply and singularly to the actions of individuals does not allow the possibility of poverty being influenced by other factors, and takes no account of the large-scale structural (social, political and economic) forces that shape people's lives. The causes of poverty are multi-faceted. Third, on closer analysis, what appear to be 'individual-level' factors often reflect underlying social and economic processes. For example, the understanding that poverty is transmitted down through generations of the same family is often perceived to be a problem of the individual, when more correctly it should be viewed as a social and economic factor. As James McCormick argued so persuasively many years ago in an earlier CPAG publication, poor places keep people poor.[1] Fourth, focusing on individual behaviour as a cause of poverty risks distracting attention from the social, economic and political factors over which it is possible for policy makers to exert influence and which, therefore, hold most potential for eradicating poverty. Finally, there is a numerical challenge to those who argue that poverty is the fault of individuals. According to the Scottish government, 940,000 people experience poverty in Scotland (Figure 5.4). There can be no credibility in the argument that one-sixth of the population in Scotland experience poverty on account of their own personal failings.

Social factors

As Chapter 7 demonstrates, the distribution of poverty in Scotland is uneven across social groups and place. This must not, however, lead to an explanation for Scotland's poverty that is based only on describing the changing composition of Scotland's population. Thus, for example, the changing composition of families in Scotland since the early 1970s – including the rise in lone parenthood – should not, *per se*, be used to explain the corresponding growth in poverty. It is more accurate to explain that the rise of poverty was due to the high risk of poverty faced by a group growing in size and the failure of policies to intervene to reduce this risk. There is clearly an association between these trends (and between the extent of poverty and other social trends), but this offers no insight into the root causes of poverty. Most problematically, this approach encourages scapegoating and a culture of blame – for example, lone parenthood causes poverty.

However, there are common shared characteristics among social groups that make some more susceptible to poverty and make the escape route from poverty more difficult than otherwise would be the case.

For example, the existence of gender pay gaps is at odds with longstanding government legislation and steps to promote equal pay in local authorities and national government in Scotland. The right of women to equal pay has been enshrined in UK legislation since the Equal Pay Act in 1975 and has since been strengthened by amendments, such as that in 1984 to ensure equal pay for equivalent work. More recently, in 1999, single status agreements were reached between the trade unions and local government in Scotland to ensure verifiable pay equality between men and women. The employment status of women in Scotland is similar to that in the rest of the UK: fewer women aged 16 to 64 are economically active (75.4 per cent, compared with 82.6 per cent of men between July and September 2015);[2] the concentration across occupational type is highly gendered and women tend to be under-represented in the higher paying sectors and over-represented in the lower paying sectors (almost 85 per cent of the 200,000 workers in Scotland in 'caring, personal service' occupations are women, compared with 12.6 per cent of the 190,000 in skilled trades);[3] and while equivalent numbers of men and women are employed (according to the *Annual Survey of Hours and Earnings* in 2014, 1,047,000 men and 1,152,000 women in Scotland in 2014),[4] in Scotland, men are 1.38 times more likely than women to be working full time, while women are more than three times as likely as men to be employed part time (498,000 women, compared with 146,000 men).[5] While these gender patterns in work would explain why men earn more than women, as explained in Chapter 6 (Table 6.1), what is particularly disconcerting is that the pay gap between men and women is evident across every type of occupation. For full-time work in the UK, using median pay as the comparator, the gender pay gap ranges from as low as 59.9 per cent of male earnings for 'skilled trades' up to a 94.4 per cent in customer service occupations. Across occupations, women on average earn only 82.5 per cent of their male counterparts.[6]

However, the gendered character of poverty should not be accepted as inevitable in the world in which we live. To its credit, the Scottish government is taking seriously the issue of gender pay inequality, monitoring its own gender pay gap,[7] and supporting the work of Close the Gap.[8] However, there has been no progress in closing the gender pay gap since the last edition of *Poverty in Scotland*. Clearly, more and more wide-ranging work needs to be done to close the gender pay gap in Scotland.

Political factors

Government action – or inaction – is one of the key factors that could determine the extent and level of poverty in Scotland. The questions that must be answered are: 'are our governments doing enough?' and 'how effective are our government interventions?'

UK government

The UK government retained responsibility following devolution for the main levers of control over poverty in Scotland – the social security system and taxation. Although the Smith Commission recommendations and Scotland Bill 2015 will lead to further devolution of powers in these areas,[9] the primary responsibility currently rests with the UK government.

Welfare system

While social security is undoubtedly a tool for poverty amelioration, the benefits system is not necessarily designed to provide an income that removes households without work from poverty. Indeed, although it is not one that is shared by the editors of this book, there is an ideological train of thought that social security payments must be kept at poverty levels to act as a disincentive to individuals who are disinclined to work. Proponents of this approach would argue that the social security system could eradicate poverty by ensuring that only poverty-level incomes were available to claimants – effectively, encouraging or coercing claimants to find work and escape poverty.

This thinking – that social security could eradicate poverty by encouraging claimants to move into paid employment – reflects the position of the current UK government. 'Welfare reform', the comprehensive overhaul of the UK welfare system, aims to reduce the total cost of social security and to effect cultural change (premised on the ideological position outlined above).[10] Although the welfare reforms herald a much more austere future for benefit claimants, it could be argued that the ideological position is merely an extension of that held by the previous government. In recent years, social security in the UK has not aimed to remove people from poverty; rather it has sought to facilitate moves into paid work and protect people from the worst excesses of abject poverty.

There are limitations to the way in which successive UK governments have used social security as a poverty-reduction strategy. First, benefit uprating operates in ways that exacerbate poverty and income inequality. Although not exactly a 'progressive' system at present, the UK government is now making the system an outwardly 'regressive' one as key benefits were only uprated by 1 per cent (for the 2013/14 through to the 2015/16 tax years),[11] and are now set to be frozen for four years from

April 2016.[12] The effect of this change will be to increase the intensity of poverty experienced by the UK's most vulnerable people, and to increase the number of people experiencing poverty.

Second, successive UK governments have subscribed to a welfare-to-work strategy through which it seeks to 'make work pay'. Although there is evidence that this approach has been successful in assisting people to escape poverty, this is an ineffective anti-poverty strategy for those who cannot work, for those for whom work is not available and those who undertake unpaid work. The 'work not welfare' mantra has been strongly championed by the UK government. Unfortunately, and unnecessarily, currently there seems to be much more focus placed on the punitive (making social security pay less in order to make work pay, relatively, more) than on the incentive (tangible steps to remove barriers to work – for example, childcare).

Third, the UK government has not been averse to using the social security system to effect behavioural change in a way that overrides its poverty-reduction credentials. Thus, previous administrations saw fit to withdraw some benefits from those who did not comply with employability conditions, and the current government continues to increase benefit sanctions at the same time as the number of conditions related to benefit entitlement are ratcheted up. Although there are differences of opinion over the moral legitimacy of using such punitive measures, they clearly demonstrate that the poverty-reducing value of social security can be overridden by other goals. Imposing severe poverty on errant claimants (and their families) by withdrawing social security is considered by government to be justified.

Taxation

Higher earners pay more tax than lower earners in absolute terms, although not, as we shall see, as a proportion of their income. For example, in 2013/14, the average annual amount paid by the richest fifth of non-retired households in the UK was £22,427 in direct taxation and £9,741 in indirect taxation. In contrast, the average amount paid by the poorest fifth of non-retired households in the UK was £1,488 in direct taxation and £4,205 in indirect taxation.[13]

However, two criticisms can be made against the effectiveness of current taxation policy as a means to tackle income poverty. First, taxation reduces the incomes of those on already low incomes: the poorest fifth of households in the UK typically have £5,693 deducted in tax from a gross income of £15,196 (37.5 per cent of gross income is deducted in tax).[14] In fairness, it could be argued that, to some extent, this is an administrative necessity as it would otherwise be too complex to refrain from taxing low-income groups, particularly at the point of consumption for indirect taxes. Second, although higher earners pay more in absolute sums, the lowest earning fifth of households in the UK pay a greater share of their gross income in taxation – for example, the 'tax burden' of the lowest earning fifth at 37.5 per cent is higher than that of the highest earning households (35.0 per cent of the gross income of the highest earning fifth of house-holds is deducted in tax).[15] Indirect taxes are particularly regressive. The poorest fifth pay twice the proportion of their gross income on indirect taxes (27.7 per cent, compared with 10.6 per cent).[16] It should therefore come as no surprise, as will be reported in Chapter 6, that there has been little change in income inequality in Scotland in recent years.

Scottish government and local government

Although largely unable to dictate who receives cash benefits, the Scottish government can influence the extent and level of poverty in Scotland: through using its limited tax-varying powers; by wholesale area regenera-tion; by creating the conditions necessary to facilitate the labour market participation of those without work; by early intervention and improved early years provision; by effective service delivery and intervention in the fields of education, training and health; by promoting take-up of benefits and tax credits; by ensuring people have access to advice and information on maximising their incomes; by ameliorating negative impacts of the withdrawal of UK government services and support; and by intervening to provide benefits in kind. Local government is responsible for direct provi-sion of key services and supports people experiencing poverty (and others living on a low income) by providing an array of benefits in kind. The extent to which these devolved 'tools' have been, and can be, used to tackle poverty is explored more fully in Section Four.

In recent years, the Scottish government's approach to tackling poverty in Scotland has been twofold. First, it has positioned itself against welfare reform and has sought to better understand the impact of these reforms in Scotland and provide direct support to mitigate the impact of these reforms. Ministers are obliged to present an annual report to the Scottish Parliament on the impact of the UK Welfare Reform Act in Scotland until 2017.[17]

Second, the Scottish government continues to operate its main anti-poverty programmes – ie, Achieving Our Potential (2008–) and the Child Poverty Strategy for Scotland (refreshed in 2014). At the heart of both approaches is a concordat with local government through which local government has responsibility for determining and addressing local anti-poverty priorities. Although many of the drivers are conceived as local, a Ministerial Advisory Group on Child Poverty has been formed and an annual report on the Child Poverty Strategy published.[18] Welcome as this work is to address welfare reform and child poverty, it might be argued that relatively less focus and prominence is currently being given to the overarching Achieving Our Potential framework. On the other hand, an independent adviser was appointed in 2015 to scrutinise and make recommendation on Scottish government policy to tackle poverty and inequality[19] and ministers have embarked on 'a national discussion about how the country can be a fairer and more equal place to live' to inform an 'action plan' with 'milestones' towards a fairer Scotland, to be published in early 2016.[20]

Economic factors

The performance of the macro-economy is one possible reason for the existence of poverty in Scotland. The logic is that there will be an inverse relationship between the economy and the extent and level of poverty – that is, the stronger the economy, the lower the intensity and extent of poverty.

Gross domestic product (GDP) is a measure of the value of the goods and products being produced in a nation state in any one year, and is widely accepted as a robust measure of economic growth.[21] Prior to the economic slowdown, Scotland's economy had grown for many years, with peaks in the rate of growth in 2004 and 2007.[22] Poverty remained stubbornly high throughout this period. However, from 2007 Scotland's economic growth first slowed down, before entering a period of economic decline from the end of 2008 to the end of 2009.[23] Poverty was stable during this period. Although subsequent growth rates have been unremarkable, the Scottish economy has since stabilised and has registered many more quarters of modest growth than it has quarters of no growth or contraction, with growth reported in every quarter since the final quarter of 2012.[24] Poverty has been unstable during this period, with increases registered between 2012 and 2013, and falls registered between 2013 and

2014. There is clearly no strong coupling of general economic growth and rates of poverty.

Employment (of 16–64-year-olds in Scotland) peaked at an all-time high of almost 75 per cent of the working-age population in 2007 (April–June), only to fall steadily to 70 per cent by the end of 2009.[25] Although an unwelcome trend in itself, it is notable that during this time employment rates in Scotland were the highest of all national regions in the UK. The employment rate in Scotland has since recovered to 73.5 per cent in the early part of 2014, although this was still lower than at any time since the end of 2002. Employment rates have been higher than Wales and Northern Ireland for more than a decade, and have been slightly better than England since 2013.

Contrary to what the public might perceive, the number and proportion of Scotland's population claiming benefits had been on a downward trend since the start of the millennium. In the middle of 1999, almost one in five adults of working age were claiming some form of benefit (615,680 or 19.6 per cent).[26] Although the numbers fluctuated, the trend was clearly downward until the middle of 2008, by which time the number of claimants had fallen to one in six (519,090). However, a steady increase in the number of claimants followed, peaking at 583,270 at the start of 2010. Claimant numbers have since fluctuated, with the trend towards a reduction in claimant numbers (estimated at just below 500,000 in May 2015).

Adding to these economic trends has been a steady increase in Scotland's real gross disposable household income throughout this period. This sum of all household income in Scotland suggests a steady year-on-year rise in household income in Scotland from £51.1 billion in 1999 to £90.8 billion in 2013.[27] Although it would be foolish to overstate the point (as the economic vitality of Scotland will clearly impact on household poverty), taken together, these economic trends suggest that household income is not solely determined by the economy alone, otherwise far more significant reductions in poverty would have been evident in recent years. Poverty cannot be reduced to the macro-economy; economy is not the only factor explaining why people are living in poverty in Scotland.

Although not irreducible to poverty, the broader economic context sets the parameters within which distributional mechanisms will create, ameliorate or eradicate household poverty – that is, the economy determines the size of the cake that is to be shared. In times of economic growth, there is less resistance to progressive distribution. Under more stricken financial conditions, people experiencing poverty are particularly vulnerable, as those living beyond poverty seek to protect, and in the case of the better off, increase their share of overall income resource in Scotland.

What do people in Scotland think are the main reasons for poverty?

In some respects, wider public opinion in Scotland is consistent with the arguments being presented in this chapter. Using the example of child poverty, attitudinal research suggests that people in Scotland acknowledge that there are multiple causes and that 'structural' factors (such as inequality in society) contribute to the problem. On the other hand, attitudinal research also suggests that people in Scotland are still inclined to attribute poverty to individual factors and, in particular, to individual 'failings', and more inclined to do so than those residing in other parts of Britain. That 25 per cent of Scots apparently think parents' alcoholism, drug or other substance abuse is the *main* cause of child poverty in Scotland (surveyed in 2014) suggests that the wider public in Scotland is too ready to acknowledge 'individual failing' in making sense of the poverty in Scotland.[28]

Conclusion

We have identified four broad multi-faceted factors, which account for the prevalence of poverty in Scotland. Although *some* individuals may contribute to their own poverty, we would contend that structural explanations are of far greater significance in explaining the extent of Scotland's poverty. Neither are poverty trends closely aligned with economic trends. Thus, political intervention and social factors must also be considered. Between 1998 and 2010 the UK government has made commitments to tackle poverty, devised strategies and introduced policy interventions that, albeit intermittently, had an important positive impact, particularly in relation to child and pensioner poverty. Scottish government policy focus and action has also had an impact. However, the persistence of poverty for many social groups, current UK government tax and benefit policy, and the tendency for the wider public to seek explanation in ways that focus on the individual, lead to the conclusion that a positive direction of travel can no longer be assumed and that there is a need for a renewed focus to better understand and address the root causes of poverty in Scotland.

Notes

1   C Philo and J McCormick, 'Poor Places and Beyond: summary findings and policy implications', in C Philo (ed), *Off the Map: the social geography of poverty in the UK*, CPAG, 1995, pp175–88

2   Office for National Statistics, 'HI11 – Headline Indicators for Scotland', *Regional Labour Market Statistics, November 2015*, Webtable HI11, www.ons.gov.uk/ons/publications/re-reference-tables.html?edition=tcm%3A77-381809

3   Data for April to June 2013 for the UK as a whole. Office for National Statistics, *Women in the Labour Market*, available at www.ons.gov.uk/ons/dcp171776_328352 .pdf

4   Annual Survey of Hours and Earnings, 2014, Table 15 (Region by Occupation), available at www.ons.gov.uk/ons/publications/re-reference-tables.html?edition=tcm%3A77-400776

5   See note 4

6   See note 4, Table 6.1

7   See Annex J of the *Equality Outcomes and Mainstreaming Report*, available at www.gov.scot/publications/2013/04/2397/14

8   See www.closethegap.org.uk

9   See www.scottish.parliament.uk/parliamentarybusiness/currentcommittees/83008.aspx

10 See www.gov.uk/government/policies/simplifying-the-welfare-system-and-making-sure-work-pays

11 See www.gov.uk/government/publications/social-security-benefits-uprating-order-2013

12 www.cpag.org.uk/content/welfare-reform-and-work-bill-2015

13 Office for National Statistics, *The Effects of Taxes and Benefits on Household Income 2013/14*, 2015, Table 6, available at www.ons.gov.uk/ons/rel/household-income/the-effects-of-taxes-and-benefits-on-household-income/2013-2014/index.html

14 See note 13

15 See note 13

16 See note 13

17 See www.gov.scot/topics/people/fairerscotland/annualreport/annualreport2013

18 See www.gov.scot/publications/2013/09/2212

19 http://news.scotland.gov.uk/news/first-minister-appoints-poverty-adviser-1a68.aspx

20 http://news.scotland.gov.uk/news/-creating-a-fairer-scotland-1a45.aspx

21 One of Scotland's purpose targets is to raise Scotland's GDP growth rate to match that of the UK and small independent countries of the European Union.

22 Drawn from the economic purpose target web pages. See www.gov.scot/
about/performance/scotperforms/purposes/economicgrowth

23 Scottish government, *Gross Domestic Product*, Statistical Bulletin Economy
Series, Second Quarter 2015, available at www.gov.scot/Resource/0048/
00487381. pdf

24 See note 23

25 Scottish Government, *High Level Summary of Statistics Trend: employment rate
(population aged 16–64)*, accessed 5 November 2015, www.gov.scot/ topics/
statistics/browse/labour-market/trenddata

26 All data drawn from the Department for Work and Pensions data tabulation tool
at: http://tabulation-tool.dwp.gov.uk/100pc/wa/ccdate/ccgor/a_carate_r_cc
date_c_ccgor.html

27 See www.gov.scot/about/performance/scotperforms/purpose/solidarity

28 Data accessed from www.britsocat.com/Home

Section Three

Poverty in Scotland:
the evidence

Five
Is poverty falling?

John H McKendrick

Summary

- The latest data, for 2013/14, show that after housing costs are taken into account, more than one in five of Scotland's children live in poverty (22 per cent, or 210,000 children). Almost one in seven children in Scotland live with income poverty/material deprivation combined (13 per cent, or 130,000 children).
- Official statistics suggest that relative poverty has remained stable in Scotland in recent years. In both 2010/11 and 2013/14, the number of children considered to be living in relative poverty was 210,000, the number of working-age adults living in relative poverty only fluctuated between 570,000 and 600,000, and the number of people of pension age living in relative poverty was 120,000.
- Scotland did experience significant reductions in the number of children living in poverty between 1999/00 and 2011/12 (from 350,000 to 190,000).
- For more than a decade after 1995/96, the reduction in absolute poverty in Scotland was much more marked than the reduction in relative poverty. This suggests that although overall standards of living may have risen, the incomes of many households still fell substantially behind those on median incomes and above. Since 2004/05, absolute child poverty has remained stable, while relative child poverty fell significantly, before increasing in recent years.
- Scotland has lower rates of child poverty and overall poverty than other parts of the UK.
- Comparing *Households Below Average Income* data for Scotland with data used to estimate child poverty across the European Union would suggest that the child poverty risk in Scotland is among the lowest in Europe. However, Scotland fares less favourably when compared with those European nations (for example, Scandinavian countries) against which it often seeks to compare its national performance.
- There has been evidence of increasing levels of 'severe' poverty and acute income crisis among Scottish households.

Introduction

Chapter 3 described the pre-eminence of household income as a means of measuring poverty in Scotland. In this chapter, the Scottish analysis of the *Households Below Average Income* (HBAI) data is used to estimate the number of people living in poverty in Scotland and to assess whether poverty is falling, remains static or is increasing.[1] In recent years, interpretation of these data has become much more complex and their pre-eminence is now being challenged by the UK government. In this chapter, the focus is on the total number of people living in poverty – first for children and then for the population as a whole. Estimates of the number of people living in poverty from sub-groups of the population (for example, by family type or by local authority area) are considered in Chapter 7.

Child poverty

Following a period of steady growth in levels of child poverty in Scotland and the UK as a whole over the last few decades of the twentieth century, came a commitment to reduce the number of children living in poverty. Since the mid-1990s, four phases can be identified in Scottish child poverty trends. First, the UK government's historic commitment in 1999 to reduce child poverty within a generation led to actions that accelerated a trend that had started in 1996/97. From 360,000 children in Scotland living in relative poverty in 1996/97, child poverty fell in six of the following eight years to reach 250,000 in 2004/05 (after housing costs are taken to account) (see Figure 5.1). This was equivalent to a fall in the rate of child poverty from 33 per cent in 1996/97 to 25 per cent in 2004/05, but still meant that child poverty was far higher than it had been in the late 1970s and early 1980s.

Second, rates of child poverty in Scotland stabilised during the next five years, with relative poverty counts of either 240,000 or 250,000 in each year between 2004/05 and 2009/10. For both of these phases, the broad trends were characteristic of both relative poverty counts and absolute poverty counts. However, between 2009/10 and 2011/12, recorded rates of relative poverty fell (from 240,000 in 2009/10 to 190,000 in 2011/12), while rates of absolute poverty were stable (220,000 in both 2009/10 and 2011/12). This would suggest that although incomes were not improving

Figure 5.1:

Proportion of children living in absolute poverty and relative poverty (after housing costs), Scotland, 1994/95 to 2013/14

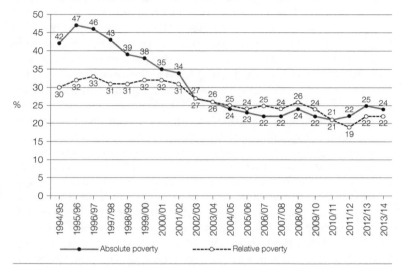

Source: Scottish Government, *Poverty and Income Inequality in Scotland: 2013/14*, 2015, Tables A1 and A2

Notes:

1. Figures are derived from the Family Resources Survey.
2. The modified OECD equivalisation scale has been used in the calculations and the figures refer to income after housing costs have been deducted.
3. See Table 3.1 for definitions of absolute poverty (low income) and relative poverty (low income).

as a whole, low-income households with children saw their incomes protected relative to those on median incomes and above. Previous government decisions to invest in child benefits and tax credits helped to reduce relative poverty, even through a period of economic crisis.

Finally, recent trends are less stable, with a sharp rise in both absolute and relative poverty between 2011/12 and 2012/13 and more modest falls between 2012/13 and 2013/14 (for example, the number of children counted as living in relative poverty in Scotland for the last three years has been 190,000, 220,000 and 210,000). While single year figures need to be treated with caution, the overall trend appears to be an increase in child poverty since 2011/12. Independent modelling by the Insititute for Fiscal Studies[2] and, more recently, the Resolution Foundation[3] suggests this trend is likely to worsen markedly, with massive increases in child poverty by 2020.

As of 2013/14, according to these Scottish government figures, 210,000 children living in Scotland are part of households whose income is so much lower than the typical income for households in Scotland that they are considered to be living in poverty (ie, they live in a household with below 60 per cent of median equivalised income, after housing costs are considered). In terms of proportions, and using the same Scottish government figures, more than one in five children in Scotland (22 per cent) live in relative poverty. Even using the 'before housing costs' measure that is used, for reasons highlighted in Chapter 3, by the government when measuring progress against child poverty targets, almost one in seven children in Scotland (140,000) are considered to be living in relative poverty.

Although the Scottish HBAI has now several years' worth of data on the 'tier 3' measure of child poverty (Table 3.1 in Chapter 3, measuring the combination of low household income and material deprivation), changes in the items used to measure deprivation in 2010/11 make it difficult to draw clear conclusions about rates and trends over time. However, this measure of child poverty tends to suggest that there has been growth in poverty/material deprivation among children in Scotland in recent years. Whereas 90,000 children were estimated to experience poverty/material deprivation combined (9 per cent of children) in 2011/12, this has risen by 20,000 in each of the last two years.

As all the above figures show, child poverty persists at a disturbingly high level in Scotland.

Figure 5.2 compares the percentage of children living in households with incomes of below 60 per cent median earnings in Scotland (relative poverty), using the after housing costs measure, with those from other Government Office regions[4] and national regions in the UK for 2013/14: Scotland has the lowest proportion of children living in poverty in the UK.

Figure 5.3 compares the percentage of children living in households with incomes of below 60 per cent median earnings in their own nation (relative poverty) across the European Union for 2014, using the before housing costs measure that is favoured by the European Union.

In contrast to the situation just a few years ago, Scotland now has a significantly lower proportion of its children living in poverty than in the European Union as a whole. Children in Scotland only fare worse than those growing up in the Nordic countries, Netherlands and Cyprus.

Figure 5.2:

Children living in low-income households in Scotland and other parts of the UK, 2013/14

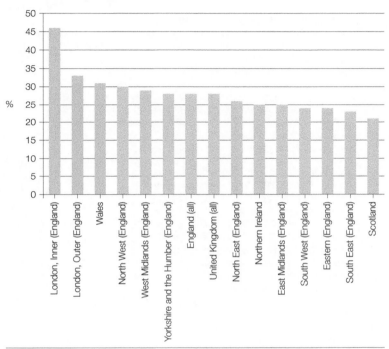

Source: Department for Work and Pensions, *Households Below Average Income: an analysis of the income distribution 1994/95 – 2013/14*, 2015, Table 4.6db

Notes:
1. Low household income is defined as below 60 per cent UK median income, after housing costs and including self-employed.
2. The modified OECD equivalised scale has been used (three-year average).

Overall poverty in Scotland

Although children and pensioners have been the primary focus of the UK and Scottish governments' anti-poverty activity, a fuller understanding of poverty in the UK requires a more broadly based analysis of poverty among the population as a whole.

Figure 5.3:

Children living in low-income households in European nations, 2014

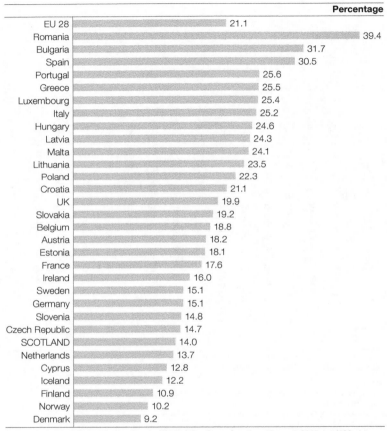

Percentage

Nation	Percentage
EU 28	21.1
Romania	39.4
Bulgaria	31.7
Spain	30.5
Portugal	25.6
Greece	25.5
Luxembourg	25.4
Italy	25.2
Hungary	24.6
Latvia	24.3
Malta	24.1
Lithuania	23.5
Poland	22.3
Croatia	21.1
UK	19.9
Slovakia	19.2
Belgium	18.8
Austria	18.2
Estonia	18.1
France	17.6
Ireland	16.0
Sweden	15.1
Germany	15.1
Slovenia	14.8
Czech Republic	14.7
SCOTLAND	14.0
Netherlands	13.7
Cyprus	12.8
Iceland	12.2
Finland	10.9
Norway	10.2
Denmark	9.2

Source: Eurostat, *At Risk of Poverty Rate by Detailed Age Group (less than 18 years), 2015*, tessi120, data updated 30 October 2015

Notes:
1. Low household income is defined as below 60 per cent national median income after social transfers, before housing costs and including self-employed.
2. The modified OECD equivalised scale has been used.
3. Not all 2012 data were available for European nations at the time of writing. 2011 data are presented for Estonia, Iceland and Ireland.
4. As is normal for international comparisons, the Eurostat UK data use the before housing costs measure, whereas the UK data in Figure 5.2 used the after housing costs measure (see Chapter 3 for explanation).
5. Scotland data are from Scottish Government, *Poverty and Income Inequality in Scotland: 2013/14*, 2015, Table A1 (before housing costs). Comparison of Scotland and European countries must be made with caution, as these are drawn from different data sources.

Mirroring the presentation of evidence for child poverty, Figure 5.4 shows the number of individuals in Scotland who have been living in poverty since 1994/95.

According to these figures, over one million individuals in Scotland are currently living in households regarded as experiencing 'absolute poverty' (more than 60 per cent below median equivalised household income, after housing costs have been deducted, at 2011/12 levels). 940,000 individuals in Scotland are living in households regarded as experiencing 'relative poverty' (60 per cent below median equivalised household income at current levels, after housing costs have been deducted). In terms of proportions, around one in five individuals in Scotland live in poverty, whether defined as a relative measure (18 per cent) or an absolute measure (20 per cent).

Figure 5.4:

Number of individuals living in absolute poverty and relative poverty (after housing costs), Scotland, 1994/95 to 2013/14

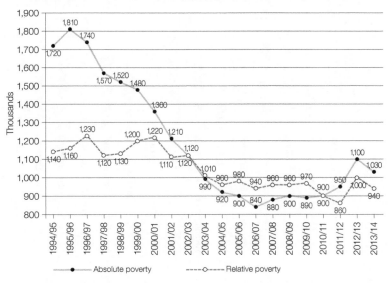

Source: Scottish Government, *Poverty and Income Inequality in Scotland: 2013/14*, 2015, Tables A1 and A2

Notes:
1. Figures are derived from the Family Resources Survey.
2. The modified OECD equivalisation scale has been used in the calculations and the figures refer to income after housing costs have been deducted.
3. See Table 3.1 for definitions of absolute poverty (low income) and relative poverty (low income).

These figures show that it is not only child poverty that is a problem in Scotland. The late 1990s and early 2000s were not characterised by the same scale of progress in reducing poverty for the population as a whole in Scotland, and there was no reduction at all in the risk of poverty for working-age adults without children. Nevertheless, some progress was evident at this time. Between 1995/96 and 2006/07, the number of individuals living in absolute poverty in Scotland fell from 1,810,000 (36 per cent) to 840,000 (17 per cent). Similarly, a fall in relative poverty can be observed – from 1,230,000 (25 per cent) in 1996/97 to 940,000 (19 per cent) in 2006/07. The later years of the first decade of the twenty-first century were characterised by the same stagnation in the level of poverty that

Figure 5.5:

Individuals living on a low income in Scotland, and other parts of the UK, 2013/14

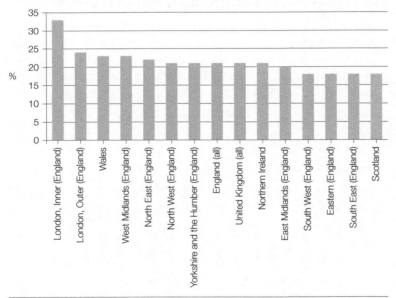

Source: Department for Work and Pensions, *Households Below Average Income: an analysis of the income distribution 1994/95 – 2013/14*, 2015, Table 3.6db

Notes:
1. Low household income is defined as below 60 per cent UK median income, after housing costs and including self-employed.
2. The modified OECD equivalised scale has been used.

is evident for children. Similarly, in more recent years, the official statistics on relative poverty report an overall, but slight, reduction in the number of people living in poverty in Scotland.

Figure 5.5 compares the percentage of individuals living in households with incomes of below 60 per cent median earnings in Scotland, after housing costs have been deducted (relative poverty), with those from other Government Office regions and national regions in the UK for 2013/14.

As for children (Figure 5.2), there is evidence to suggest that the level of poverty in Scotland compares favourably with that in other parts of the UK. Poverty in Scotland, on the whole, is lower than in Wales, England and Northern Ireland and in all English regions, except for the East of England, South East and South West (with which it shares the same level of poverty).

Once again though, although UK comparative data cast Scotland in a positive light, this should not be allowed to obscure the fact that many thousands of people in Scotland are currently living in poverty – 1,030,000 people if the measure of absolute poverty is used, or 940,000 if we adopt the relative measure of poverty (Figure 5.4).

Figure 5.6 compares whole-population poverty across Europe using the same approach (and with the same caveats) as Figure 5.3 did for children. In contrast to evidence for children, Scotland has rates of overall poverty that is slightly above the European Union average. There are far more countries in the European Union that have a lower incidence of overall poverty than Scotland than there are that have a higher incidence of overall poverty than Scotland.

Acute poverty is on the increase

Although almost one million people living in poverty in Scotland, including one in five children, could never be presented as a positive state of affairs, recent official statistics on income poverty do not suggest a situation that has worsened dramatically in recent years. On the other hand, and in contrast, recent trends also suggest that there has been an increase in material deprivation (and income poverty combined) among children in Scotland. More generally, the sense that poverty is intensifying, with an increasing number of people facing an immediate and acute income crisis, is one that is consistent with the observations of research activists from the third sector,[5] and with the rising level of demand on food banks.[6]

Figure 5.6:

Individuals living in low-income households in European nations, 2014

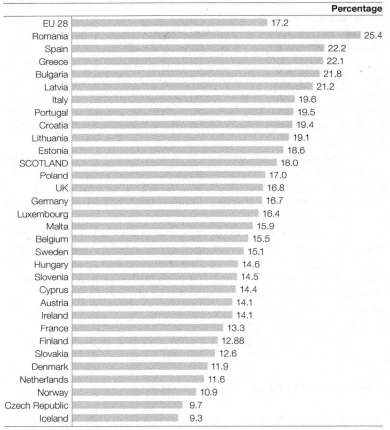

Percentage

EU 28	17.2
Romania	25.4
Spain	22.2
Greece	22.1
Bulgaria	21.8
Latvia	21.2
Italy	19.6
Portugal	19.5
Croatia	19.4
Lithuania	19.1
Estonia	18.6
SCOTLAND	18.0
Poland	17.0
UK	16.8
Germany	16.7
Luxembourg	16.4
Malta	15.9
Belgium	15.5
Sweden	15.1
Hungary	14.6
Slovenia	14.5
Cyprus	14.4
Austria	14.1
Ireland	14.1
France	13.3
Finland	12.88
Slovakia	12.6
Denmark	11.9
Netherlands	11.6
Norway	10.9
Czech Republic	9.7
Iceland	9.3

Source: Eurostat, *At Risk of Poverty by Poverty Threshold, Age and Sex – [ilc_li02]*, 2015, data updated 30 October 2015

Notes:
1. Low household income is defined as below 60 per cent national median income, before housing costs and including self-employed.
2. The modified OECD equivalised scale has been used.
3. Data from 2011 are used (in preference to 2012), as 2012 data were not available for all European nations at the time of writing.
4. As is normal for international comparisons, the Eurostat UK data use the before housing costs measure, whereas the UK data in Figure 5.6 used the after housing costs measure (see Chapter 3 for explanation).
5. Scotland data are from Scottish Government, *Poverty and Income Inequality in Scotland: 2013/14*, 2015, Table A1 (before housing costs). Comparison of Scotland and European countries must be made with caution, as these are drawn from different data sources.

Figure 5.7:

Intensity of poverty among those in relative poverty (after housing costs), by age group, Scotland, 2010/11 to 2012/13

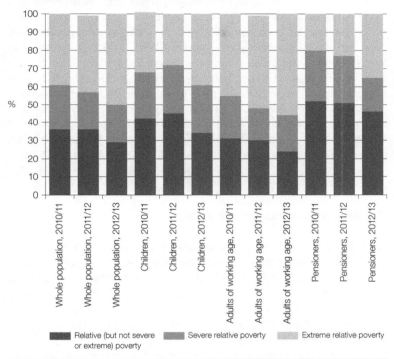

Relative (but not severe or extreme) poverty   Severe relative poverty   Extreme relative poverty

Source: Scottish Government, *Severe Poverty in Scotland*, 2015, Charts 2, 4, 6 and 8

Notes:
1. Figures are derived from the Family Resources Survey.
2. The modified OECD equivalised scale has been used in the calculations and the figures refer to income after housing costs have been deducted.
3. See Table 3.1 for definitions of absolute poverty (low income) and relative poverty (low income). Severe poverty is defined as those experiencing relative poverty whose household income is below 50% of the UK median income; those experiencing extreme poverty have household incomes below 40% of the UK median income.

Further analysis of income poverty trends seems to suggest that these contrasting accounts are not inconsistent. Experimental Scottish government analysis in 2015 introduced two new poverty thresholds: a severe poverty threshold and an extreme poverty threshold – households with incomes below 50 per cent and 40 per cent of the median income respectively.[7] The analysis demonstrates that while overall rates of poverty have been fairly stable in recent years, there has been a significant intensification of poverty among those who experience it (Figure 5.7). Thus, for children, working-age adults and pensioners, the proportion of those living in poverty who experience *extreme* poverty was estimated to have risen dramatically in recent years, although Scottish government analysis has subsequently identified concerns with these data. The nature of poverty in Scotland seems to be changing, in ways that can only make life much more difficult for already the most vulnerable people in Scotland.

Poverty measures under threat

On 1 July 2015, Iain Duncan Smith, the UK Secretary of State for Work and Pensions, gave notice of a 'new and strengthened approach to tracking the life chances of Britain's most disadvantaged children'. If passed, the UK government's Welfare Reform and Work Bill will repeal most of the Child Poverty Act 2010, and see the abandonment of UK poverty-reduction targets and the introduction of new 'measures of poverty' that do not include income.[8]

Reaching the point where measures of child poverty are enshrined in law was a hard-fought gain for those concerned with tackling poverty in the UK, which if lost, as proposed by the UK government, will be much lamented. However, these data will continue to be published (alongside 'new' and as yet unspecified indicators of child poverty). These poverty numbers have a central role in monitoring progress and measuring success and it is incumbent upon the anti-poverty sector to give the same prominence to making sense of these numbers, as has been characteristic of the last few decades.

Conclusion

The figures in this chapter have outlined the broad trends in poverty using the key measure of household income. All the data show that income poverty remains a significant problem in Scotland, although not all data point to worsening conditions. Significant falls were evident in child and pensioner poverty from 1998. More recent falls in levels of poverty from 2008/09 to 2011/12, at a time of broader economic stress, reflect the positive impact of providing social protection through inflation-linking benefit levels. However, with a decoupling of benefit uprating from inflation and severe cuts to social security now proposed, without adequate measures to fully compensate workers on low incomes, it seems likely that following a period of real progress there will now be a return to rapidly increasing rates of poverty in the years ahead. There is clearly a need to reappraise how poverty is tackled in Scotland if the UK and Scottish government aims (as stated and however measured) are to reduce the numbers living in poverty. As will be shown in Chapter 7, some groups in Scottish society are at even greater risk of poverty than these aggregate figures suggest.

Notes

1   Scottish Government, *Poverty and Income Inequality in Scotland: 2013/14*, 2015
2   Modelling (January 2014) by the Institute for Fiscal Studies suggests that up to 100,000 children will be pushed into poverty by 2020, with the proportion of children living in poverty in Scotland forecast to increase to 26.2% by 2020, after housing costs are taken into account. See www.ifs.org.uk/publications/ 7054, Appendix, Table B2
3   See www.resolutionfoundation.org/publications/a-poverty-of-information-assess ing-the-governments-new-child-poverty-focus-and-future-trends
4   Government Offices for the English regions were abolished in 2011, having been established in 1994. However, English regional data on poverty are still published for these areas.
5   For example, see F McHardy, *What's Going on in Glasgow?* Research Welfare Trackers Briefing Number 3, Poverty Alliance, 2014, and CPAG in Scotland's Early Warning System, www.cpag.org.uk/scotland/early-warning-system
6   www.cpag.org.uk/sites/default/files/Cpag_Food_Bank_Report.pdf
7   Scottish Government, *Severe Poverty in Scotland*, 2015, available at www.gov. scot/resource/0047/00473036.pdf
8   See http://services.parliament.uk/bills/2015-16/welfarereformandwork.html

Six

Is income inequality reducing?

John H McKendrick

Summary

- The Scottish government aims to reduce income inequality by 2017.
- Income inequality has not reduced in Scotland over the last decade.
- Recent and projected trends for the key identified drivers of change for income inequality are largely positive, although these do not seem to be impacting on levels of income inequality in Scotland.
- Now that it is unlikely that income inequality in Scotland will reduce dramatically by 2017, substantial changes in policy, practice and strategy are required if this national purpose target is to be recalibrated as a future goal.

Introduction: failure to deliver on income inequality despite its centre-stage billing

In 2007, the Scottish government set itself the target of reducing income inequality in Scotland. As noted in Chapter 2, the high-level Solidarity Purpose Target commits Scotland 'to increase overall income and the proportion of income earned by the three lowest income deciles as a group by 2017'. The Scottish government's commitment to reduce income inequality (the distribution of income) is set within a commitment to increase overall income for Scotland as a whole. Thus, the aim is for the poorest Scots to receive a bigger share of a bigger cake. For the overall income component of this measure, the Scottish government uses Office for National Statistics estimates of gross disposable household income, which suggests that household income in Scotland has risen consistently year on year over the last decade – from £51.1 billion in 1999 to £90.80 billion in 2013 (2013 prices).[1]

However, the central focus of the Solidarity Purpose Target is the distribution of household income. Not only does this imply analysis of the contemporary estimate and direction of change of income inequality in Scotland, it also involves consideration of 'direction of change' evidence for the key drivers of income inequality. According to the Scottish government, income inequality will be tackled by: the accessibility of employment opportunities, especially for those on lower incomes; opportunities for the lower paid to improve their skills; changes in the income differential between the lowest and highest paid occupations; and entitlement to, and take-up of, benefits.[2] This chapter presents evidence on the current state of income inequality in Scotland and the key drivers that may influence it.

Income inequality: a persistent problem in Scotland

The big, bad picture in Scotland

Income inequality in Scotland is stark. The 'poorest' third of Scotland's households share only 14.4 per cent of Scotland's income.[3] Although a broader population than that which is living in poverty, this is the group that is the focus of the Scottish government's Solidarity Purpose Target. While this group's share of Scotland's total income rose by 0.3% in 2013/14, it fell in the two years preceding that and has not improved over all since 2004/05 (Figure 6.1).

However, strictly speaking, according to the Scottish government criterion, income inequality has neither reduced nor increased in Scotland in recent years. The Solidarity Purpose Target specifies that income inequality is increasing if the income share of the poorest 30 per cent in Scotland falls by one percentage point or more (or if total income falls). Income inequality is improving if the same group increases its share of income by one percentage point or more (and total income does not fall). These targets are set against a baseline for 2006/07, when the poorest 30 per cent of individuals in Scotland shared only 13.9 per cent of income. Although the income share of this group was below this baseline level for the next three years, it did not fall below 12.9 per cent (baseline minus 1 per cent) and thus income inequality is not considered to have increased according to the definition of the Solidarity Purpose Target. Similarly, the percentage point rise over the next year to 14.5 per cent in 2010/11 did not exceed the 14.9 per cent that would be required to denote progress in tackling income inequality.

Figure 6.1:

Share of total income by three lowest income groups (deciles) in Scotland (the Solidarity Purpose Target), 1999/00 to 2013/14

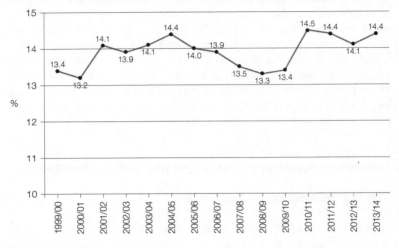

Source: Scottish Government, Solidarity Purpose Target, available at www.gov.scot/about/performance/ scotperforms/purpose/solidarity#chart

It is also significant that the Solidarity Purpose Target focuses on the poorest 30 per cent in Scotland. This includes individuals who would not be defined as living in income poverty (14 per cent of all individuals using the before housing costs relative income poverty measure, favoured by the Scottish government). Figure 6.2 compares the family work status profile of different groups that are the focus of the Solidarity Purpose Target in Scotland across the lowest income deciles.

In contrast to the focus on people living in poverty (largely, the population of the lowest two deciles in Figure 6.2), the Scottish government's approach to 'income inequality' (with its focus on the poorest 30 per cent) broadens the range of target groups. In theory, compared to a narrower focus on people experiencing poverty, this means that: relatively more attention is given to low-paid households; relatively less focus is given to workless households in which the head or spouse is unemployed; and relatively less focus is given to self-employed households.

Figure 6.2:

Profile of bottom three income deciles in Scotland, 2013/14

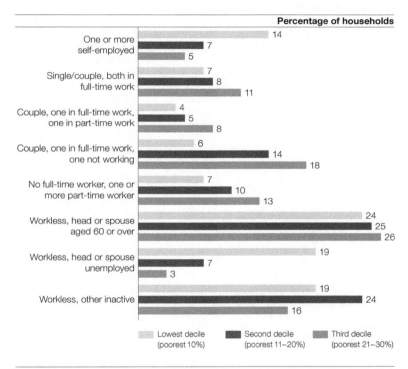

Percentage of households

	Lowest decile (poorest 10%)	Second decile (poorest 11–20%)	Third decile (poorest 21–30%)
One or more self-employed	14	7	5
Single/couple, both in full-time work	7	8	11
Couple, one in full-time work, one in part-time work	4	5	8
Couple, one in full-time work, one not working	6	14	18
No full-time worker, one or more part-time worker	7	10	13
Workless, head or spouse aged 60 or over	24	25	26
Workless, head or spouse unemployed	19	7	3
Workless, other inactive	19	24	16

Source: Scottish Government, *Poverty and Income Inequality in Scotland: 2013/14*, 2015, Table A12

Other ways of measuring income inequality also confirm the lack of progress in tackling income inequality. The Scottish government estimate of our *Gini* co-efficient (a widely used measure of overall income inequality for nations) suggests that Scotland's distribution of income has not changed since 2004/05.[4] On the other hand, the same analysis demonstrates that Scotland has, consistently, had a more equitable distribution of income, compared to Great Britain and the UK as a whole.

Figure 6.3:

Income inequality in European nations, as measured by the *Gini* co-efficient, 2014

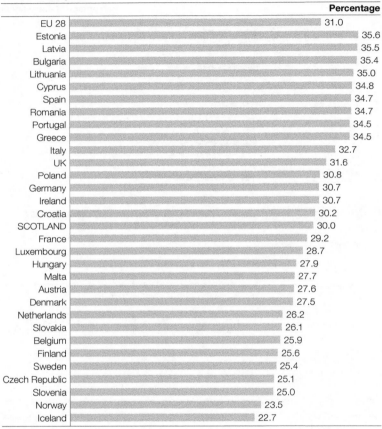

	Percentage
EU 28	31.0
Estonia	35.6
Latvia	35.5
Bulgaria	35.4
Lithuania	35.0
Cyprus	34.8
Spain	34.7
Romania	34.7
Portugal	34.5
Greece	34.5
Italy	32.7
UK	31.6
Poland	30.8
Germany	30.7
Ireland	30.7
Croatia	30.2
SCOTLAND	30.0
France	29.2
Luxembourg	28.7
Hungary	27.9
Malta	27.7
Austria	27.6
Denmark	27.5
Netherlands	26.2
Slovakia	26.1
Belgium	25.9
Finland	25.6
Sweden	25.4
Czech Republic	25.1
Slovenia	25.0
Norway	23.5
Iceland	22.7

Source:

1. EU data: European Union Statistics on Income and Living Conditions (EU-SILC). Drawn from the Eurostat Data Explorer Tool. Data table tessi190, 2015

2. Scottish data: drawn from Scottish government analysis of the *Households Below Average Income* dataset, www.gov.scot/topics/statistics/browse/social-welfare/incomepoverty/coreanalysis/additionalpovertytables

Notes:

1. Higher numbers represent higher levels of income inequality.

2. In the Scottish government's analysis of *Households Below Average Income* data, the Great Britain *Gini* co-efficient was described as 34.0. The EU-SILC estimate for the UK is lower than this estimate. Although this may reflect Great Britain/UK differences, it may also suggest that the Scottish *Gini* co-efficient would be slightly lower if robust data were available through the EU-SILC.

Scotland in context

Although European Union data to estimate income inequality does not directly compare Scotland to other European Union nations, with due caution the Scottish government estimates can be used to position ourselves in the wider European context; income inequality in both Scotland and the UK as a whole is not far removed from the typical income distribution in Europe.[5]

Gender pay gap

Income inequality is measured for households. However, income inequality in Scotland comes in different guises. Among the most significant of the income inequalities that exist among the population in Scotland is the gender pay gap. Regrettably, the gender pay gap has been an ever-present feature in earlier editions of *Poverty in Scotland*.

Table 6.1 shows that women working in full-time paid employment earn just over £4 for every £5 that men earn (82.5 per cent of men's earnings). Expressed differently, at present levels of pay, women would need to work almost a 50-hour week to earn the same amount as men working a 40-hour week in Scotland. A significant gender pay gap for full-time workers is evident for all occupational groups, with women's pay falling to almost three-fifths of that of men's for 'skilled trades'.[6] The gender pay gap is more complex for part-time workers, with inequity being less marked and several examples of women appearing to be paid more than men in some occupational sectors.[7] More optimistically, if the Scottish Living Wage Campaign continues to extend its reach, this may contribute toward the reduction in the gender pay gap, given that women are over-represented in jobs that currently fail to pay at living wage rates.

Key drivers of change for income inequality in Scotland

In this section, we focus on the drivers of income inequality that are acknowledged by the Scottish government as areas for which, at least in part, it has responsibility. Social security and taxation policies have perhaps

Table 6.1:

Gender gap in weekly gross earnings of full-time and part-time employees by occupational group, Scotland, 2014

	Gross median weekly earnings					
	Full time			Part time		
	Men £	Women £	Women as a % of men	Men £	Women £	Women as a % of men
Managers, directors and senior officials	831.40*	642.90	77.3%	***	***	***
Professional occupations	731.50	667.70	91.3%	264.00**	330.90	125.3%
Associate professional and technical	610.80	527.80	86.4%	***	245.20*	***
Administrative and secretarial	432.10	379.80	87.9%	152.80**	189.70	124.1%
Skilled trade	495.00	337.40*	68.2%	186.60*	158.40**	84.9%
Caring, leisure and other service	395.50	346.00	87.5%	164.10**	186.60	113.7%
Sales and customer service	332.30	313.80	94.4%	150.40*	133.10	88.5%
Process, plant and machine operatives	471.10	339.70*	72.1%	151.70**	***	***
Elementary	367.50	280.80	74.6%	125.00*	117.00	93.6%
All occupations	558.40	460.60	82.5%	153.00	177.50	116.0%

Source: *Annual Survey of Hours and Earnings, 2014, Provisional Results*, Table 3.1a, available at
www.ons.gov.uk/ons/publications/re-reference-tables.html?edition=tcm%3A77-337425

Notes:
1. Employees on adult rates whose pay was not affected by absence for the survey period.
2. * Treat estimate with caution
   ** Treat estimate with high caution
   *** Insufficient sample size to estimate

the greatest power to transform income inequality in Scotland, and although a degree of additional responsibility for both is set to be devolved to Scotland, at present, the key levers rest with the UK.

Employment opportunities

It is widely understood that the Scottish labour market is in the midst of a period of flux and adjustment, with the loss of public sector jobs and a consequent structural shift away from public sector employment. A further round of contraction in public sector employment is expected in 2016 and 2017. In terms of the anticipated impact of these changes on income inequality, all that can be said with certainty is that it is not at all clear whether the changing landscape of employment opportunities will reduce, maintain or exacerbate income inequality in the medium term.

However, the contraction of public sector employment in recent years has not led to significant increases in levels of unemployment in Scotland. Indeed, unemployment levels in Scotland have fallen steadily – for both men and women, and for all age groups – over the last few years: from 8.1 per cent between July 2011 to June 2012 to 5.9 per cent between July 2014 and June 2015.[8] Although this is to be welcomed, it also raises doubt over the extent to which simply increasing levels of employment in Scotland can positively impact on poverty and income inequality, given the lack of progress in both these areas as rates of unemployment have fallen.

Skill development

Enhancing the skills of those traditionally at greater risk of lower income is recognised by the Scottish government as one means of tackling income inequality. Skills Development Scotland promotes a series of initiatives, each of which is designed to improve earning and employment prospects in Scotland.[9] Furthermore, in an advanced economy, one key means to improve career-earning prospects is through positive educational outcomes.

At school level, 'positive destinations' are defined as leaving school to either enter higher or further education, or to start training, employment, voluntary work or an activity agreement. Just over nine of every 10 school leavers in 2014 were reported to be in a positive destination in March 2015 (91.7 per cent), the second successive annual rise.[10] There has also been an increase in positive destinations for leavers from Scotland's most deprived areas. Although still lower than the Scottish average, 85 per cent of 2014 leavers from Scotland's 20 per cent most deprived areas were reported to be in a positive destination in March 2015.[11] This is particularly welcome, given the persistence and depth of the attainment gap between pupils from more and less deprived areas. For example, half as many pupils (39 per cent) from Scotland's 20 per cent most deprived areas gained at least one Level 6 qualification in 2013/14 (equivalent to an A–C in a Scottish Higher), compared to pupils from the least deprived areas (79.7 per cent).[12]

In 2012/13, 238,805 students were undertaking courses at one of Scotland's colleges,[13] while in 2013/14, 279,495 students were undertaking a higher education course in Scotland.[14] These numbers suggest high levels of skills and personal development in Scotland. However, for the last five years, there has been a year-on-year reduction in the number of students at Scotland's colleges: the student population is less than two-thirds of 2007/08 (63 per cent), although the 'full-time equivalent' totals are similar (reflecting the fact that more students are now studying full time).[15] Furthermore, there was a 3 per cent reduction in the number of students entering Scottish higher education institutions between 2010/11 and 2013/14.[16] Perhaps of equal importance to summary levels of participation, is consideration of whether or not participation is socially progressive – ie, are students from disadvantaged backgrounds as, more or less likely than those from non-disadvantaged backgrounds to study in further education or higher education? Despite efforts to widen participation, the proportion of Scottish-domiciled entrants to higher education from the 20 per cent most deprived areas has only increased by one percentage point in the last decade (15.9 per cent in 2013/14, an under-representation of 3.4 percentage points against the population).[17]

Making work pay

Providing opportunities to work and enhancing the skills that will increase the chances of finding work (and finding better paid work) will only impact on income inequality if work is sufficiently well paid across the labour market. At present, work does not pay well for everyone. Table 6.1 has already demonstrated that women in full-time employment are less well paid than men. This table also highlights the scale of the differences in typical pay across occupational groups. For example, men working full time in 'sales and customer service' in Scotland are typically paid £332.30 per week; men in 'professional occupations' are paid more than double this amount (£731.50 per week). Incidentally, the typical weekly pay for a man in 'sales and customer services' is well below the poverty threshold for a couple with two children aged five and 14 (Table 3.2). It is not insignificant, given the current UK government's concerns about tax credits, that such families are currently reliant either on the state to lift them out of poverty (for example, through child benefit or tax credits) or on a second household income.

There has been growing recognition among the anti-poverty sector that low pay is a significant problem in its own right. A 'living wage' in

November 2015 was defined as £8.25 per hour,[18] a figure in excess of the 'national living wage' for over 25s that will be introduced in April 2016, following announcements in the summer 2015 Budget. Albeit welcome for those eligible to receive it, the introduction of what is essentially an enhanced national minimum wage for some will still fail to ensure that Scotland's lowest paid workers are remunerated at a level that allows them to sustain a decent standard of living. The Scottish Living Wage Campaign seeks to address this problem and in 2015 presented evidence that almost 470 employers in Scotland had been 'accredited' as living wage employers.[19] Nevertheless, research in Scotland by KPMG estimates that one in every five workers in Scotland (441,000) are remunerated below the living wage, with the highest proportion of jobs below the living wage found in East Renfrewshire (32 per cent of jobs in this district), despite its being one of the most affluent parts of Scotland.[20] It should also be noted that the living wage, as defined by the Living Wage Campaign, is set using a methodology that assumes employees will also receive all the in-work benefits and tax credits to which they are entitled.[21]

Welfare benefit entitlement and take-up

The explicit goal of welfare reform is to undermine the supposed comfort of 'living on benefits' and facilitate moves into employment.[22] These changes have not been well received by anti-poverty campaigners, many economists and, indeed, the Scottish government. Impact analysis has demonstrated that, through welfare reform, those people who rely on benefits and tax credits will be less well off in the years ahead.[23] UK government analysis demonstrates that the overall impact of recent tax and benefit policies are largely regressive – reducing the incomes of those in the lower half of the income distribution while increasing those in most of the top half.[24]

Notwithstanding the difficulties these changes will present to the most financially vulnerable, the purported 'simplification' of the benefits system that is part of welfare reform could, in theory, offer the means to tackle one of the most persistent and perplexing problems that exacerbate income inequality – low take-up of welfare benefits. The Department for Work and Pensions (DWP) estimates that, for the UK as a whole a pounds sterling take-up rate of: between 67 per cent and 73 per cent for pension credit; 78 per cent and 82 per cent for income support and employment and support allowance; 59 per cent and 66 per cent for jobseeker's allowance; and 85 per cent and 88 per cent for housing benefit.[25] Clearly, then, there is a significant problem of non-take-up of welfare benefits in the UK. This, along with the low financial value of benefits to which people are entitled, is undoubtedly exacerbating income inequality, despite the efforts of the Scottish government to invest in welfare rights advice and protect citizens from selected cuts – for example, the underoccupancy penalty or 'bedroom tax' and cuts to the help available for council tax.

Conclusion

Income inequality has been a persistent problem in Scotland. There is no sign of this inequality lessening, although there is some positive evidence in terms of the direction of travel for what are currently identified to be the primary drivers of change. This would tend to suggest that, without more radical and significant shifts in policy, practice and strategy to address low pay, skills gaps, tax policy, social security adequacy and benefit take-up, there will be no significant reduction in income inequality in the years ahead. However, even in a time of overall pay restraint and labour market 'restructuring', it may be possible to make progress against the Solidarity Purpose Target if sufficient attention is paid to protecting and increasing the relative share of overall pay, and wider income distribution, of those in the bottom three deciles. Less optimistically, current welfare reform and the inadequacy of current proposals to boost the incomes of all the lowest paid workers makes it more likely that the relative share of overall income will reduce for the least affluent in the next few years.

Notes

1   See www.gov.scot/about/performance/scotperforms/purpose/solidarity
2   See note 1
3   See note 1. From 2004/05, four years of increasing income inequality were followed by two years of reducing income inequality. For the three years since 2010/11, income inequality in Scotland has been stable.
4   Access additional analysis, downloading Excel datasheet at www.gov.scot/topics/statistics/browse/social-welfare/incomepoverty/coreanalysis
5   Note that this comparison used Scottish government data and compares them with Eurostat data. See table notes for more details.

6   Caution is required with this statistic, given that it is based on a low number of women providing income data.

7   There is a need for cautious interpretation of these data, with low returns for all occupational groupings.

8   Office for National Statistics, *Regional Labour Market HI11: headline indicators for Scotland, October 2015*, Table 2(2), available at www.ons.gov.uk/ons/publications/ re-reference-tables.html?edition=tcm%3A77-381057

9   See www.skillsdevelopmentscotland.co.uk/what-we-do

10 Scottish Government, *Summary Statistics for Attainment, Leaver Destinations and Healthy Living, Number 5: 2015 Edition*, 2015, Table 2, available at www.gov.scot/publications/2015/06/2579/0

11 See note 10, Table 3

12 See note 10, Table 6

13 See www.scotland.gov.uk/topics/statistics/browse/lifelong-learning/trendfe students

14 Scottish Funding Council, *Higher Education Students and Qualifiers at Scottish Institutions 2013/14*, 2015, available at www.sfc.ac.uk/web/files/statistical_publications_sfcst042015_highereducationstudentsandqualifiersat/sfcst042015_he_students_and_qualifiers_2013-14.pdf

15 See note 13

16 See note 14

17 Scottish Funding Council, *Higher Education Students and Qualifiers at Scottish Institutions*, 2013/4, Table 25a

18 See http://slw.povertyalliance.org/about

19 See http://scottishlivingwage.org/accreditation/find_living_wage_employers

20 Markit Group Ltd, *Living Wage Research for KPMG*, 2015, available at www.kpmg.com/UK/en/issuesandinsights/articlespublications/documents/pdf/latest%20news/kpmg-living-wage-research-2015.pdf

21 www.lboro.ac.uk/media/wwwlboroacuk/content/crsp/downloads/reports/Uprating%20the%20out%20of%20London%20Living%20Wage%20in%202015. pdf

22 Department for Work and Pensions, *Universal Credit: welfare that works*, Cm 7957, 2010, available at www.gov.uk/government/publications/universal-credit-welfare-that-works

23 See www.gov.scot/publications/2014/05/7146

24 http://cdn.hm-treasury.gov.uk/budget2013_distributional_analysis.pdf, Chart 2F

25 Department for Work and Pensions, *Income-related Benefits: estimates of take-up, financial year 2013/14 (experimental)*, 2015, available at www.gov.uk/government/uploads/system/uploads/attachment_data/file/437501/ir-benefits-take-up-main-report-2013-14.pdf

Seven

Who lives in poverty?

John H McKendrick

Summary

- Children are at greater risk of poverty than both working-age adults and pensioners, with one in five of Scotland's children growing up in poverty in 2013/14 (22 per cent), compared with 19 per cent of working-age adults and 12 per cent of pensioners.
- Since 1994/95, the overall number of adults of working age who are living in poverty in Scotland has increased.
- In the UK, lone parents are almost twice as likely to be living in poverty than couples with children.
- Gender-based poverty is most marked among people of pensionable age.
- It is important to consider both the risk of poverty and the composition of poverty if group differences are to be fully understood.
- Poverty is unevenly distributed across Scotland. The highest numbers of people living in poverty are found in Scotland's largest cities, particularly Glasgow, although poverty is also prevalent in rural Scotland.

Introduction

This chapter identifies the likelihood of living in poverty in Scotland for different groups (risk rate) and how much of Scotland's poverty is experienced by these groups (poverty composition). The risks of poverty are not spread evenly and, as was discussed in Chapter 4, there are many causes of poverty, some of which impact more strongly on particular groups.

Poverty varies across the lifecycle, by family and household type, by social status and according to where we live. The distribution of poverty across each is considered for different groups of the population. Children, youth, working-age adults and pensioners are considered for the *lifecycle*; lone parents, partnered parents and childless adults are considered for *families and households*; work status, gender, ethnicity and disability are considered for *social status*; and local authorities, urban/rural areas and data zones (very small areas) are considered for *place*.

It is important to remember that no group is homogenous and that real people share characteristics across these groupings that may increase or reduce the amount of poverty that they encounter. For example, although children in lone-parent households are, on the whole, at greater risk of experiencing poverty than children in two-parent households (41 per cent of children in lone-parent households are living in poverty, compared with 24 per cent of children in two-parent households – see Table 7.2),[1] the risk rate of a child experiencing poverty is far lower in a lone-parent household in which the lone parent works full time, than it is in a couple household in which both adults do not work (20 per cent, compared with 76 per cent – see Table 7.2). Similarly, it must also be understood that belonging to one of the groups with a higher at-risk rate of poverty does not in itself cause poverty. As Chapter 4 explained, poverty is caused by the interaction of political, social, economic and personal factors. Thus, lone parenthood, in itself, does not cause poverty. Rather, the way in which the labour market, taxation and welfare system operate in Scotland (and the UK) mean that lone parents are more likely to experience poverty. Poverty is not an inevitable outcome for lone-parent families.

Where possible, Scottish poverty data are used. Most importantly, this chapter uses the Scottish government's analysis of the *Households Below Average Income* (HBAI) data series. This provides a measure of income poverty for children, working-age adults and pensioners in Scotland.[2] Its additional analysis on the 2013/14 dataset, which has been published online, provides detail on poverty for a wider range of groups.[3] Where there is an absence of readily available data for Scotland, reference is made to the original HBAI data for the UK to describe variation within groups – for example, to identify groups of children that are at greatest risk of experiencing poverty in Scotland.[4] Although using UK data to understand poverty in Scotland is not unproblematic, commentary is limited to that data which is considered to provide insight into poverty in Scotland. Finally, reference is also made to more broadly based measures of area-based multiple deprivation in Scotland. Once again, these data are used carefully, as they do not strictly describe poverty, but rather communities with high levels of household deprivation.

Poverty across the lifecycle

Overview

People's risk of poverty and the particular barriers to escaping that poverty vary considerably over the lifecycle (Table 7.1). Although children are at highest risk of poverty, there are particular problems associated with each age stage. Least progress has been made in reducing poverty among working-age adults, while the last of the four substantial drops in the rate of pensioner poverty (from 1996/97, 2002/03, 2003/04 and 2007/08) was more than five years ago. However, we should avoid over-simplifying poverty to simple statements of particular challenges to be faced at a set of discrete life stages – experience of poverty at one stage in the life cycle can also have a significant impact on an individual's risk of poverty later on. These figures also remind us that policy interventions can impact favourably on rates of poverty: while children and pensioners benefited from governments' anti-poverty targets and strategies that were characteristic of New Labour's early years in government, those of working age did not.

Children

Despite significant improvements over time that were discussed in Chapter 5, children are still at greater risk of poverty than either working-age adults or pensioners, with more than one in five of Scotland's children growing up in poverty in 2013/14 (22 per cent), compared with 19 per cent of working-age adults and 12 per cent of pensioners (Table 7.1).

However, as Table 7.2 shows, the risk of children experiencing poverty in the UK varies hugely on account of family type, number of siblings, the work status of parents or carers, and the age of the mother. Risk rates are particularly high in lone-parent households (41 per cent), especially when that lone parent is not working (58 per cent), in couple households with part-time (but not full-time) work (56 per cent in the UK), in couple households in which no one works (76 per cent) and in households with three or more children (35 per cent).

Higher risks of poverty need to be understood in the context of the overall numbers of children experiencing poverty in the UK. Thus, it is also important to note that: almost two-thirds of children in poverty live in

Table 7.1:

Age-based variation in population living in households with below 60 per cent UK median income (after housing costs), including the self-employed, Scotland, 1994/95 to 2013/14

Year	Children	Working-age adults	Pensioners	All individuals
	%	%	%	%
1994/95	30	18	29	23
1995/96	32	18	31	23
1996/97	33	19	33	25
1997/98	31	18	28	22
1998/99	31	19	27	23
1999/00	32	20	28	24
2000/01	32	22	25	24
2001/02	31	19	24	22
2002/03	27	20	25	22
2003/04	26	18	20	20
2004/05	25	18	16	19
2005/06	24	19	16	20
2006/07	25	18	15	19
2007/08	24	18	15	19
2008/09	26	19	11	19
2009/10	24	19	12	19
2010/11	21	18	12	17
2011/12	19	17	12	16
2012/13	22	21	11	19
2013/14	22	19	12	18

Source: Scottish Government, *Poverty and Income Inequality in Scotland: 2013/14*, 2015, Table A1

Notes:
1. Figures are derived from the Family Resources Survey.
2. The modified OECD equivalisation scale has been used in the calculations and the figures refer to income after housing costs.

households in which an adult is working (62 per cent of children experiencing poverty); most children experience poverty in households headed by a couple (66 per cent); and most child poverty is found in households with either one or two children (66 per cent) (Table 7.2). Indeed, it is only when households are classified according to the age of youngest child that the risk rate and proportionate share of children experiencing poverty coincide – poverty is clearly more likely to be a characteristic feature of households with very young children (Table 7.2).

Table 7.2:

Variation among children living in households with less than 60 per cent of contemporary median household income (after housing costs), UK, 2013/14

	Risk rate	Children in low-income households
	%	%
Family type		
Lone parent	41	34
Couple	24	66
Family type and work status		
Lone parent, in full-time work	20	4
Lone parent, in part-time work	32	8
Lone parent, not working	58	22
Couple, one or more full-time self-employed	28	13
Couple, both in full-time work	5	3
Couple, one in full-time work, one in part-time work	9	6
Couple, one in full-time work, one not working	33	19
Couple, one or more in part-time work	56	9
Couple, both not in work	76	16
Number of children in household		
1	26	27
2	25	39
3 or more	35	34
Age of youngest child in household		
Under 5	30	48
5 to 10	25	27
11 to 15	28	18
16 to 19	27	7

Sources: Department for Work and Pensions, *Households Below Average Income: an analysis of the income distribution 1994/95 – 2013/14*, 2015, Tables 4.3-4.6

Notes:
1. UK figures are derived from the Family Resources Survey.
2. The modified OECD equivalisation scale has been used in the calculations and the figures refer to income after housing costs.

Working-age adults

Adults of working age in contemporary Scotland are no less likely to be living in poverty than their counterparts in the mid-1990s (Table 7.1). As for children, risk rates vary among adults of working age and are higher in the UK among the youngest adults – 54 per cent of adults with children and aged under 25 years of age are living in poverty (Table 7.3).

Table 7.3 also shows that being a parent – and, in particular, being a lone parent – and being in a household with less work, are associated with living in poverty for adults of working age in the UK (41 per cent of lone parents are living in poverty). These conclusions are predictable, but the poverty risk rate of working-age adults in workless households is notable: more than two-thirds living in households with unemployed adults are living in poverty (68 per cent).

Yet, once again, we must guard against reducing our understanding of poverty in the UK to the most at-risk groups. More than half of working-age adults living in poverty are from households without children (57 per cent), one-third of whom are living as a couple (19 per cent of all adults living in poverty). One-half of working-age adults living in poverty live in households in which at least one adult works (51 per cent). Similarly, working-age adult poverty is not limited to youth: among family heads living in poverty, one-quarter are in their forties (23 per cent) or fifties and older (26 per cent).

Pensioners

There has been no reduction in the risk of pensioners living in poverty in the last five years although their risk of poverty in Scotland has been markedly reduced from 33 per cent to 12 per cent since 1996/97 (Table 7.1).

Families and households

Lone parents

Lone parents are disproportionately represented among families experiencing poverty in the UK. They are almost twice as likely to live in poverty compared with couples with children (Table 7.3). The routes into lone parenthood are many and the characteristics of lone-parent families are varied. There are around 150,000 lone parents with dependent children in Scotland, one in four of all family households in Scotland.[5] However, lone parenthood is often not a permanent status, but is rather a stage in family life, lasting on average around five and a half years.[6] It has been estimated that one-third to one-half of all children in Scotland will spend some time in a lone-parent family.[7] The vast majority of lone parents are women (confirming common understanding), but often the reality of lone parenthood is at odds with some popular perceptions, with most lone parents having previously been married and the typical age of lone parents being 36 (contrasting the image of lone parents as single young mums).[8] At any point in time, less than 3 per cent of lone parents are teenagers and only 15 per cent have never lived with the father of their child.[9]

Partnered parents

Although lone-parent households are more likely to experience poverty (Table 7.3), the poverty experienced in two-parent households is equally important. For example, poverty is experienced in more than one in every five two-parent households in the UK (Table 7.3). Furthermore, one-third of the adults living in poverty in the UK are living in two-parent households (33 per cent) – more than three times the number of adults living in poverty in lone-parent households (10 per cent) (Table 7.3). Thus, although the risk rate of poverty is higher for lone parenthood, there is more poverty in two-parent households in the UK.

Table 7.3:

Variation among working-age adults living in households with less than 60 per cent of contemporary median household income (after housing costs), UK, 2013/14

	Risk rate %	Working-age adults in low-income households %
Presence of children in household		
None	19	57
Some	24	43
Couple and child status		
Couple, no children	12	19
Lone man, no children	26	22
Lone woman, no children	28	16
Couple, with children	22	33
Lone parent	41	10
Work status		
Single/couple, one or more full-time self-employed	23	13
Single/couple, both in full-time work	6	11
Couple, one in full-time work, one in part-time work	7	5
Couple, one in full-time work, one not working	25	13
Single/couple, no full-time, one or more in part-time work	32	14
Workless, one or more aged over 60	35	5
Workless, one or more unemployed	68	12
Workless, other inactive	54	28

Age of head of family	No child	With child	No child	With child
16–19	28	54	4	4
20–24	25		12	
25–29	15	33	5	5
30–34	13	24	3	7
35–39	17	24	3	8
40–44	22	21	4	8
45–49	16	18	5	6
50–54	17	23	6	4
55 and over	19	26	14	2

Source: Department for Work and Pensions, *Households Below Average Income: an analysis of the income distribution 1994/95 – 2013/14*, 2015, Tables 5.4, 5.5, 5.7 and 5.8

Notes:
1. Figures are derived from the Family Resources Survey.
2. The modified OECD equivalisation scale has been used in the calculations and the figures refer to income after housing costs.

Social status

Patterns of poverty are not only determined by the stage in life at which we are at, or our family status. Cross-cutting these factors are a range of social factors that are associated with the likelihood of living in poverty. Significant here is the impact of work status, gender, ethnicity and disability.

Workers/non-workers

Those in work in the UK are less likely to face poverty. Unsurprisingly, the risk of poverty is lower for households that are 'work-rich' (all adults working) than for households which are 'work-poor' (no-earner couples or for couples where part-time work is the only experience) (Table 7.3). Indeed, almost half of the adults of working age who are living in poverty are not in work (45 per cent), with the risk rate of poverty being even more marked (at 68 per cent) for households in which no adult works and at least one adult is unemployed (Table 7.3).

However, these observations should not be taken to imply that poverty is absent from households with work. After all, more than half of adults of working age who are living in poverty in the UK are from households with work (55 per cent). This poverty is spread across a range of household types (defined by work status), with a significant proportion of 'all households in poverty made up of adults of working age' being of the self-employed (13 per cent); where one is working full time and the other is not working (13 per cent); and where no one is engaged in full-time work, but one or more adults is engaged in part-time work (14 per cent). It is also significant to note that a number of adults experiencing poverty in the UK reside in households in which all adults are engaged in full-time work (11 per cent). Adult poverty is not solely a result of worklessness (entry into the labour market does not guarantee a route out of poverty).

Gender

In Scotland, more adult women live in poverty than adult men, although the risk of poverty is only marginally greater for women (18 per cent for women, compared with 16 per cent for men). There has been little change in the risk rate of poverty by gender over the last decade. Although risk rates are similar, the number of women living in poverty in Scotland is greater, which can be explained by the fact that women live longer than men. For far too many women, later life is one that is characterised by poverty. Furthermore, the Scottish government estimates suggest that 17 per cent of female pensioners living alone are in poverty, compared with only 9 per cent of male pensioners who live alone.[10] The same analysis suggests that while the risk of poverty for single female pensioners in Scotland has increased in the last two years (from 11 to 17 per cent), the risk has fallen for single male pensioners (from 16 to 9 per cent). Gender dynamics for pensioner poverty in Scotland appear to be particularly regressive for women at the current time. This may reflect women's vulnerability in not having the same level of protection as a result of historically poorer provision of private pensions and lower national insurance contributions.[11]

Disability

As for gender, disability also increases the risk of poverty in Scotland. Having a disabled adult in the family is estimated by the Scottish government to increase the risk of living in poverty from 16 per cent to 23 per cent.[12]

Ethnicity

Information about poverty and minority ethnic populations in Scotland is still scarce, hampered by the small number of respondents to the social surveys from which estimates are drawn, which in turn reflects the small size of minority ethnic populations in Scotland. However, the Scottish government estimates that, compared with the 17 per cent of those in Scotland whose ethnicity can be described as 'White British' who are living in poverty, higher risk rates are found for minority ethnic groups – ie, 21 per cent for 'Other White' populations, 20 per cent for 'Asian/Asian British' and 31 per cent for 'Mixed, Black/Black British', Chinese and Other' populations.[13] Although there is clearly an ethnic complexion to poverty in Scotland, caution is urged given the diverse populations that comprise these very general ethnic groupings.

Tenure

Arguably, the greatest gulf in the experience of poverty that cuts across social status is housing tenure. The Scottish government estimates that fewer than one in ten people who own their property are currently living in poverty (9 per cent of those who own with a mortgage and 8 per cent for those who own outright), compared with one in three of those who rent (32 per cent for those renting privately and 37 per cent of those who rent from either a council or a housing association).[14]

Place

Local authorities

It is well established that Glasgow has far more than its fair share of Scotland's poverty, whatever estimate we use.[15] However, more generally, we are poorly served with robust and regular estimates of the distribution of poverty across Scotland. The next iteration of the Scottish Index of Multiple Deprivation is due to be published in 2016 (current data pertains to 2011) and, although Bramley and Watkins have recently completed a modelling exercise for the Improvement Service, which presents fresh perspectives of the geography of poverty in Scotland,[16] there remains a pressing need for data to inform local poverty intelligence across Scotland.

The End Child Poverty coalition commisions Loughborough University to provide local estimates of child poverty across the UK[17] – the latest ones of which are presented as Figure 7.1. Predictably, Glasgow heads the list, with one in three children estimated to be living in poverty in the city. However, poverty is prevalent in many other authorities and evident in them all. Even in the Shetland islands, it is estimated that one in ten children are living in poverty.

Small area concentrations of poverty

The widespread adoption and utilisation of the Scottish Index of Multiple Deprivation has cemented the idea that Scotland's poverty is particularly concentrated in small areas. In particular, it demonstrates that Glasgow's problems are highly concentrated – in 2011, approaching one-half of small areas in Glasgow were found to be among the 15 per cent 'most deprived areas in Scotland' (41.6 per cent), with almost one-quarter of small areas in Glasgow being among the 15 per cent 'most deprived areas in Scotland' (29.6 per cent).[18]

Figure 7.1 also suggests that small area concentrations of poverty are characteristic across Scotland, with the longer bar denoting the electoral ward in each of Scotland's 32 local authorities that is estimated to have the highest incidence of child poverty. Indeed, there are local areas in the most affluent parts of Scotland (such as East Renfrewshire, East Dunbartonshire and Aberdeenshire) where one in every four children is currently living in poverty.

Urban and rural

As the discussion of poverty across Scotland's local authorities and wards emphasises, poverty is most prevalent in urban settings, although there are rural dimensions of poverty that must be acknowledged. The Scottish government's own analysis of HBAI suggests that, although relative poverty is higher in urban than rural Scotland (19 and 12 per cent, respectively), the extent of poverty in rural areas does not suggest that Scotland should only be concerned with poverty in urban areas – 130,000 people are estimated to be living in poverty in rural Scotland.[19] Sight must also not be lost of the fact that one-quarter of Scotland's poor live between the extremes of city and country – poverty is also experienced in Scotland's small towns, accessible and remote to larger centres of population.

Figure 7.1:

Local estimates of child poverty, Scottish local authorities and wards, after housing costs, 2013

| Local authority (ward with highest child poverty) | Percentage |

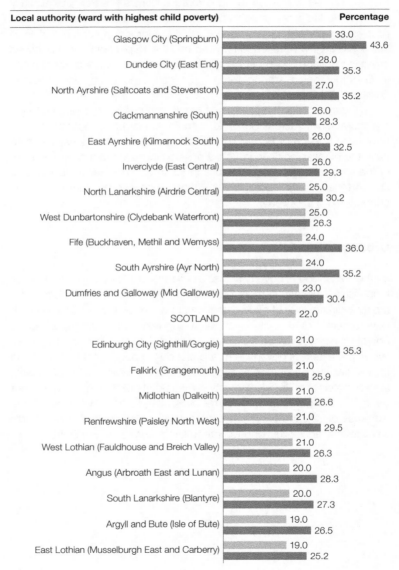

Glasgow City (Springburn) — 33.0 / 43.6
Dundee City (East End) — 28.0 / 35.3
North Ayrshire (Saltcoats and Stevenston) — 27.0 / 35.2
Clackmannanshire (South) — 26.0 / 28.3
East Ayrshire (Kilmarnock South) — 26.0 / 32.5
Inverclyde (East Central) — 26.0 / 29.3
North Lanarkshire (Airdrie Central) — 25.0 / 30.2
West Dunbartonshire (Clydebank Waterfront) — 25.0 / 26.3
Fife (Buckhaven, Methil and Wemyss) — 24.0 / 36.0
South Ayrshire (Ayr North) — 24.0 / 35.2
Dumfries and Galloway (Mid Galloway) — 23.0 / 30.4
SCOTLAND — 22.0
Edinburgh City (Sighthill/Gorgie) — 21.0 / 35.3
Falkirk (Grangemouth) — 21.0 / 25.9
Midlothian (Dalkeith) — 21.0 / 26.6
Renfrewshire (Paisley North West) — 21.0 / 29.5
West Lothian (Fauldhouse and Breich Valley) — 21.0 / 26.3
Angus (Arbroath East and Lunan) — 20.0 / 28.3
South Lanarkshire (Blantyre) — 20.0 / 27.3
Argyll and Bute (Isle of Bute) — 19.0 / 26.5
East Lothian (Musselburgh East and Carberry) — 19.0 / 25.2

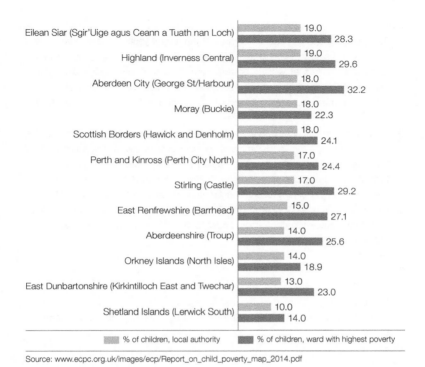

| | % of children, local authority | % of children, ward with highest poverty |

Eilean Siar (Sgir'Uige agus Ceann a Tuath nan Loch) — 19.0 / 28.3
Highland (Inverness Central) — 19.0 / 29.6
Aberdeen City (George St/Harbour) — 18.0 / 32.2
Moray (Buckie) — 18.0 / 22.3
Scottish Borders (Hawick and Denholm) — 18.0 / 24.1
Perth and Kinross (Perth City North) — 17.0 / 24.4
Stirling (Castle) — 17.0 / 29.2
East Renfrewshire (Barrhead) — 15.0 / 27.1
Aberdeenshire (Troup) — 14.0 / 25.6
Orkney Islands (North Isles) — 14.0 / 18.9
East Dunbartonshire (Kirkintilloch East and Twechar) — 13.0 / 23.0
Shetland Islands (Lerwick South) — 10.0 / 14.0

Source: www.ecpc.org.uk/images/ecp/Report_on_child_poverty_map_2014.pdf

Conclusion

This chapter has highlighted how the risk of poverty for people in Scotland is related to their age, the kinds of households in which they live, their social status and the places where they live. Marked and important variations are apparent across these factors. However, it is also clear that poverty impacts on people to a greater or lesser extent regardless of how old they are, who they live with, their gender, ethnicity, work status or geographical location. It is, therefore, important to examine risk of poverty alongside the overall proportion of the population who make up these different groups and places – the people and places with the highest risk of poverty do not necessarily account for the greatest numbers of people living in poverty.

Notes

1 This poverty gap has reduced significantly in recent years, as lone parents' risk of poverty has fallen significantly. In *Poverty in Scotland 2007*, the respective risk rates of poverty that were reported were 48% compared with 20%; and in *Poverty in Scotland 2011*, the risk rates were reported as 50% and 24%.

2 Scottish Government, *Poverty and Income Inequality in Scotland: 2013/14*, 2015

3 www.gov.scot/topics/statistics/browse/social-welfare/incomepoverty/coreanalysis

4 Department for Work and Pensions, *Households Below Average Income: an analysis of the income distribution 1994/95–2013/14*, 2015

5 http://nationalrecordsofscotland.gov.uk/statistics-and-data/statistics/statistics-by-theme/households/household-estimates/2014/list-of-tables, Table 10

6 One Parent Families Scotland, *One Parent Families: a profile*, 2009, available at www.opfs.org.uk/wp-content/uploads/2013/10/one-parent-families_a-profile_2009.pdf

7 See note 6

8 See note 6

9 See note 6

10 See Note 3

11 D Thurley, *Married Women and State Pensions*, SN 1910, House of Commons Library, 2014

12 See note 3

13 See note 3

14 See note 3

15 JH McKendrick, 'Place', in JH McKendrick, G Mooney, J Dickie, G Scott and P Kelly (eds), *Poverty in Scotland 2014: the independence referendum and beyond*, CPAG, 2014, pp127–33

16 G Bramley and D Watkins, *Local Incomes and Poverty in Scotland: developing local and small area estimates and exploring patterns of income distribution, poverty and deprivation*, Improvement Service, 2013

17 See www.ecpc.org.uk/images/ecp/Report_on_child_poverty_map_2014.pdf

18 Scottish Government, *Scottish Index of Multiple Deprivation 2012*, 2012

19 See note 3

Eight

What is life like for people experiencing poverty?

John H McKendrick

Summary

- Low-income households report far lower levels of financial wellbeing, relative to high-income households.
- Exposure to the risk of fuel poverty is highly skewed by household income, with virtually all households with the lowest income experiencing fuel poverty, in contrast to virtually none of the highest earning households.
- For both adults and children, low-income living is associated with a range of poorer health outcomes.
- It is problematic to 'blame the poor' for adverse health outcomes, with low-income living not always associated with adverse health behaviours – for example, there are equivalent levels of alcohol consumption among high- and low-income households.
- Living in a deprived area is generally associated with less neighbourhood satisfaction.
- Children from deprived areas are consistently reported to have poorer access to local opportunities for safe play and to participate in fewer activities, compared with children living beyond these areas.

Introduction

This chapter considers the experience of living in poverty in contemporary Scotland, one of the wealthiest countries in the world. It focuses on the here and now. It does not speculate on the long-term consequences of living in poverty, or claim that people currently experiencing poverty will be forevermore condemned to a life of adversity. The experience of poverty and deprivation in Scotland is described in terms of financial wellbeing, health, community life and children's leisure lives. It primarily draws on household income data and data comparing people living in and beyond multiply deprived areas. Without identification of the point at which low income reflects poverty for different household types, caution is required when using distribution of household income data to represent poverty. Similarly, living in a multiply deprived area does not imply living in poverty (nor does living outside a multiply deprived area imply an absence of poverty). Care is taken in interpreting these data when discussing poverty in Scotland. The chapter is based largely on quantitative data. Numbers cannot fully capture the reality of what life is like for people living in poverty. In particular, the numbers that are available to us are unable to tell us what people think or how people experiencing poverty make sense of this condition. However, numbers are not without value. The numbers that are reported in this chapter summarise the collective experiences of people experiencing poverty. They provide insight into the scale of the problem that persists in Scotland and the injustice that negative life experiences are more likely to be encountered by those living in poverty. It should always be acknowledged that behind every number is a real life. Testimony from people experiencing poverty in Scotland is used to illustrate the impact of poverty on everyday life.

Financial wellbeing

For people living on a low income, a lack of money leads to a fragile existence that involves the ever-present threat of falling into debt, being forced to choose between one necessity and another, going without, being trapped in 'dead-end' jobs, and being unable to save money.

National survey data reinforce these observations. Although more people from low-income households report that they 'manage financially well' than 'do not manage well' (33 per cent, compared with 24 per cent, for those households with an annual net income of less than £10,000), it is much more likely that those in Scotland who report that they are not managing their finances well are from low-income households (the 24 per cent compares with only 2 per cent from those in households with more than £30,000 annual net income).[1] It is more difficult to manage money well when working with a very low income. Similarly, while one-third of those from Scotland's (20 per cent) most deprived areas report that they are 'managing well', more than half of those living outside these areas report likewise (34 per cent, compared to 57 per cent, respectively).[2]

Of course, 'managing well' does not necessarily imply an easy life, as tough choices often have to be made when living in poverty, as this unnamed Poverty Truth Commissioner acknowledges:[3]

'I have to switch off my electric in the winter as I cannot afford to put money in the meter. Three days before my giro payment it comes down to "heat or eat", as often I cannot afford to do both.'

As Figure 8.1 suggests, households with the lowest annual net income are four times as likely not to have savings or investments (41 per cent of those with an annual income of less than £10,000, compared with 9 per cent of those with an annual income of £30,000 or above). Thus, an unacceptable and disproportionate share of low-income households in Scotland do not

Figure 8.1:

Absence of savings and investments by annual household income, Scotland, 2014

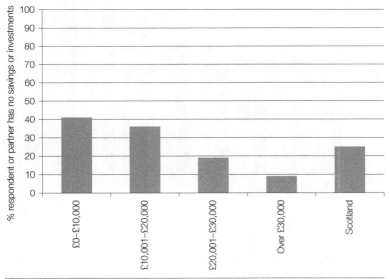

Source: Scottish Government, *Scotland's People Annual Report: results from the 2014 Scottish Household Survey*, 2015, Figure 6.4

Note: Without identification of the point at which low income reflects poverty, distribution of household income data does not measure poverty. Furthermore, the income data presented in this table are not equivalised. Care has to be taken in interpreting these data when discussing poverty in Scotland.

have the financial means that provides stability and enables them to fend off unforeseen financial crises.

Living on a low income is also associated with less ready access to those resources that are important to participate fully in contemporary Scotland, including those helpful in accessing the world of work. As Figure 8.2 shows, households in Scotland with lower net incomes are most likely not to have home internet access, and not to have access to a car for private use. Thus, the majority of households with an annual net income of less than £6,000 do not have access to a car for private use (56 per cent) compared with a tiny minority of households with an annual income of over £40,000 (3 per cent). Many also do not have access to the internet at home (in this instance, 39 per cent, compared with 1 per cent, respectively).

Figure 8.2:

Aspects of consumption by annual household income, Scotland, 2014

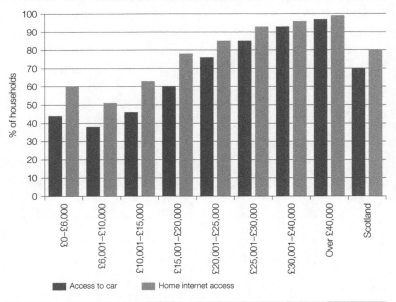

Source: Scottish Government, *Scotland's People Annual Report: results from 2014 Scottish Household Survey*, 2015, Table 7.2 and Figure 8.2

Note: Without identification of the point at which low income reflects poverty, distribution of household income data does not measure poverty. Furthermore, the income data presented in this table are not equivalised. Care has to be taken in interpreting these data when discussing poverty in Scotland.

Consumption that is pertinent to accessing the world of work does throw a consistent 'glitch' at the lower end of the household income scale in that those on the very lowest income (£0 to £6,000 per annum) have higher consumption than those with a 'slightly higher' low income (£6,001 to £10,000).[4]

Not having a car does not mean that transport costs can be avoided. Meeting the cost of public transport can be a significant financial challenge for people experiencing poverty, which can lead them to withdraw or not avail themselves of key services that would provide support, as Robbie and Donna explain in CPAG's *Hard Choices* report:[5]

> '… it was too expensive for the two of us to go [to the advice service] … it would be £7.60 or £10.50 depending on the [bus] driver if we had to pay for the kids or not. So that is too much money, money that we could have used for something else rather than going to the advice shop.'

If we step back to consider the basic necessities of existence, we find unacceptable deprivations among Scotland's poorest people. For example, the Scottish government estimates that 100,000 more households are living with fuel poverty in 2013, compared with 2012.[6] Two of every five households in Scotland are now estimated to be living with fuel poverty (39.1 per cent), with one in 10 considered to be experiencing 'extreme fuel poverty' (10.5 per cent). As might be expected, those on the lowest incomes are more vulnerable, although fuel poverty is almost absent among households in Scotland with a net weekly income of over £700 (2 per cent). In sharp contrast, it seems to be a universal experience for all with a net weekly income of less than £200 (94 per cent) and for the vast majority of those households with a net weekly income of between £200 and £299 (69 per cent of households).[7]

Health

The problems caused by low-income living extend far beyond the ability to consume, with people living in poverty sensing that their worth is often rated (adversely) on account of living in poverty. Being seen to be poor is to be seen to be less worthy, and leads to low self-esteem. People living on a low income experience stigmatisation on account of their poverty, a lack of emotional and practical support that could be provided by those in more powerful positions, and a feeling of being unable to participate fully in one's community.[8]

Mental wellbeing is, not surprisingly, less than satisfactory among low-income households in Scotland. Table 8.1 presents evidence of the three indicators that are used in Scotland to gauge the psychological health of adults using standard measurement tools from the Scottish Health Survey. For example, signs of psychological disorder are shown by 26 per cent of women and 25 per cent of men in the households with the lowest income. Differences between men and women become more marked at the very lowest end of the income spectrum – for example, for men, there is a sharp difference between quintile four (14 per cent showing signs of a psychological disorder) and those living in households with the very lowest household income levels (25 per cent).

Physical ill health is also much more prevalent in low-income, compared to high-income, households.

Clearly, deprivation and low income prevent men and women from enjoying healthy lives. However, it does not follow that people in low-income households are making free choices that are leading to less healthy outcomes. For example, and in sharp contrast to the public persona of someone experiencing poverty, alcohol is consumed to similar levels of risk across the income spectrum (Table 8.2).

Even though the evidence is that the level of alcohol consumption is not so different for people experiencing poverty, such consumption nevertheless can attract criticism. It is important to acknowledge the factors that lead people to seek solace in alcohol; as this worker from a housing and support organisation acknowledges, the drivers are not typically hedonistic:[9]

'We have seen an observable increase in alcohol consumption in our client group due to the despondency and fear created by the changes and difficulties of navigating the benefit and accommodation systems.'

The complexities of understanding the relationship between low income and health outcomes is further demonstrated in Table 8.3, which considers healthy weight issues. Girls from low-income households are more likely than boys from low-income households to be overweight (45 per cent, compared with 30 per cent for those from the 20 per cent lowest income households); men are no more likely than women to be overweight from this same household income group (64 per cent for men and 66 per cent for women). For both boys and girls, there is a marked increase in the

Table 8.1:

Mental and physical health by household income groups (quintiles), across age and sex, Scotland, 2014

	20% highest income household %	Quintile 2 %	Quintile 3 %	Quintile 4 %	20% lowest income household %
Adults, self-assessed general health as 'bad or very bad'					
Men	2	4	6	10	21
Women	4	3	6	10	19
Adults, 'possible presence of psychological disorder' from General Health Questionnaire					
Men	10	11	12	14	25
Women	13	16	16	19	26
Children, wellbeing					
Boys, SDQ of 14 or more	6	19	14	26	22
Girls, SDQ of 14 or more	1	3	0	11	21
Adults, longstanding illness					
Men	34	45	41	47	64
Women	40	44	47	50	56
Children, longstanding illness					
Boys	14	22	21	28	16
Girls	11	16	23	24	18

Source: D Campbell-Jack and others, *Scottish Health Survey 2014*, Scottish Government, 2015, supplementary web tables, W3, W23, W167, W171, and W815, available at www.gov.scot/topics/statistics/browse/health/scottish-health-survey/publications/supplementary2014

Notes:
1. Without identification of the point at which low income reflects poverty, distribution of household income data does not measure poverty. Furthermore, the income data presented in this table are not equivalised. Care has to be taken in interpreting this data when discussing poverty in Scotland.
2. Adults aged 16 and over were asked to rate their general health on a five-point scale ranging from 'very bad' through a mid-point of 'fair' to 'very good'.
3. The General Health Questionnaire consists of 12 questions on mental distress and psychological ill health. A point is allocated for every time an experience is described as occurring 'more than usual' or 'much more than usual' over the last few weeks. A score of four or more is taken as sign of a possible psychiatric disorder.
4. The Strengths and Difficulties Questionnaire (SDQ) was answered by parents on behalf of children aged four to 12 years. The SDQ comprises 25 questions covering aspects such as consideration, hyperactivity, malaise, mood, sociability, obedience, anxiety and unhappiness. These can be condensed into five component symptom scores corresponding to emotional symptoms, conduct problems, hyperactivity, peer problems and pro-social behaviour, ranging in value from zero to 10. A total SDQ score (referred to here as a total deviance score) was calculated by summing the scores from each domain, with the exception of pro-social behaviour, ranging from 0 to 40. An SDQ of 14 or more reflects borderline or abnormal total difficulties.
5. Respondents reporting that they (or their child) had a physical or mental health condition that had lasted, or was likely to last, for 12 months or more were considered to have a long-term condition.

incidence of being overweight between those from lowest income households and highest income households (45 per cent, compared with 33 per cent for girls, and 30 per cent, compared with 21 per cent for boys).

Table 8.2:

Selected food and drink consumption by household income groups (quintiles), across sex and age, Scotland, 2014

	20% highest income household %	Quintile 2 %	Quintile 3 %	Quintile 4 %	20% lowest income household %
Drinking, men					
Low-risk drinking or abstinence	76	75	76	83	72
Hazardous drinking	20	24	19	15	22
Harmful drinking	0	1	4	1	2
Possible alcohol dependence	3	1	1	1	3
Drinking, women					
Low-risk drinking or abstinence	89	90	86	87	87
Hazardous drinking	9	10	13	10	10
Harmful drinking	2	1	1	2	2
Possible alcohol dependence	0	–	–	1	1
Likelihood of boys aged 2–15 consuming selected foodstuffs					
Oily fish, at least weekly	20	19	14	12	15
Drink whole milk	30	20	33	37	46
Drink non-diet soft drinks, daily	25	33	39	43	40
Chips, at least twice weekly	28	43	55	49	52

Source: D Campbell-Jack and others, *Scottish Health Survey 2014*, Scottish Government, 2015, supplementary web tables, W499, W511, W535, W555, and W699, available at www.gov.scot/topics/statistics/browse/health/scottish-health-survey/publications/supplementary2014

Notes:
1. Without identification of the point at which low income reflects poverty, distribution of household income data does not measure poverty. Furthermore, the income data presented in this table are not equivalised. Care has to be taken in interpreting these data when discussing poverty in Scotland.
2. The *Scottish Health Survey* uses the UK government's recommendations that women should not drink more than 2 to 3 units of alcohol per day and men should not exceed 3 to 4 units per day.
3. The *Scottish Health Survey* uses the AUDIT questionnaire to determine alcohol risks. Ten questions are asked, with respondents answering on a five-point scale ranging from 0 (never) through to 5 (four or more times per week). A score of 0–7 is low risk, 8–15 is defined as hazardous, 16–19 as harmful and 20 or more as 'warrants further investigation for possible alcohol dependence'.

Table 8.3:

Overweight/obese by household income groups (quintiles), across sex and age, Scotland, 2014

	20% highest income household %	Quintile 2 %	Quintile 3 %	Quintile 4 %	20% lowest income household %
Boys	21	25	33	31	30
Girls	33	29	30	35	45
Men	71	71	70	70	64
Women	53	63	63	69	66

Source: D Campbell-Jack and others, *Scottish Health Survey 2014*, Scottish Government, 2015, supplementary web table W803, available at www.gov.scot/topics/statistics/browse/health/scottish-health-survey/publications/supplementary2014

Notes:
1. BMI is used to define underweight and overweight (either side of the healthy BMI range of 18.5 to 25). Refer to section 7.2.3 of the source report for details.
2. Without identification of the point at which low income reflects poverty, distribution of household income data does not measure poverty. Furthermore, the income data presented in this table are not equivalised. Care has to be taken in interpreting these data when discussing poverty in Scotland.
3. Children are aged 2–15. Men are aged 16 or over.

Community life and environment

People experiencing poverty are more likely to be living in deprived areas with inadequate services and facilities and, as Table 8.4 shows, they are more likely to feel unsafe in their neighbourhood.

Table 8.4 uses information from the *Scottish Household Survey* to compare perceptions of night-time safety at home and in the wider neighbourhood. On the whole, the majority of people in Scotland perceive themselves to be safe in their own homes at night, and there is little significant difference between those living in the most deprived areas and the rest of Scotland in the proportion who feel unsafe in their own home. However, there is a marked difference in perceived safety in the wider neighbourhood at night. More than twice as many people from the most deprived areas in Scotland do not feel safe walking alone at night in their neighbourhood (27 per cent, compared with 11 per cent of those living outside the most deprived areas).

Table 8.4:

Perceptions of personal safety by deprivation area status, Scotland, 2014

	20% most deprived areas %	Rest of Scotland %	Scotland %
How safe respondent feels walking alone in neighbourhood at night			
Safe (very, fairly)	72	88	85
Unsafe (bit, very)	27	11	14
Don't know	1	1	1
Base	*1,810*	*7,500*	*9,310*
How safe respondent feels at home at night			
Safe (very, fairly)	96	98	98
Unsafe (bit, very)	4	2	2
Don't know	0	0	0
Base	*1,920*	*7,880*	*9,800*

Source: Scottish Government, *Scotland's People Annual Report: results from the 2014 Scottish Household Survey*, 2015, Table 4.13

Note: Living in a multiply deprived area does not imply living in poverty (nor does living outside a multiply deprived area imply an absence of poverty). Care has to be taken in interpreting these data when discussing poverty in Scotland.

Local area differences extend beyond perceptions of safety. As Table 8.5 shows, people living in the most deprived areas of Scotland (also the areas with a disproportionate share of people experiencing poverty in Scotland) are more likely to express displeasure over anti-social behaviour in their neighbourhood (16 per cent have experienced rowdy behaviour, compared with 'only' 8 per cent expressing such concern outside areas of deprivation). Similarly, residents of multiply deprived areas are more likely to acknowledge environmental incivilities (30 per cent reported rubbish or litter lying around, compared with only 20 per cent of those living outside deprived areas).

Table 8.5:

Experience of neighbourhood problems, by deprivation area status, Scotland, 2014

	20% most deprived areas %	Rest of Scotland %	Scotland %
General anti-social behaviour			
Vandalism, graffiti, damage to property	9	4	5
Groups or individual harassing others	6	2	3
Drug misuse or dealing	12	4	6
Rowdy behaviour	16	8	9
Neighbour problems/environmental incivilities			
Noisy neighbours/loud parties	16	8	9
Neighbour disputes	7	4	5
Rubbish or litter lying around	30	20	22
Animal nuisance, such as noise or dog fouling	37	31	32

Source: Scottish Government, *Scotland's People Annual Report: results from the 2014 Scottish Household*, *Survey*, 2015, Table 4.9

Note: Living in a multiply deprived area does not imply living in poverty (nor does living outside a multiply deprived area imply an absence of poverty). Care has to be taken in interpreting these data when discussing poverty in Scotland.

Growing up in poverty and in deprived areas

It is widely recognised that having adequate opportunities to play and participating in a range of activities is beneficial for children. Indeed, as Fiona McHardy has demonstrated, it is particularly important for children living in poverty.[10]

Compared with other children, those from deprived areas in Scotland are reported to have less ready access to different types of play space in their local area; there are greater parental concerns for children's safety travelling to these play spaces; there is more concern for children's safety in these play areas; and children must reach an older age before parents consider it to be safe for them to visit these areas without supervision (Table 8.6). Clearly, there are more concerns over children's play in Scotland's most deprived areas.

Children from deprived areas are reported to be disadvantaged at every turn. Of particular note is the dearth of access to natural and wooded areas for play (only 28 per cent have local access to such space, compared with 51 per cent of those from non-deprived urban areas). This may be disconcerting to play professionals given the value of natural play environments.

Table 8.6:

Opportunities for children's play, by deprived area status, 2014

	Playground %	Park %	Games pitch (including football) %	Field/open space %	School playground %	Natural/wooded area %	Access to at least one play area/street play %	Base %
Availability of play area								
Deprived urban area	54	67	48	45	31	28	89	*280*
Rest of urban areas	59	67	46	55	39	51	91	*790*
Safe for children to walk or cycle to play area on their own								
Deprived urban area	47	45	55	56	64	31	53	*90*
Rest of urban areas	62	58	61	56	56	39	55	*320*
Safe to visit play area with two or three friends								
Deprived urban area	53	52	57	64	62	35	56	*90*
Rest of urban areas	68	66	65	62	60	44	58	*320*
Concerns of bullying by children in play area								
Deprived urban area	55	58	50	53	41	72	36	*90*
Rest of urban areas	32	37	37	36	33	38	24	*320*
Concerns of children being harmed by adults in play area								
Deprived urban area	52	58	52	58	41	82	35	*90*
Rest of urban areas	31	34	35	37	32	50	25	*320*

Source: Scottish Government, *Scotland's People Annual Report: results from the 2014 Scottish Household*, *Survey*, 2015, Tables 14.1–14.5

Note:

1. Data in these tables report findings from households containing a child aged between 6 and 12 years old.
2. Living in a multiply deprived area does not imply living in poverty (nor does living outside a multiply deprived area imply an absence of poverty). Care has to be taken in interpreting these data when discussing poverty in Scotland.
3. Deprived areas are defined as those in the lowest 20% of data zones for the SIMD.
4. Column heading 'Access to at least one play area' pertains to the rows on 'Availability of play area'.

Disadvantage is not only associated with playspace. Parents also report that children and young adults from deprived areas participate less frequently in a whole range of leisure activities (Table 8.7). Together, while less than a quarter outside deprived parts of urban Scotland do not participate in any activity (23 per cent), almost one-third within deprived areas experience no activities (29 per cent). We should also acknowledge that everyday evidence of child poverty is often masked and that the absence of public expressions does not mean that someone is doing without, as Moira explains:[11]

'I had six children. I am lucky to say my kids never went to bed hungry, but my husband and I did... and we were working. When I just had my kids we were not in debt, but once I had the grandkids to look after I got a lot of debt. There was so much going against them. I am still trying to pay off the debts.'

Table 8.7:

Activities of young people aged 8 to 21, by deprivation area status, Scotland, 2014

Activity	20% most deprived urban areas %	Rest of urban areas %	Scotland %
Music or drama	20	29	26
Other arts	8	7	7
Sports or sporting	47	56	55
Other outdoor activity	14	19	19
Other groups or clubs	19	25	24
Representing young people's views	1	4	3
Mentoring or peer education	3	5	5
Base	*490*	*1,380*	*2,390*

Source: Scottish Government, *Scotland's People Annual Report: results from the 2014 Scottish Household, Survey*, 2015, Table 14.7

Note: Living in a multiply deprived area does not imply living in poverty (nor does living outside a multiply deprived area imply an absence of poverty). Care has to be taken in interpreting these data when discussing poverty in Scotland.

Conclusion

This chapter has demonstrated that low income and living in deprived areas have far-ranging impacts on Scotland's adults and children. A lack of money leads directly to insecurity, and an inability to meet life's basic necessities. Poverty also strips people of their dignity and is associated with poorer mental health. The experience of trying to take steps to escape poverty can sometimes leave people feeling more vulnerable and less worthy:[12]

> 'You used to come out the of the jobcentre happy if you had found a job. Now you come out pleased if you haven't got a sanction.'

> 'I've seen me fill in application forms and I'll put down I live in Govan. But I'm then told "No, you don't put down Govan. Write Glasgow, because if you say Govan, no one is going to employ you." They are even saying that at the jobcentre.'

Physical ill health is also more prevalent among the men, women, boys and girls of Scotland's lower income households. Scotland's more deprived communities are more likely to be less pleasant places in which to live, in which concerns for personal safety are heightened. Finally, children from more deprived areas in Scotland are consistently disadvantaged in terms of access to safe play and participation in activities.

Although a bleak picture has been portrayed of life on a low income and in deprived places in contemporary Scotland, we should not lose sight of the continuing resilience of people living in some of Scotland's poorest communities. As well as highlighting the difficulties people face, we must also recognise the quality in many people's lives, their desire to get on, get heard and overcome. The present conditions that many experience need not determine their futures, if we can find effective means to support and enable Scotland's most disadvantaged communities and tackle the underlying poverty that too often undermines their resilience. Or in the words of Tricia from the Poverty Truth Commission:[13]

> 'When people in poverty are listened to, change happens.'

Notes

1 Scottish Government, *Scotland's People Annual Report: results from the 2014 Scottish Household Survey*, 2015, Figure 6.2

2 See note 1, Table 6.4

3 Poverty Truth Commission, *Turning up the Volume on Poverty*, 2014, p9

4 The glitch may reflect difficulties in obtaining accurate data for the most severely income deprived households. More generally, the problem of obtaining accurate household income estimates is acknowledged in the technical report that accompanies the substantive research findings report (S Hope and I Nava-Ledezma, 'Limitations of the Data', *Scottish Household Survey: methodology and fieldwork outcomes, 2011*, 2012, section 6). Thus, it is possible that the glitch is an anomaly and that there is generally lower consumption at the lower end of the household income spectrum.

5 J Perry and H McCulloch, *Hard Choices: reducing the need for food banks in Scotland*, CPAG in Scotland, 2014, p14

6 G Mueller and others, *Scottish House Conditions Survey: key findings 2013*, Scottish Government, 2014, Figure 22. The definition of fuel poverty that is used was specified by the Scottish Executive in the Fuel Poverty Statement of 2002. Households are defined as 'fuel poor' if they would be required to spend more than 10 per cent of household income on fuel. Households in extreme fuel poverty would be required to spend more than 20 per cent of their household income on fuel. See T Wilson and others, *Fuel Poverty Evidence Review: defining, measuring and analysing fuel poverty in Scotland*, Scottish government, 2012 for more detailed discussion.

7 See note 6, Figure 22 and Table 37

8 R Tennant, *No Light at the End of the Tunnel: tracking the impact of welfare reform across Glasgow*, Poverty Alliance, 2015, p8

9 S Payne, *Mental Health, Poverty and Social Exclusion*, Poverty and Social Exclusion Conceptual Note 9, 2012

10 F McHardy, *Play In and Around the Home: play and poverty in Fife*, Poverty Alliance, 2015, available at http://povertyalliance.org/article/play_poverty_fife; B Manwaring and C Taylor, *The Benefits of Play and Playwork*, SkillsActive, 2007

11 See note 3, p3

12 See note 3, p11 and p15

13 See note 3, p2

Section Four

Tools for tackling poverty in Scotland

Nine

Knowledge as a tool to tackle poverty

John H McKendrick

Knowing poverty

The *Poverty in Scotland* series is premised on an understanding that knowledge of poverty needs to be re-appraised and updated regularly, and that this should involve not only a consideration of the fundamental nature of poverty (Section Two) and a description of recent trends (Section Three), but also an awareness of how poverty is impacting upon, and being tackled by, different populations and interest groups in Scottish society. This is best achieved by listening to those with expertise and interest in these issues.

The expert voices in this latest edition of *Poverty in Scotland* focus on 'tools for tackling poverty', still considering groups and pertinent issues, but in the specific context of the levers at the disposal of government and civil society to ameliorate or eradicate poverty in Scotland. The eleven tools that we consider are introduced at the end of this chapter.

Although the knowledge shared in *Poverty in Scotland 2016* furthers an understanding of poverty and provides insight into how best to tackle it, much more has been learned since 2014, when the last edition was published to inform debate in advance of the election of a Scottish government. Arising from the belief that 'knowledge is a tool to tackle poverty', we introduce this collection of 'tools for tackling poverty' by signposting some of the ways in which our understanding of poverty in Scotland has been refreshed, supplemented and expanded since 2014.

Refreshing knowledge

As Chapter 5 has shown, poverty in Scotland is not fixed and the nature and extent of poverty has changed through time. Although caution must be taken when interpreting apparent changes from one year to the next, it is important to keep abreast of recent and emergent trends. Updating understanding is a worthwhile goal in its own right.

The primary source of information about poverty in Scotland is the Scottish government's annual analysis of the *Households Below Average Income* data, the key findings from which have been summarised in Section Two of this book.[1] This authoritative source is occasionally supplemented with additional analysis for a wider range of population groups.[2] In 2015, a simplified version of the annual report was published in conjunction with the Poverty Truth Commission, which also included testimony from people experiencing poverty.[3] Also in 2015, the Scottish government published reports on wealth[4] and severe poverty,[5] and a trio of short briefings on poverty and inequality.[6]

Regular authoritative commentary on poverty in Scotland is not restricted to government reports. The New Policy Institute, on behalf of the Joseph Rowntree Foundation, publishes biennial reviews of poverty in Scotland under the *Monitoring Poverty and Social Exclusion* series, with the 2015 report providing reviews of poverty and ill health, education inequalities, low-paid work and housing.[7] Similarly, researchers from Heriot-Watt University and the University of Glasgow are part of a UK-wide team that has been conducting the decennial update of the seminal poverty and social exclusion surveys, and which has already generated an understanding of attitudes of people in Scotland toward necessities.[8]

The referendum in 2014 also afforded an opportunity to reflect on poverty in Scotland. In addition to a referendum-focused edition of this *Poverty in Scotland* series in 2014 to inform this debate,[9] the New Policy Institute also published a series of referendum briefings[10] and the Poverty Alliance produced a discussion paper.[11]

The particularities of the referendum debate should not detract from the reality that poverty is an everyday issue for many people in Scotland and overviews of poverty in recent years have been published by, and for, a range of interest groups, including the Church of Scotland[12] and multi-faith collectives.[13] Several reviews of specific aspects of poverty have also been published – for example, Energy Action Scotland (fuel poverty),[14] National Union of Students (student poverty),[15] NHS Health Scotland (child poverty),[16] Community Food and Health Scotland (food poverty),[17] STV Children's Appeal (attitudes toward child poverty),[18] and the Children and Young People's Commissioner Scotland (poverty and education).[19] Similarly, growing interest in local responses to poverty has also given rise to a series of local reviews – for example, Dundee (Fairness Commission),[20] Fife (Fairer Fife)[21] and Glasgow (Indicators project),[22] which complement the reviews of more established groups concerned to tackle poverty locally in Scotland – ie, Employability in Scotland[23] and the Scottish Local Government Forum Against Poverty.[24]

More generally, the Poverty Truth Commission[25] and the Poverty Alliance[26] regularly update an understanding of poverty in Scotland, the latter most notably with the re-introduction of its quarterly journal, the *Scottish Anti-Poverty Review*.[27] There is a tradition in Scotland of research that aims to convey directly the experiences of people experiencing poverty[28] and several projects have furthered our understanding of contemporary experiences, such as the participatory research instigated by the Wheatley Group to consider young people's experiences of housing,[29] CPAG's work to understand the underlying causes of food bank use,[30] Poverty Alliance's exploration of the experience of poverty among lone parents in Fife,[31] while the Poverty Truth Commission produced a more wide-ranging review on a range of issues impacting on a range of people experiencing poverty in Scotland.[32]

Supplementing knowledge

Although much is known about the ways in which poverty impacts adversely on the lives of people in Scotland, new studies extend our understanding of the reach of poverty in Scotland.

It is well established that people experiencing poverty are often stigmatised, often on account of being perceived to be the sole architects of the condition they experience. Focusing on Glasgow, Hancock and Mooney have extended an understanding of poverty and stigmatisation by considering the way in which disadvantaged communities are constructed as 'welfare ghettos' by those in power.[33] Poverty and place has also been the focus of two recent essays on regeneration – ie, Robertson's retrospective on the shortcomings of regeneration work to tackle poverty and McKendrick's articulation of how Common Weal principles might reconfigure area regeneration work in Scotland.[34] The geographies of poverty has also been the focus of work by Kavanagh and others[35] who describe the suburbanisation of poverty in Glasgow (echoing earlier work by Pacione[36]), arguing that regeneration strategies are not best-placed to address what they portray as a 'new geography', while Rae[37] has described the concentration and persistence of labour market deprivation across Scotland using data from the Scottish Index of Multiple Deprivation.

Once more focusing on Glasgow as a case study, Anderson and Whalley describe the role of public libraries in facilitating access to the internet, a timely reminder of the ways in which everyday public services serve a multiplicity of functions to those without private means.[38] Also considering provision of support in Glasgow, was Piacentini, who reviewed the anti-poverty work of migrant and refugee community organisations in the city.[39]

Fuel poverty has been a longstanding concern for the Scottish government and the anti-poverty sector and recent government reports and briefings have been published to keep interested parties abreast of recent trends.[40] Reviewing anti-poverty strategies as a whole has also remained a key focus for academics and commentators, with a wide range of papers reviewing recent work: child poverty, in particular, has received much attention.[41] The well-established links between poverty and crime were refreshed in a special edition of *Social Justice Matters* in November 2015, which focused on poverty, inequality and justice.[42]

The introduction of the Scottish government's 'attainment challenge', which aims to 'close the equity gap' by raising the attainment of children living in deprived areas[43] will provide further impetus to an issue that has continued to attract the attention of education researchers in Scotland in recent years.[44] The Children and Young People's Commissioner Scotland has also added to the range of studies and reviews of educational outcomes by commissioning Susan Elsley[45] to report on young people's views on the links between poverty and education, while the Educational Institute of Scotland has published a guide for classroom teachers and other educational practitioners to help raise awareness of the different ways in which poverty may present in Scottish schools, which also offers concrete advice on how this might be tackled.[46]

Taulbut and Walsh have also explored life for children in Scotland, finding little evidence that parenting and risk of poverty account for poorer health outcomes for young children in Glasgow, relative to those in Liverpool and Manchester.[47] Somewhat in contrast, Treanor analyses Growing Up in Scotland data and finds that 'high maternal social assets and financial vulnerabilities separately are associated with higher and lower levels of child social, emotional and behavioural development', leading to the conclusion that:[48]

> … mothers, families and children living in poverty would benefit from policy and practice interventions that support geographical proximity of family and friends, that foster close and supportive wider family relationships, and that

promote access to credit that does not lead to unmanageable debt and detrimental levels of additional financial stress.

Clearly, more work is required to better understand the ways in which impoverished early childhood environments impact upon children's development and wellbeing.

Evidently, our understanding of the ways in which poverty impacts upon people in Scotland is being furthered in many fields and for many issues. However, it is in the field of health where the greatest range of studies has been completed in recent years, particularly with regards to exploring the extent to which living in deprived areas is associated with poorer health outcomes and receipt of poorer health services. Adding to the evidence base that living in a deprived area is associated with poorer outcomes have been studies of older people living in deprived neighbourhoods,[49] mortality rates in areas that are persistently among the most deprived,[50] all-cause mortality rates across Scotland,[51] visual acuity before cataract operations,[52] general hospital emergency admissions, A&E attendances and psychiatric hospital admissions for men and women, and for maternity hospital admissions for women,[53] proximal humeral fractures,[54] and day-case tonsillectomy for children in Glasgow.[55] On the other hand, deprivation and poverty were not found to be a key determinant of the excess mortality that is evident in Glasgow (when compared to Belfast),[56] confirming the conclusions reached in a seminal review of mortality in Glasgow by Walsh.[57] Neither was deprivation associated with risk of traumatic dental injury.[58]

The association between deprivation and environmental conditions thought not be conducive to negative health outcomes has also been explored. Morrison and others found that soil metal concentration is correlated to deprivation in Glasgow, concluding that the legacy of environmental pollution remains in impoverished parts of post-industrial Glasgow long after the industry has declined.[59] Maantay has also found a link between deprivation and an impoverished environment, in her analysis of derelict land in Glasgow.[60] She concludes with suggestions as to how evidence might be used to inform priorities to promote social justice in neighbourhood regeneration.

Similarly, further evidence that living in a deprived area is associated with inadequacies in health service provision has been observed for antibiotic prescribing (with significantly higher rates of prescribing being evident for deprived areas in Scotland).[61] On the other hand, deprivation and poverty were not found to a determinant of the ethnic differences that were observed in breast cancer screening uptake across ethnic groups,[62] access to treatment for colorectal cancer in southwest Scotland[63] and success of renal transplantation.[64] Interestingly, although Mercer and others' key finding in their west of Scotland study is that physician empathy is most important if patient enablement (empowerment) is to be facilitated in both affluent and deprived areas, they also noted that emotional distress has an additional negative effect on enablement in deprived areas.[65] Similarly, Campbell and others identify higher rates of both referral and diagnosis of autism in early childhood among children in Glasgow.[66] Unable to identify environmental factors that would have accounted for this, they conclude that area differences in care pathways is likely to explain these area differences.

Expanding knowledge

Writing on poverty in Scotland has not been limited to updating or extending existing knowledge. The boundaries of understanding are also being furthered with new lines of inquiry. For example, Andreadis and colleagues have demonstrated through their work in Dundee that city level solar installation programmes can help eliminate fuel poverty in Scotland at an acceptable cost.[67] Tackling poverty was also the focus of work by Naven and Egan who evidence the financial gains, as well as support for housing and childcare, that can be provided by nurses and midwifes when their remit is extended to provide information pathways to money and welfare advice services.[68] More generally, the Common Weal project opens debate on a wider range of ways of tackling poverty than tends to be considered within the mainstream political arenas.[69] Also challenging convention was the study of Matthews and Besemer, who demonstrate that far from being pioneers of gentrification, there is actually a disproportionate concentration of non-heterosexual people in the most deprived places in Scotland.[70] McHardy also rethinks the reach of anti-poverty work by exploring the importance of poverty and play with a group of lone parents in Fife.[71] Work from the Glasgow School *for* Business in Society in North Lanarkshire also challenged the understanding of austerity cuts as a straightforward issue of service provision or financial resourcing, instead rethinking this as part of a risk shift through which vulnerable people and communities were tasked with bearing a greater burden of risk as the state shifted responsibilities toward them.[72] Even our understanding of how we conceptualise and measure local area deprivation has been questioned: researchers from Heriot-Watt University responded to the brief of the Improvement Service to envisage alternative ways of measuring local area deprivation,[73] and CPAG has investigated the cost of the school day in Glasgow, identifying the key financial barriers to participation for children from low-income households and children's views on the best ways to overcome them.[74]

New understanding has also been furthered in response to changes in the way that poverty is experienced, generated and tackled in Scotland. Most notably, and adding to the CPAG work referred to earlier that explored the experiences of food bank users,[75] Douglas and colleagues have produced a wide-ranging report and review of food availability and poverty in Scotland.[76] The ongoing in-work poverty research project should also be expected to soon yield new understanding of what is also emerging as a key feature of poverty in contemporary Scotland.[77] The referendum, as noted above, also provided an opportunity to question the taken-for-granted political settlement and to consider whether alternative configurations would reduce or increase poverty in Scotland.[78] Above all, the studies commissioned by the Scottish government[79] to appraise the impact of welfare reform in Scotland, in addition to the work of CPAG through its 'early warning system'[80] and Poverty Alliance through its 'welfare trackers' research[81] are ensuring that interested parties are kept abreast of what might be described as the most serious threat to the welfare of Scotland's most vulnerable people and communities in recent years.

What might life beyond poverty look like? It is perhaps fitting to end this review of new knowledge about poverty in Scotland by recommending the thinkpiece by Peter Kelly and Laura Darling, which summarises what a Scotland free of poverty would mean to communities and individuals who live with poverty on a daily basis in Scotland.[82]

Introduction to the 'tools to tackle poverty'

Although tax and social security have tended to be portrayed as more marginal to the analysis of what should be done in Scotland to tackle poverty, the reconfiguration of the devolution settlement will determine that the Scottish government could use these anti-poverty tools to greater effect if it so chooses in the years ahead. David Eiser (University of Stirling) and Hanna McCulloch (CPAG Scotland) consider these issues in turn at the start of the collection. However, making better use of procedures and mechanisms outside Scotland should also be considered as part of the effort to tackle poverty in Scotland, as Pauline Nolan (Inclusion Scotland) argues in a consideration of the contribution of human rights frameworks. Much attention has been paid to living wage campaigns in recent years, acknowledging the importance of remuneration in tackling poverty. Peter Kelly (Poverty Alliance) considers this in a more wide-ranging review of how work might be used to tackle poverty in Scotland. Core services are not only important in their own right, it is also argued that education (Andrea Bradley, Educational Institute of Scotland), childcare and early years services (Gill Scott), health (Jackie Erdman, Greater Glasgow and Clyde Health Board) and housing (Paul Bradley, Shelter) are also important tools for tackling poverty. Mary Anne MacLeod addresses the issue of food security, evaluating the extent to which food banks are an effective tool for tackling poverty in Scotland. Finally, the strategic interventions of the third sector (Martin Sime, SCVO) and local government (Annabelle Armstrong-Walter, Renfrewshire Council) are appraised.

Notes

1 Scottish Government, *Poverty and Income Inequality in Scotland: 2013/14*, 2015; *Scottish Government, Poverty and Income Inequality in Scotland: 2012/13*, 2014; Scottish Government, *Poverty and Income Inequality in Scotland: 2011/12*, 2013; Scottish Government, *Poverty and Income Inequality in Scotland: 2010/11*, 2012. All available at www.gov.scot/topics/statistics/browse/social-welfare/incomepoverty

2 See www.gov.scot/topics/statistics/browse/social-welfare/incomepoverty/core analysis

3 Scottish Government and the Poverty Truth Commission, *Poverty in Scotland*, 2015, available at www.gov.scot/resource/0048/00480340.pdf

4 Scottish Government, *Wealth and Assets in Scotland 2006–2012*, 2015, available at http://www.gov.scot/publications/2015/03/2333/0

5 Scottish Government, *Severe Poverty in Scotland*, 2015, available at www.gov.scot/publications/2015/03/4673/0

6 See www.gov.scot/topics/statistics/browse/social-welfare/incomepoverty

7 P Kenway, T MacInnes and H Aldridge, *Monitoring Poverty and Social Exclusion in Scotland 2013*, Joseph Rowntree Foundation, 2013, available at http://npi.org.uk/files/3513/7477/5908/poverty-exclusion-scotland-summary.pdf; P Kenway, S Busche, A Tinson and TB Born, *Monitoring Poverty and Social Exclusion in Scotland 2015*, Joseph Rowntree Foundation, 2015, available at http://npi.org.uk/files/6914/2736/4937/MPSE-scotland-full.pdf

8   N Bailey and G Bramley, *The Poverty and Social Exclusion in the UK Survey 2012: headline results for Scotland*, PSE-UK, 2013; M Gannon and N Bailey, 'Attitudes to the 'Necessities of Life': would an independent Scotland set a different poverty standard to the rest of the UK?', *Social Policy and Society*, Vol. 13, No. 3, 2014, pp321–36

9   JH McKendrick, G Mooney, J Dickie, G Scott, and P Kelly, *Poverty in Scotland 2014: the independence referendum and beyond*, CPAG, 2014

10 H Aldridge and P Kenway, *Referendum Briefing: child poverty in Scotland*, Joseph Rowntree Foundation, 2014

11 Poverty Alliance, *Constitutional Reform and Poverty: some key questions*, 2012, available at http://povertyalliance.org/userfiles/files/briefings/PA_Discussion_Constitution-FINAL230812.pdf

12 www.churchofscotland.org.uk/speak_out/poverty_and_economics

13 www.jointpublicissues.org.uk/truthandliesaboutpoverty

14 www.eas.org.uk/key_issues_fuel_poverty.php

15 www.nus.org.uk/en/take-action/welfare-and-student-rights/stop-student-poverty

16 www.healthscotland.com/uploads/documents/20578-childpovertybriefingmarch 2013_1.pdf

17 www.communityfoodandhealth.org.uk/our-work/food-poverty-access

18 JH McKendrick, *Attitudes Toward Child Poverty in Contemporary Scotland*, The Hunter Foundation, 2014

19 www.cypcs.org.uk/publications/poverty

20 www.dundeepartnership.co.uk/content/dundee-fairness-commission

21 www.fifedirect.org.uk/minisites/index.cfm?fuseaction=page.display&pageid=6EE 8041B-E387-D685-6DBE9BE4D5C06929&siteID=6EE6DD98-ED66-5C2C-CFE 1A79C6D975A5D

22 www.understandingglasgow.com/indicators/poverty/overview

23 www.employabilityinscotland.com/barriers/poverty

24 www.scottishpovertyforum.org.uk

25 www.faithincommunityscotland.org/poverty-truth-commission

26 http://povertyalliance.org/index.php

27 http://povertyalliance.org/news_and_publications/scottish_anti_poverty_review

28 M Green, *Voices of People Experiencing Poverty*, Joseph Rowntree Foundation, 2007, available at http://cdn.basw.co.uk/upload/basw_92538-8.pdf

29 F McHardy and others, *Beyond 4 Walls: participatory youth research project*, Wheatley Group, 2015, available at http://povertyalliance.org/article/b4w_report

30 J Perry and H McCulloch, *Hard Choices: reducing the need for food banks in Scotland*, CPAG in Scotland, 2014, available at www.cpag.org.uk/sites/default/files/CPAG_Food_Bank_Report.pdf

31 F McHardy, *Surviving Poverty: the impact of lone parenthood*, Poverty Alliance,

2013, available at http://povertyalliance.org/userfiles/files/EPIC/Reports/EPIC_Research_Surviving_Poverty2013.pdf

32 Poverty Truth Commission, *Turning Up The Volume on Poverty*, 2014

33 G Mooney and L Hancock, "Welfare Ghettos" and the "Broken Society": territorial stigmatization in the contemporary UK', *Housing, Theory and Society*, Vol. 30, No. 1, 2013, pp46–64

34 D Robertson, *Regeneration and Poverty in Scotland: evidence and policy review*, Centre for Regional Economic and Social Research, Sheffield Hallam University, 2014; JH McKendrick, *A Red Road to Regeneration in Scotland?* Common Weal, 2014, available at www.allofusfirst.org/library/a-red-road-to-regeneration-in-scotland-2014

35 L Kavanagh, D Lee, and G Pryce, *Poverty in Suburbia: has Glasgow gone the way of American cities?* AQMeN Research Briefing No. 5, University of Edinburgh, 2014, available at www.research.ed.ac.uk/portal/files/18805757/RB5_poverty_suburbia.pdf

36 M Pacione, 'A Tale of Two Cities: the migration of the urban crisis in Glasgow', *Cities*, Vol. 7, No. 4, 1990, pp304–14

37 A Rae, 'Spatial Patterns of Labour Market Deprivation in Scotland: concentration, isolation and persistence', *Local Economy*, Vol. 27, Nos. 5–6, 2012, pp593–609

38 G Anderson and J Whalley, 'Public Internet Access in Areas of Deprivation: the case of Glasgow', *Paper Presented at the 24th European Regional Conference of the International Telecommunication Society*, Florence, 20–23 October 2013, available at www.econstor.eu/bitstream/10419/88489/1/773083448.pdf

39 T Piacentini, 'Missing From the Picture? Migrant and refugee community organizations' responses to poverty and destitution in Glasgow', *Community Development Journal*, Vol. 50(3), 2015, pp433–47

40 G Liddell, *Fuel Poverty in Scotland*, Financial Scrutiny Unit Briefing 15/13, SPICe, 2015; T Wilson, J Robertson and L Hawkins, *Fuel Poverty Evidence Review: defining, measuring and analysing fuel poverty in Scotland*, Scottish House Condition Survey and the Scottish government, 2012

41 G Mooney, C Morelli and P Seaman, 'Tackling Inequality and Disadvantage in the Devolved Scotland', in M Leith, I McPhee and T Laxton (eds), *Scottish Devolution and Social Policy: evidence from the first decade*, Cambridge Scholars, 2012, pp115–34; JH McKendrick and S Sinclair, 'Tackling Child Poverty: the contribution of devolution', in M Leith, I McPhee and T Laxton (eds), *Scottish Devolution and Social Policy: evidence from the first decade*, Cambridge Scholars, 2012, pp161-90; S Sinclair and JH McKendrick, 'From Social Inclusion to Solidarity: anti-poverty strategies under devolution', in G Mooney and G Scott (eds), *Social Justice and Social Welfare in Contemporary Scotland*, Policy Press, 2012, pp61–80; S Sinclair and JH McKendrick,

'Tackling Child Poverty Locally: principles, priorities and practicalities in challenging times', *Scottish Affairs*, Vol. 23, No. 4, pp454–85; JH McKendrick and S Sinclair, *Local Action to Tackle Child Poverty in Scotland*, Save the Children, 2012, available at www.savethechildren.org.uk/resources/online-library/local-action-tackle-child-poverty-scotland

42 See http://scottishjusticematters.com/the-journal/poverty-inequality-and-justice-november-2015

43 See www.educationscotland.gov.uk/inclusionandequalities/sac/index.asp

44 SJ McKinney, S Hall, K Lowden, M McClung and L Cameron, 'Poverty and Prospects for Young People in Glasgow', *Open House*, Vol. 240, 2014, pp14–15; SJ McKinney, S Hall, K Lowden, M McClung and L Cameron, 'The Relationship Between Poverty and Deprivation, Educational Attainment and Positive School Leaver Destinations in Glasgow Secondary Schools', *Scottish Educational Review*, Vol. 44, No. 1, 2012, pp33–45; A Pirrie and E Hockings, *Poverty, Educational Attainment and Achievement in Scotland: a critical review of the literature*, SCCYP, 2012; C Iannelli, E Smyth and M Klein, 'Curriculum Differentiation and Social Inequality in Higher Education Entry in Scotland and Ireland', *British Educational Research Journal*, 2015, available at http://onlinelibrary.wiley.com/doi/10.1002/berj.3217/epdf

45 S Elsley, *Learning Lessons: young people's views on poverty and education in Scotland*, SCCYP, 2014, available at www.cypcs.org.uk/ufiles/learning-lessons.pdf

46 Educational Institute of Scotland, *Face Up to Child Poverty*, 2015, available at www.eis.org.uk/public.asp?id=3066&parentid=0&dbase=2

47 M Taulbut, and D Walsh, *Poverty, Parenting and Poor Health: comparing early years experiences in Scotland, England and three city regions*, Glasgow Centre for Population Health, 2013

48 M Treanor, *Exploring the Impacts of Assets and Vulnerabilities of Families Experiencing Multidimensional Poverty and Income Inequality on Children's Early Cognitive, Social, Emotional and Behavioural Developmental Outcomes in Scotland*, PhD thesis, University of Edinburgh, 2013, p3

49 R Mõttus, CR Gale, JM Starr and IJ Deary, 'On the Street Where You Live: neighbourhood deprivation and quality of life among community-dwelling older people in Edinburgh, Scotland', *Social Science and Medicine*, Vol. 74, No. 9, 2012, pp1368-74

50 DJ Exeter, PJ Boyle and P Norman, 'Deprivation (Im) mobility and Cause-specific Premature Mortality in Scotland', *Social Science and Medicine*, Vol. 72, No. 3, 2011, pp389–97

51 S Sridharan, J Koschinsky and JJ Walker, 'Does Context Matter for the Relationship Between Deprivation and All-cause Mortality? The West vs. the rest

of Scotland', *International Journal of Health Geographics*, Vol. 10, No. 1, 2011, pp33–46

52 PY Chua, MS Mustafa, NW Scott, M Kumarasamy and A Azuara-Blanco, 'Relationship Between Socioeconomic Deprivation or Urban/Rural Residence and Visual Acuity Before Cataract Surgery in Northern Scotland', *European Journal of Ophthalmology*, Vol. 23, No. 6, 2013, pp831–35

53 G McCartney, I Tamvakas, D Millard, L Smith and L Renwick, *The Patterning of Hospital Discharges and Bed-days by Deprivation in Scotland, 2011/12*, NHS Health Scotland, 2015, available at www.scotpho.org.uk/downloads/scotpho reports/scotpho150319-hospital-discharges-and-bed-days-Scotland-by-depriv ation-2011-12.pdf

54 ND Clement, MM McQueen and CM Court-Brown, 'Social Deprivation Influences the Epidemiology and Outcome of Proximal Humeral Fractures in Adults for a Defined Urban Population of Scotland', *European Journal of Orthopaedic Surgery and Traumatology*, Vol. 24, No. 7, 2014, pp1039–46

55 WA Clement, 'Day-case Tonsillectomy for Children in Glasgow: the impact of changing indications and deprivation', *The Journal of Laryngology and Otology*, Vol. 127, No. 4, 2013, pp392–98

56 P Graham, D Walsh and G McCartney, 'Shipyards and Sectarianism: how do mortality and deprivation compare in Glasgow and Belfast?, *Public Health*, Vol. 126, No. 5, 2012, pp378–85

57 D Walsh, *An Analysis of the Extent to Which Socio-economic Deprivation Explains Higher Mortality in Glasgow in Comparison With Other Post-industrial UK Cities, and an Investigation of Other Possible Explanations*, PhD thesis, University of Glasgow, 2014

58 O Rhouma, AD McMahon and R Welbury, 'Traumatic Dental Injury and Social Deprivation in Five-year-old Children in Scotland 1993–2007', *British Dental Journal*, Vol. 214, No. 10, 2013, E26

59 S Morrison, FM Fordyce and EM Scott, 'An Initial Assessment of Spatial Relationships Between Respiratory Cases, Soil Metal Content, Air Quality and Deprivation Indicators in Glasgow, Scotland, UK: relevance to the environmental justice agenda', *Environmental Geochemistry and Health*, Vol. 36, No. 2, 2014, pp319–32

60 JA Maantay, 'The Collapse of Place: derelict land, deprivation, and health inequality in Glasgow, Scotland', *Cities and the Environment (CATE)*, Vol. 6, No. 1, 2013, Article10, available at http://digitalcommons.lmu.edu/cgi/viewcontent.cgi? article=1130&context=cate

61 JR Covvey, BF Johnson, V Elliott, W Malcolm and AB Mullen, 'An Association Between Socioeconomic Deprivation and Primary Care Antibiotic Prescribing in Scotland', *Journal of Antimicrobial Chemotherapy*, Vol. 69, No. 3, 2014,

pp835–41; JR Covvey, 'Deprivation Leads to Increased Antibiotic Use in Scotland', *PharmacoEconomics and Outcomes News*, Vol. 691, 2013, pp7–16

62 N Bansal, RS Bhopal, MFC Steiner and DH Brewster, 'Major Ethnic Group Differences in Breast Cancer Screening Uptake in Scotland are not Extinguished by Adjustment for Indices of Geographical Residence, Area Deprivation, Long-term Illness and Education', *British Journal of Cancer*, Vol. 106, No. 8, 2012, pp1361–66

63 HM Paterson, BJ Mander, P Muir, HA Phillips and SH Wild, 'Deprivation and Access to Treatment for Colorectal Cancer in Southeast Scotland 2003–2009', *Colorectal Disease*, Vol. 16, No. 2, 2014, ppO51–O57

64 E Aitken, N Dempster, C Ceresa, C Daly and D Kingsmore, 'The Impact of Socioeconomic Deprivation on Outcomes Following Renal Transplantation in the West of Scotland', *Transplantation Proceedings*, Elsevier, 2013, Vol. 45, No. 6, pp2176–83

65 SW Mercer, BD Jani, M Maxwell, SYS Wong and GCM Watt, 'Patient Enablement Requires Physician Empathy: a cross-sectional study of general practice consultations in areas of high and low socioeconomic deprivation in Scotland', *BMC Family Practice*, Vol. 13, No. 6, 2012, available at www.biomedcentral.com/content/pdf/1471-2296-13-6.pdf

66 M Campbell, L Reynolds, J Cunningham, H Minnis, and C Gillberg, 'Autism in Glasgow: cumulative incidence and the effects of referral age, deprivation and geographical location', *Child: Care, Health and Development*, Vol. 39, No. 5, 2013, pp688–94

67 G Andreadis, S Roaf, and T Mallick, 'Tackling Fuel Poverty with Building-integrated Solar Technologies: the case of the city of Dundee in Scotland', *Energy and Buildings*, Elsevier, Vol. 59, 2013, pp310–20

68 L Naven, and J Egan, 'Addressing Child Poverty in Scotland: the role of nurses: findings from the Healthier, Wealthier Children project, with a focus on service user outcomes and impact on NHS workforce practice', *Primary Health Care*, Vol. 23, No. 5, 2013, pp16–22

69 M Danson and K Trebeck, *No More Excuses: how a Common Weal approach can end poverty in Scotland*, The Jimmy Reid Foundation, 2013, available at http://reidfoundation.org/wp-content/uploads/2013/08/Poverty1.pdf

70 P Matthews and K Besemer, 'The "Pink Pound" in the "Gaybourhood"? Neighbourhood deprivation and sexual orientation in Scotland', *Housing, Theory and Society*, Vol. 32, No. 1, 2015, pp94–111

71 F McHardy, *Play In and Around the Home: play and poverty in Fife*, Poverty Alliance, 2015, available at http://povertyalliance.org/userfiles/files/Play%26Poverty_in_Fife_FINAL_March15.pdf

72 D Asenova, JH McKendrick, C McCann and R Reynolds, *Redistribution of*

Social and Societal Risk: the impact on individuals, communities and their networks in Scotland, Joseph Rowntree Foundation, 2015, available at www.jrf. org.uk/report/redistribution-social-and-societal-risk

73 www.improvementservice.org.uk/assets/local-incomes-poverty-scotland.pdf

74 S Spencer, *The Cost of the School Day*, CPAG in Scotland, 2015, available at http:// www.cpag.org.uk/sites/default/files/CPAG-Scot-Cost-Of-School-Day-Report (Oct15)_0.pdf

75 J Perry and H McCulloch, *Hard Choices: reducing the need for food banks in Scotland*, CPAG in Scotland, 2014, available at www.cpag.org.uk/sites/ default/ files/CPAG_Food_Bank_Report.pdf

76 F Douglas, O-Z Ejebu, A Garcia, F MacKenzie, S Whybrow, L McKenzie, A Ludbrook, and E Dowler, *The Nature and Extent of Food Poverty*, NHS Health Scotland, 2015, available at www.abdn.ac.uk/ heru/documents/reports_etc/ Nature_and_extent_of_food_poverty_report_May_2015.pdf; D Crichton, A Parrett and AL Garcia, 'A Mapping Study of Food Availability in an Area of Deprivation: Viewpark, North Lanarkshire, Scotland', *Proceedings of the Nutrition Society*, Vol. 70, No. OCE1, E25, 2011

77 http://in-work-poverty-scotland.info

78 D Comerford and D Eiser, 'Constitutional Change and Inequality in Scotland', *Oxford Review of Economic Policy*, Vol. 30, No. 2, 2014, pp346–73; D Bell and D Eiser, *Inequality in Scotland: trends, drivers, and implications for the independence debate*, ESRC, 2013; P Dempsie, *A Stark Choice: widening inequality or a fairer, more prosperous Scotland*, 2013; G Mooney and G Scott, 'The 2014 Scottish Independence Debate: questions of social welfare and social justice', *Journal of Poverty and Social Justice*, Vol. 23, No. 1, 2015, pp5–16

79 See www.gov.scot/Topics/People/fairerscotland/analysis

80 See www.cpag.org.uk/scotland/early-warning-system; www.cpag.org.uk/content/ case-studies-meet-families

81 R Tennant, *No Light at the End of the Tunnel: tracking the impact of welfare reform across Glasgow*, Poverty Alliance, 2015, available at www.gcvs.org. uk/wp-content/uploads/2015/10/No-Light-at-the-End-of-the-Tunnel_Tracking-the-Impact-of-Welfare-Reform-across-Glasgow.pdf

82 P Kelly and L Darling, *A Scotland Without Poverty*, Poverty Alliance, 2015, available at www.povertyalliance.org/article_publications/scotland_without_poverty

Ten

Tackling poverty through taxation: options for the Scottish government

David Eiser

In the UK, almost 40p of every pound earned is taken in tax. The way the tax system is designed clearly has major consequences for the distribution of income: some taxes, particularly the direct taxes on earnings, explicitly aim to achieve redistributional objectives. Indirect taxes, like VAT, are not designed with redistribution in mind, but can have distributional consequences.

A tax system which effectively alleviates poverty is clearly one which does not impose an undue burden of taxation on the poorest in society. But it is also one which does not trap people in poverty by creating high rates of marginal taxation that influence decisions over employment, education and careers. Achieving these two goals simultaneously is not easy.

This chapter considers the role that taxes can play in alleviating poverty. It starts by reviewing some of the redistributional effects of tax changes made by the UK government during the 2010–2015 Parliament. It then considers taxation in Scotland. It discusses the effect of the Scottish government's council tax freeze, and considers the scope for more fundamental reform of property taxation in Scotland. The chapter finishes by discussing some of the options that income tax devolution may provide the Scottish government to use the tax system to tackle poverty.

Tax changes by the UK coalition government, 2010 to 2015

At UK level, the primary fiscal policy objective of the coalition government during the 2010–2015 Parliament was to reduce the deficit. Most of the consolidation came through spending cuts rather than tax rises, although the coalition did make significant tax changes during the Parliament.

Some of these tax changes had significant distributional impacts, particularly in relation to income tax changes. The personal allowance was increased significantly, to £10,000 (it would only have reached £7,800 if it had been uprated in line with inflation).[1] This took 2.6 million people out of income tax, and reduced the income tax bill of those earning above the personal allowance by £567. The higher rate threshold, however, was not uprated in line with inflation. By 2015, it was £42,000, significantly below the £53,000 it would have been had it been indexed to prices.[2] This resulted in some two million taxpayers moving into the higher rate band. The additional rate was reduced, from 50 per cent to 45 per cent, although this affects less than 1 per cent of taxpayers – ie, those earning over £150,000.

Perhaps surprisingly, these income tax changes were not particularly progressive across the whole income distribution. The lowest earning 40 per cent of adults already earn too little to be liable for income tax, and so do not benefit from the rise in the personal allowance. Households in the middle and upper middle of the distribution gained more from these changes, particularly in households in which there are two earners. It is only households in the top 10 per cent of the distribution that are paying more income tax (as a percentage of income) than they would have been doing if thresholds had been linked to inflation (and within this group, the losses for the top 1 per cent are offset by the reduction in the additional rate).

Other tax changes had mixed effects. Changes to national insurance contributions, including a rise in both the rate and threshold, were (slightly) progressive – although the threshold for paying national insurance contributions did not rise in real terms (the threshold at which employees begin making contributions is £8,000, whereas the income tax personal allowance was £10,000 by the end of the Parliament). The rise in VAT from 17.5 per cent to 20 per cent in 2011 is regressive to the extent that poorer households pay a larger proportion of their income as VAT than richer households (given that poorer households spend a larger proportion of their income).

While the effects of tax changes at different parts of the income distribution were somewhat mixed, the distributional effects of tax and benefit changes combined during the last Parliament were largely regressive. Poorer households experienced larger percentage falls in their net incomes than households in the middle and upper middle of the distribution, as tax cuts were more likely to be offset by reductions in means-tested benefits.[3]

The Scottish government's council tax freeze and scope for reform

The existing council tax system is regressive, charged at a lower percentage of property value for high value properties than for low value properties. Discounts for second homes and unused homes encourage inefficient use of the housing stock. And it is based on property values in 1991, favouring properties that have seen disproportionate rises since then.

The Scottish government has maintained the council tax freeze since 2008/09. The average Band D council tax in 2015, at £1,149, is around £200 per year less than it would have been had council tax increased in line with inflation since 2008.

Is freezing council tax a progressive or regressive tax policy? The answer depends, in part, on rates of take-up of council tax reduction (which has replaced council tax benefit). If there were no council tax reduction, then council tax itself would be a very regressive tax, with poorer households paying a higher proportion of their income in tax than richer households. Council tax reduction is designed to offset the regressive nature of council tax. But take-up rates are quite low: around a third of eligible households do not claim. This non take-up of council tax reduction means that council tax remains regressive across the whole of the income distribution. Because of this, a rise in council tax further exacerbates its regressive impact and thus a freeze, which is equivalent to a real-terms cut, is inequality reducing, as poorer households benefit proportionately more than richer households. So, although the Scottish government could make the case that its council tax freeze is a progressive policy, this outcome occurs, in part, because of low take-up of council tax reduction.

Moreover, it does not address the fact that council tax itself is a poorly designed tax. Rather than freezing it – which reduces the resources available to the Scottish government and local authorities – it would be far better to undertake a more comprehensive reform of local taxation. One way to reform council tax would be to replace it with a tax that is proportional to property value. For example, a tax of less than 1 per cent of the value of property is likely to be revenue neutral for the government (in the longer term, it may be preferable to base the tax on land value rather than property value, but basing the tax on property value would be more practicable in the short term). This and other options for reform were considered by the Commission on Tax Reform, which reported later in November

2015.[4] Both the cross-party Commission on Tax Reform and the Conservative-instigated Independent Commission for Competitive and Fair Taxation in Scotland argued for a fairer, more progressive system of local property taxation.[5] This is, of course, not the first time that calls for council tax reform have been made. But whether these reports will kick-start serious reform of the flawed council tax, or simply lead to further political prevarication, remains to be seen.

Tax powers being devolved to the Scottish Parliament

The Scottish government's powers over tax are expanding. In 2015, stamp duties were transferred to Scotland. The Scottish government replaced stamp duties with a new 'land and buildings transactions tax'. This does represent an improvement on the previous stamp duty system, setting a more progressive rate structure. But the tax remains a tax on transactions, which is inefficient (transactions taxes discourage people from making beneficial exchanges). If the Scottish government reformed property taxation more fundamentally, it could eliminate the land and buildings transactions tax entirely.

In 2016, the Scottish government gains partial control over income tax in Scotland, following the recommendations of the Calman Commission which were implemented by the Scotland Act 2012. Under the Scotland Act powers, the Scottish government can increase or decrease income tax rates, but each rate must be changed by the same amount. So it could increase the additional rate by 1p to 46p, but only by simultaneously increasing the higher rate by 1p to 41p, and the basic rate to 21p. It is probably fair to say that the income tax powers of the Scotland Act 2012 do not provide the Scottish government much leverage to influence the income distribution, although a 1p rise in each of these bands would be slightly progressive.[6]

In the longer term, the Scottish government will gain almost full control over income tax, including the ability to vary rates and thresholds without constraint, if the recommendations of the Smith Commission are implemented. It is not particularly obvious how this power might be exercised to alleviate poverty given that, as mentioned above, the lowest earning 40 per cent of adults (and almost 20 per cent of the lowest paid workers) already face no income tax liability; so, the case for further rises to the personal allowance is not as clear cut as politicians sometimes imply. (Raising the personal allowance from £10,000 to £11,000 in 2016 will cost the UK government £1 billion, with most of the gain going to households in the middle and upper part of the income distribution – it would be more sensible to keep the personal allowance fixed and use the revenue to reverse the proposed cuts to tax credits.) Regarding inequality more generally, the Scottish government would have the ability to increase tax rates on those with the highest incomes. The risk is that such policy might induce some high-income earners to relocate themselves (or their earnings) to the rest of the UK, depriving the Scottish government of tax revenues. There is much uncertainty around the extent to which such income relocation might happen in response to tax increases in Scotland.[7] But the Scottish government will certainly have some leeway to adopt a more progressive rate structure, if it has the political will to do so.

Conclusions

A well designed tax system can ensure that the poorest in society do not face an undue burden of taxation, at the same time as generating the revenues needed to invest in the social infrastructure needed to prevent poverty. But it must do so in a way that does not disincentivise households from taking up employment opportunities. In this respect, design of the tax system should be considered alongside the benefit system.

Under the Smith Commission proposals, the Scottish government will gain almost full control over income tax, which will open the possibility of a more progressive rate system in Scotland. Arguably however, the area where there is greater scope for reform is in relation to property taxation. This is an area that is already under the control of the Scottish government, but to date the emphasis has been on tinkering with the existing system rather than addressing the underlying deficiencies.

Notes
1 This personal allowance is now £10,600. Income earned between £10,600 and £42,385 is taxed at the basic income tax rate of 20%.
2 Currently, income earned between £42,385 and £150,000 is taxed at the higher tax rate of 40%.
3 For further discussion of the distributional effects of the coalition government's tax and benefit changes, see P de Agostini, J Hills and H Sutherland, *Were We Really All In It Together? The distributional effects of the UK coalition govern-*

ment's tax-benefit policy changes, London School of Economics, 2014, available at http://sticerd.lse.ac.uk/dps/case/spcc/WP10.pdf; and S Adam, J Browne and W Elming, 'The Effect of the Coalition Government's Tax and Benefit Changes on Household Incomes and Work Incentives', *Fiscal Studies* 36(3), 2015, pp375–402, available at http://onlinelibrary.wiley.com/doi/10.1111/j.1475-5890.2015.12058/abstract

4   See http://localtaxcommission.scot/download-our-final-report

5   See www.comtax.org/wp-content/uploads/2016/01/A-Dynamic-Scotland-FINAL. pdf

6   See http://centreonconstitutionalchange.ac.uk/blog/scottish-rate-income-tax-progressive-or-regressive

7   D Bell and D Eiser, *Addressing Inequality in Scotland: what can be done?* Paper for the David Hume Institute, 2015, available at www.davidhumeinstitute.com/wp-content/uploads/2015/07/Inequality-in-Scotland.pdf

Eleven

Social security: a tool for tackling poverty

Hanna McCulloch

The efficiency of social security as a tool for reducing poverty was clearly demonstrated in the UK between 1998 and 2010, during which time the number of children living in poverty fell by 1.1million.[1] In Scotland alone, 160,000 children were lifted out of poverty.[2] While this period also saw investment in childcare, improved access to employment and the creation of a national minimum wage, the Institute for Fiscal Studies notes that the dramatic decrease in child poverty was 'largely as a result of very significant additional spending on benefits and tax credits'.[3]

The impact of this investment in social security, along with wider support for low-income families, was reflected in the wellbeing of children as well as in poverty statistics. Between 1998 and 2010:[4]

> Educational attainment improved. Housing conditions improved and child homelessness fell… There was even evidence that adolescent mental health improved as did the happiness and overall life satisfaction of children.

Investment in social security was thus shown to be an important part of reducing poverty and improving child wellbeing. Indeed, analysis shows that social security plays a key role in reducing and preventing poverty across developed economies, although high levels of pre-tax and benefit income inequality mean that the UK is more reliant than most other countries on its redistributive effect.[5]

The 2010–2015 coalition government, however, was not convinced. Elected with a mandate to cut the deficit in the wake of the global financial crisis, it made it clear it believed that the existing approach to social security was not a solution to child poverty; it was part of the problem. It proclaimed that: 'a system that was originally designed to support the poorest in society is now trapping them in the very condition it was supposed to alleviate.'[6] Instead, the UK government set out its vision of a system intended to radically simplify entitlement, 'make work pay' and cut costs associated with what it saw as an overly generous approach to welfare.

The vehicle for most of these changes was the Welfare Reform Act 2012. As well as introducing the flagship benefit, universal credit, the legislation laid out a series of reforms that included the creation of the 'bedroom tax' and the benefit cap. In addition to these poverty-creating provisions, subsequent measures reduced entitlement to tax credits and child benefit, chipping away at previous investments to reduce child poverty. Although it received little attention at the time, one of the most significant changes concerned limiting the rate at which benefits were uprated. This meant that, despite the cost of living rising by more than 10 per cent between 2010 and 2015, the value of benefits stagnated. This measure alone is thought to have cost low-income Scottish households around £230 million per year.[7]

While previous investment in benefits and tax credits continued to provide protection for low-income families, by 2013 independent modelling forecast that up to 100,000 more children in Scotland were likely to be pushed into poverty by 2020, primarily as a result of social security cuts.[8]

Families with children were not the only group affected. For disabled people, 'welfare reform' meant increasingly stringent eligibility criteria and increased use of medical assessments. New procedures, along with changes to the review system, resulted in extended delays, reduced income and stress for many vulnerable people.[9]

The introduction of new medical assessments formed part of the shift towards increased conditionality and an arguably more punitive approach to social security. Though sanctions were in place under previous governments, their use increased dramatically under the coalition.[10] At the same time, rapid changes to the structure of the social security system coupled with a failure to develop effective delivery mechanisms appear to have resulted in extended delays, errors and maladministration on the part of the Department for Work and Pensions, HM Revenue and Customs, local authorities and the growing number of private contractors.[11] Errors, delays and sanctions not only contribute to increased relative poverty, they are also the key drivers of income crisis and the increased food bank use in the UK.[12]

The next five years

At UK level there is little evidence that the government is planning an about-turn on social security. Signs of improvement, such as a reduced rate of sanctioning, are dwarfed by ever-deeper cuts. Even universal credit, once considered to be a poverty-reducing measure,[13] is likely to reduce many household incomes further as a result of ongoing cuts.[14]

Furthermore, the Welfare Reform and Work Bill 2016 will freeze the value of benefits for the next four years, reduce the benefit cap to £20,000 and exclude third children from universal credit. Projections produced by the Resolution Foundation in the wake of the summer 2015 Budget suggest that these measures will contribute to a further dramatic rise in child poverty.[15]

However, since 2010, the Scottish government has been outspoken in its rejection of the UK government's approach to social security and has repeatedly raised concerns about the impact on poverty rates.[16] This has created an expectation that devolved aspects of social security might be used to reduce poverty, and to protect the health and wellbeing of vulnerable families.

The Scottish government's track record on social security

The Scottish government already has limited power in relation to social security. While the council tax reduction scheme and the Scottish Welfare Fund represent little more than 2 per cent of the social security spend in Scotland,[17] the extent to which they have been used to reduce poverty might be telling in terms of the Scottish government's willingness to put its principles into practice.

Control over both the Scottish Welfare Fund and council tax reduction was transferred to the Scottish Parliament in 2013. In both cases, power was preceded by a reduction in funding. In response, the Scottish government and the Convention of Scottish Local Authorities stepped up to the mark and, having already invested significantly to help mitigate the impact of the 'bedroom tax', invested an additional £40 million a year in reversing the 10 per cent cut to council tax benefit and an additional £9.2 million in the Scottish Welfare Fund. This has helped to avert the scenario unfolding in parts of England, where cuts were made to both council tax benefit and local welfare assistance schemes, resulting in the emergence of a shambolic postcode lottery of delivery.[18]

While the Scottish government has taken a laudable approach to ensuring consistency and transparency in the administration of devolved benefits, aspects of their delivery has triggered some alarm bells. While the previous UK discretionary social fund only delivered cash awards, in Scotland there has been a move towards making awards 'in kind'. This can include delivery of goods, such as carpets, vouchers and store cards. While recent legislation has placed important safeguards on when it is appropriate to make non-cash awards, there is still unease, particularly in the third sector, about the effect this approach will have on the dignity of claimants.[19]

Furthermore, in a year in which demand for emergency food aid has risen by 40 per cent,[20] applications to the Scottish Welfare Fund – a fund intended to provide assistance to those experiencing crisis – appear to have fallen.[21] This suggests that there are thousands of families in crisis who are either unaware of, or choosing not to use, the Fund. A strong Scottish safety net is only effective if people are aware of its existence.

Scotland's future social security powers

Although new powers relate to only 17 per cent of social security spend in Scotland,[22] there is no doubt that they could allow for a markedly different approach to tackling poverty.

As drafted, the Scotland Bill will enable the Scottish government to top up the income of households already in receipt of reserved social security benefits. A significant step would be to use this power to top up child benefit and other family benefits. New powers might also be used to boost maternity benefits, augmenting family finances at a time when low-income families are at risk of experiencing poverty. Increasing the rates at which housing and disability benefits are paid could also dramatically reduce rates of poverty in Scotland.

However, it is clear that in order to use the social security system to reduce poverty, difficult political choices are required. In all likelihood, significant poverty reduction will necessitate the use of existing and future tax-raising powers. While creating a more redistributive system of tax and social security in Scotland will be constrained by the limits of devolved power and will not be easily achieved, it is by no means impossible. Few modern governments experience the level of public support currently enjoyed by the SNP, and the government's unprecedented popularity provides a rare opportunity for it to lead public opinion, allowing it to take meaningful steps towards poverty eradication.

There is also a great deal that could be done to improve the social security system without a dramatic increase in spending. The government in Scotland must build on the principles it set out in late 2015,[23] as well as embrace the new approach to social security advocated by civic organisations such as the Scottish Campaign on Welfare Reform.[24] This must involve careful design to ensure administrative errors and delays are minimised. Ensuring that benefits are delivered in a way that promotes, rather than undermines, the dignity of the claimant could also have a transformative effect. Above all, building equality and fairness into the heart of the system is vital. In relation to newly devolved powers this will mean, for example, ensuring that entitlement to disability and carers' benefits is established nationally in order to avoid varying standards, complexity and the emergence of a postcode lottery.

Conclusion

The Scottish government's use of its limited social security powers to date suggests that its willingness to use these to address poverty extends beyond mere rhetoric. Wider social security powers create even greater opportunities for meaningful change for children and families in Scotland, including the potential to top up child and other family benefits.

Furthermore, the Scottish government must invest time and expertise in ensuring systems designed to deliver the new powers are workable, intuitive and easy to use, especially for the most vulnerable claimants. Both UK and Scottish benefit delivery has demonstrated that overlooking important details creates cracks in the system through which claimants can easily fall.

Notes

1 Before housing costs. Department for Work and Pensions, *Households Below Average Income 1994/95–2010/11*, 2014, Table 4.3tr

2 Scottish Government, *Poverty and Inequality in Scotland: 2013/14*, 2015, Table A1, children, before housing costs, 1997/98 to 2010/11

3 R Joyce and L Sibieta, *Labour's Record on Poverty and Inequality*, Institute for Fiscal Studies, 2013

4 J Bradshaw, 'Child Wellbeing in the 2000s', in *Ending Child Poverty by 2020: progress made and lessons learned*, CPAG, 2012

5 HX Java and C Leventi, *Note on EU27 Child Poverty Rates*, Institute for Social and Economic Research, University of Essex, 2014

6 Speech by the Rt Hon Iain Duncan Smith MP, 'Welfare for the 21st Century', 27 May 2010

7 C Beatty and S Fothergill, *The Cumulative Impact of Welfare Reform on Households in Scotland*, Sheffield Hallam University, 2015, Table 1

8 J Browne, A Hood and R Joyce, *Child and Working-age Poverty in Northern Ireland Over the Next Decade: an update*, Briefing Note 144, Institute for Fiscal Studies, 2014, Appendix Table B2

9 See, for example, P Gray, *An Independent Review of the Personal Independence Payment*, DWP, 2014, Chapter 4, para 4

10 Department for Work and Pensions, *JSA and ESA Sanctions Statistics*, updated November 2015

11 Cases received through CPAG in Scotland's 'Early Warning System', for example, show consistently high rates of maladministration and error. See www.cpag.org.uk/scotland/early-warning-system.

12 J Perry, M Williams, T Sefton and M Haddad, *Emergency Use Only: understanding and reducing the use of food banks in the UK*, CPAG, Church of England, Oxfam GB and the Trussell Trust, 2015

13 D Ghelani and L Stidle, *Universal Credit: towards an effective poverty reduction strategy*, Policy in Practice, 2014

14 D Finch, *A Poverty of Information: assessing the government's new child poverty focus and future trends*, Resolution Foundation, 2015

15 See note 14

16 See, for example, Nicola Sturgeon's speech to the Poverty Alliance Conference on 13 October 2014

17 *DWP Outturn and Forecast: Autumn Statement 2014, DWP Benefit Expenditure by Region 1996/97 to 2013/14, HMRC Tax Receipts Between England, Wales, Scotland & Northern Ireland, Scottish Welfare Fund Statistics: 2013/14, Council Tax Reduction: caseload and expenditure, Scotland, 2013/14*, as summarised

in *Social Security for Scotland: benefits being devolved to the Scottish Parliament*, Scottish Government, 2015

18 CPAG response to the House of Commons Work and Pensions Committee Inquiry into a local social security safety net, November 2015

19 See, for example, the briefing circulated by the Scottish Council of Voluntary Organisations in advance of the Scottish Parliament stage three debate on the Welfare Funds (Scotland) Bill

20 The number of food parcels distributed by the Trussell Trust in Scotland increased from 71,428 in 2013/14 to 117, 689 in 2014/15: Trussell Trust annual statistics 2015

21 'Comparing April to June 2015 with the same quarter one year ago, applications for Community Care Grants decreased by 1,700 applications (–9%) whilst applications for Crisis Grants decreased by 1,200 applications (–3%)': *Scottish Welfare Fund Statistics*, Scottish Government, update to 30 June 2015

22 *Social Security for Scotland: benefits being devolved to the Scottish Parliament*, Scottish government, 2015

23 http://news.scotland.gov.uk/news/scotland-s-social-security-principles-208c.aspx

24 www.cpag.org.uk/scotland/scowr

Twelve

Using human rights to tackle poverty among disabled people

Pauline Nolan

In April 2012, less than two years after the UK government announced plans in its 2010 emergency Budget to reduce public spending and the welfare benefits paid to working-age people, including disabled people, the Scottish Campaign for a Fair Society took its concerns about the Welfare Reform Act 2012 to the United Nations' (UN) Universal Periodic Review in Geneva.[1] The Universal Periodic Review is a mechanism of the UN Human Rights Council that periodically examines the human rights performance of all member states. Our concerns centred around the actual and potential human rights infringements and abuses of disabled people in accordance with both the International Covenant on Economic, Social and Cultural Rights and the UN Convention on the Rights of Disabled People. This chapter examines the potential of using a human rights approach as a tool for tackling poverty.

The Scottish Campaign for a Fair Society's submission

The original submission to the Universal Periodic Review was a broad assessment of the limited impact on disabled people in Scotland of the various conventions signed and ratified by the UK.[2] It examined the impact of cuts to benefits and services, and also a range of policy areas, both reserved and devolved to Scotland. For example, it highlighted the development of the Self-Directed Support Strategy and Bill in Scotland,[3] praising it for its ambition, but also raising concerns about the piecemeal roll-out of direct payments and warning of the replication of inherent inequalities in the Bill's delivery.

The Campaign was invited to speak directly on the submission to the

UN Human Rights Council in Geneva. We decided to focus on the cumulative impact of the cuts on disabled people's benefits. Disability organisations, disabled people and the UK Parliament's own Joint Committee on Human Rights had all concluded that these cuts would have a devastating cumulative impact on the livelihoods of disabled people.[4]

Further cuts were also being implemented to local authority services. For example, former ballerina Ms Elaine McDonald, a Scottish stroke survivor living in London's Royal Borough of Kensington and Chelsea, lost her appeal to the Supreme Court in which she challenged the local authority's decision not to provide her with night-time care to help her use a commode, arguing that her right to a private life had been abused due to the lack of dignity of being left in a nappy at night – possibly lying in her own excrement for 12 hours at a time.

As Inclusion Scotland, drawing on Department for Work and Pensions figures, argued at the time, the potential cuts ran into millions of pounds of losses for disabled people in Scotland. Of the overall £18 billion planned cut to welfare benefits, £2 billion was to be taken out of local economies here in Scotland, and we estimated that at least half of this (£1 billion) would fall on Scottish disabled people and their families. Those with 'the broadest shoulders' were not 'bearing the greatest burden', as famously promised by Prime Minister David Cameron in his Conservative Party conference speech in 2010.

Documentary evidence was provided, showing that disabled people were, and would be, 'directly and disproportionately' impacted. It concluded:

> These cuts will push hundreds of thousands of disabled people and their families into poverty and thousands will be made homeless. Scotland's disabled people are over-represented in these numbers as there is a higher rate of impairments and long-term health conditions here.

The evidence summary we provided ended with four recommended questions for the Council to ask the UK government in its examination:

1. How does the UK government intend to measure the scale and cumulative impact of the Welfare Reform Act on disabled individuals and their families, and when will it publicise this? What action does it intend to take on the basis of these enquiries?
2. Disabled people's organisations agree that disabled people should be given increased opportunities to enter and maintain paid employment. However, there are insufficient resources to help them do this. How

does the UK government intend to ensure paid work for disabled people when it is cutting in-work benefits for disabled people (such as disability living allowance and the Independent Living Fund) and restricting what it will pay for with Access to Work funds, and when the country is in recession and already has high levels of unemployment?

3. How will the UK government guarantee the rights established by the International Covenant on Economic, Social and Cultural Rights and the UN Convention on the Rights of Disabled People as it implements cuts to a number of benefits on which disabled people rely in order to live independently and be included in their communities?

4. How will the Scottish and UK governments ensure disabled people have access to justice when they appeal incorrect benefit assessments (such as for employment and support allowance and personal independence payment)?

Using UN Convention rights as a tool for influencing policy

As a tool for addressing the impact on UK poverty, the direct effect of this submission to the UN may not have made a vast amount of difference. The only recommendation to result from the Universal Periodic Review examination that pertained to social security[5] was to enhance the 'welfare of all segments of society and protect their rights'[6] – a somewhat weak recommendation from the Nepalese UN mission, which was countered by the UK Coalition government on the grounds that the cuts were to be '*fairer*, more affordable and *better able to tackle poverty*, worklessness and welfare dependency.'[7] [emphasis added]

Of course, a submission to the Universal Periodic Review is not a standalone approach to using human rights to tackle poverty. It should be seen as part of a much broader human rights approach, in which disabled people and anti-poverty organisations attempt to influence the development of fairer policies and strategies to reduce the impact of poverty here in Scotland. This includes: awareness-raising among affected communities; the development of a human rights 'tool-kit' to independent living and information sessions on its use; actions to influence the Scottish Parliament to mitigate some of the worst effects of welfare reform; and promoting anti-poverty strategies co-produced by various stakeholders, including disabled people, at a local level.

Our experience demonstrated that fringe lobbying is essential to influence the Human Rights Council: identifying and meeting with individual country representatives who have made parallel recommendations in other countries' Universal Periodic Review examination processes; arranging fringe meetings in advance to engage; using evidence and case studies on specific issues, in particular, bringing someone whose rights are affected, who can illustrate in her/his own words the impact of the cuts on her/his own life and ability to live independently. With better use of more lobbying activities, it would have been possible to engage more fully with the Human Rights Council. We could also have maximised the impact of media coverage of the trip.[8]

Conclusion: planning a human rights campaign and embedding human rights in other work

This was the first Universal Periodic Review of the UK since the process began, and engaging with the UN Convention on the Rights of Disabled People is also a new experience for disability organisations. For the next review of the UK, a more thorough plan – from reporting through to engaging with the Human Rights Council – should be implemented, with a focus on a more inclusive and unified civil society approach. Learning from this experience can improve other organisations' approaches to reporting on individual human rights instruments, and encourage them to continue to use such opportunities to bring the impacts of the poverty caused by the cuts to the attention of the UN.

Currently, Inclusion Scotland is compiling a report to the UN Disability Committee, which includes extensive evidence of the adverse impacts of recent welfare cuts. The report will be endorsed by a wide range of disability and other civil society organisations, and the engagement with the Committee will be well planned. This work is fully funded by the Scottish government and includes a budget not only to consult widely with disabled people but for disabled people to report their experiences directly to the Committee in Geneva. Children's representative organisations have also reported on the UN Convention on the Rights of the Child and we have been involved in promoting disabled children's voices and raising concerns about child poverty in families affected by disability in these reports.[9]

There is still scope to influence governments, both in Scotland and at Westminster, on how they might pursue an anti-poverty agenda. In

Scotland, we currently have a unique opportunity to influence the new devolved powers on disability benefits and employability. We have already had relative success in doing that here in Scotland. For example, the Scottish government is also funding Inclusion Scotland to co-produce with disabled people, their organisations and local third sector organisations poverty mitigation strategies related to welfare reforms.

A human rights approach that is strengthened by recommendations from the UN can have an impact, but it needs to be part of a much wider approach to embedding human rights – for disabled people themselves and in the minds of decision makers.

Notes

1   The Campaign for a Fair Society is a UK-wide popular movement to challenge the unfair cuts that target the most vulnerable people in our society and to propose positive principles for a better system. Established in February 2011, the Scottish Campaign for a Fair Society believes everyone is equal, no matter their differences or impairments. A fair society sees each of its members as a full citizen – a unique person with a life of their own.

2   http://lib.ohchr.org/HRBodies/UPR/Documents/Session13/GB/SCFS_UPR_GBR _S13_2012_TheScottishCampaignforaFairSociety_E.pdf

3   Now the Self-Directed Support (Scotland) Act 2013

4   Human Rights Joint Committee, Twenty First Report, *Legislative Scrutiny: Welfare Reform Bill*, available at www.publications.parliament.uk/pa/jt201012/jtselect/ jtrights/233/23302.htm

5   *United Nations Universal Periodic Review Mid-term Report of the United Kingdom of Great Britain and Northern Ireland, and the British Overseas Territories, and Crown Dependencies*, https://www.gov.uk/government/uploads/ system/uploads/attachment_data/file/418272/uk-upr-mid-term-report-2014.pdf

6   Recommendation 110.42 (welfare, rights): 'continue efforts in enhancing the welfare of all segments of society and protect their rights'.

7   UK Government, *UK National Report*, 2011, available at www.justice.gov.uk/ downloads/human-rights/upr-report.pdf, p6

8   Stephen Naysmith, 'UK is breaching human rights of disabled, UN told', *The Herald*, available at www.heraldscotland.com/news/13052730.uk_is_breaching_ human_rights_of_disabled__un_told

9   See Article 12 in *I Witness: the UNCRC in Scotland*, 2015 on the implementation of the Convention, informed by young disabled people in a workshop set up by an IS member organisation, GDA; and Together: Scottish Alliance for Children's Rights, *NGO Report to UN on UNCRC Implementation in Scotland*, available at www.togetherscotland.org.uk/news-and-events/news/detail/?news=916

Thirteen

Fair work and poverty reduction

Peter Kelly

For the last twenty years the mantra that 'work is the best route out of poverty' has dominated the official discourse on poverty reduction. However, for many, the notion that any paid employment will address poverty has been seen as fanciful.[1] It is encouraging then that in recent years there has been a growing recognition, at least among the mainstream of policy makers in Scotland, of the more complex relationship between paid employment and poverty. Perhaps the clearest indication of this recognition has been the support that the living wage has received from across the political spectrum.

However, the problem of in-work poverty is about more than just low pay. Indeed, addressing low pay is only one part of creating 'fair employment' and if we are to break the link between poverty and paid employment, then a range of actions will be required. Below we consider what we mean by fair work, the context for fair work over the last few years, and what more is needed to ensure that fair work is an effective tool for tackling poverty.

What do we mean by fair work?

While some policy makers may talk as though fair work is a new discovery, notions of fair employment or 'decent' work are hardly new. Indeed, the International Labour Organisation (ILO) was set up in 1919 in order to promote social justice based on decent work. Going further back, trade unions have been organising for decent employment conditions for centuries.

Despite this long history, what constitutes fair work is still subject to some debate. Evidence to the Scottish Parliament noted that there remains no single accepted definition of what constitutes decent work,[2] and elements of employment that some may see as negative can in, other contexts, be positive for some workers. Flexible employment is a good example. Flexibility is required and needed by most employees, but some flexible arrangements (such as zero-hour contacts) can also be used in ways that negatively impact on employees.

The Fair Work Convention, established by the Scottish government in April 2015 to follow up the recommendations from the *Working Together Review*,[3] immediately set out to define what it understood to be fair work. Its working definition is 'work that provides opportunity, fulfilment, security, respect and effective voice'. Fair work should also 'generate benefits for individuals, organisations and for society.'[4] Clearly, these themes take us far beyond the confines of low-paid work.

Questions of voice, fulfilment and respect also emerged in research carried out by the Poverty Alliance, which considered what employment would look like in a Scotland without poverty. The following quotes are all from individuals who are living on low incomes and who have had a variety of employment experiences:[5]

> 'Work needs to pay a decent wage, but it also needs to be a job that is worthwhile. You should feel valued as a worker.'

> 'It (decent work) gives you more than money – it gives me qualifications and training, it builds my confidence and my self-esteem.'

> 'If employees are happy then they will be better at their jobs, they'll contribute more. Nobody wants to work where they aren't appreciated.'

These views resonate with the ILO approach to decent work, which emphasises the centrality of work to both individual and community wellbeing, as well as the dimensions of social protection, dialogue and workers' rights. Paid employment that does not fit with these varied definitions of decency – that does not provide an adequate wage, where there is little control or choice for the worker, where the work is unstable or erratic – is more likely to be associated with in-work poverty.

The context for fair work in Scotland

It was clearly shown in the last edition of *Poverty in Scotland*, published early in 2014, that the Scottish labour market was still a long way from recovery.[6] The uneven progress that was highlighted then has largely continued. Our labour market remains one in which there are divided experiences.

While employment levels continue to recover in Scotland and stood at 74.3 per cent in April 2015, higher than in Great Britain as a whole, this headline figure does not tell the whole story.[7] The STUC has noted that full-time employment at this time was still well below pre-recession levels and part-time employment had increased by 12 per cent.[8] So changes that may have been seen as part of a response to economic crisis (cutting full-time employment and replacing it to some extent with part-time) now appear to be firmly embedded in the way our labour market functions.

A similar analysis can be made for the number of people in temporary employment or on zero-hour contracts. Both have fallen back in recent years, at the UK and Scottish levels, but both remain higher than pre-recession levels. While unemployment rates had been falling on a fairly consistent basis since the start of 2012, this decline has faltered in 2015. We also need to add to this mix the growth in self-employment over this period. By April 2015, there had been a 12 per cent increase in self-employment and, although not all of this increase can be associated with poor employment, there is evidence to suggest that these newly self-employed people are more likely to earn less and work less.[9]

Low pay, while not always an indicator of bad work or of poverty, is undoubtedly closely associated with both. The proportion of employees earning less than the living wage in Scotland in 2014 was 19 per cent, around 441,000 individuals.[10] This has been relatively unchanged in recent years. This is perhaps unsurprising given that the STUC has noted that real wages have only recently begun to recover after a fall, which it refers to as 'unprecedented in modern times.'[11] Those affected by low pay remain depressingly familiar: women, young people and those from particular ethnic minorities all remain at greater risk of low pay.[12]

This mix of factors – increased levels of part-time, temporary and atypical working, stagnating unemployment, entrenched patterns of low pay – make for a difficult context in which to effectively promote decent employment as a route out of poverty. However, it is precisely this context that requires a greater focus on decent work if we are to really address poverty.

Analysis in the latest edition of *Monitoring Poverty and Social Exclusion* shows the importance of labour market changes for those entering and leaving poverty. It found that 'labour market events' – increases or decreases in earnings as a result of leaving or entering a job – were associated with more than half of all moves into or out of poverty for children. In comparison, changes to family structure were less significant. Fourteen per cent of children whose parents separated moved into poverty, although this accounted for only 1 per cent of all moves into poverty.[13]

If we are to genuinely address poverty, it is imperative that we more effectively address the labour market factors that lie behind much of the poverty that is experienced in Scotland. Creating the conditions for more 'fair work' will be central then to tackling poverty in the future.

Priorities for fair work

As outlined above, the context for fair work remains challenging. However, there have been some welcome developments in Scotland in recent years in relation to the promotion of fair work. The establishment of the Fair Work Convention in 2015, the creation of the Scottish Business Pledge, and the increasing support for the living wage through the voluntary accreditation scheme have been welcome steps forward. Taken together, these measures point to an important change in the direction of travel in Scotland. However, there is still a long way to go in reshaping our economy in order for decent work to be available to all, especially those workers living on low incomes.

The Poverty Alliance has been at the forefront of the living wage campaign in Scotland since 2007. In that time we have seen a significant shift in attitudes towards the living wage, from pronounced scepticism from policy makers at both local and national levels, to enthusiastic support. The Scottish government has placed the living wage at the heart of the Scottish Business Pledge and a number of local authorities (Dumfries and Galloway, Renfrewshire and Glasgow) all see the living wage as central to their local anti-poverty strategies.

A critical component of the living wage in Scotland has been the development of the accreditation initiative.[14] This scheme has given recognition to those employers who adopt the living wage (£8.25 an hour, at the time of writing) for all their employees and sub-contracted workers. More than 470 employers have become accredited in Scotland, with more than 2,000 across the UK. Not only has this meant pay rises for thousands of workers across Scotland, it has also opened the door for different kinds of discussions with employers about their role in promoting fair work and addressing poverty. It is to be hoped that the next Scottish government will continue to play a strong leadership role in relation to the living wage.

The Fair Work Convention should play a pivotal role in fleshing out how improvements in the experience of paid employment can be made in ways that will help address poverty. It is more understood than ever that fair work is required in order to reduce in-work poverty. There is a range of areas in which the Convention could help to focus efforts to reduce in-work poverty:

- Ensuring that the provision of business support is effectively tied to the promotion of fair work.
- Ensuring that there is a strategy to promote awareness of employment rights, particularly to vulunerable workers.
- Enhancing access to in-work training and support for low-paid workers to ensure they progress in the labour market.

There has been a welcome recognition of the central role of trade unions in promoting a fair work agenda. The stance adopted by the Scottish government and others to oppose the Trade Union Bill currently going through the UK Parliament highlights an alternative vision for the promotion of fair work in Scotland. The announcement that the Scottish government is to retain the Scottish Agricultural Wages Board, which sets pay and conditions for agricultural workers and which had been under threat, puts into practice this alternative vision.

The promotion of fair work as an effective tool to tackle poverty will require a significant degree of cultural change in Scotland. It will require a mix of efforts: encouraging and cajoling employers, promoting those who are examples of good practice, but also regulating those who continue to exploit their staff. Any anti-poverty strategies in Scotland that do not recognise the importance of fair work as a route out of poverty will be destined to fail.

Notes

1   H Ferreira and A Ferro, *Quality of Work and Employment in the EU,* European Anti-Poverty Network, 2014
2   Scottish Parliament Information Centre, *Economy, Energy and Tourism Committee Work, Wages and Wellbeing: summary of written submissions*, 2015, available at www.scottish.parliament.uk/s4_economyenergyandtourismcommittee/inquiries/summary_of_evidence.pdf
3   Scottish Government, *Working Together Review: progressive workplace policies in Scotland*, Scottish Government, 2014
4   See www.fairworkconvention.scot

5 P Kelly and L Darling, *A Scotland Without Poverty*, Poverty Alliance, 2015, available at http://povertyalliance.org/userfiles/files/Scotland_Without_Poverty_ May2015.pdf

6 S Boyd, 'Wages, the Labour Market and Low Pay' in JH McKendrick, G Mooney, J Dickie, G Scott and P Kelly (eds), *Poverty in Scotland 2014: the independence referendum and beyond*, CPAG, 2014

7 Office for National Statistics, *Regional Labour Market, April 2015*, 2015, available at www.ons.gov.uk/ons/dcp171778_401130.pdf

8 *STUC Labour Market Report*, STUC, 2015

9 J Philpott, *The Rise in Self-employment*, Chartered Institute of Personnel and Development, 2012

10 Markit Group Ltd, *Living Wage Research for KPMG: structural analysis of hourly wages and current trends in household finances*, 2015, available at www. kpmg.com/uk/en/issuesandinsights/articlespublications/documents/pdf/latest% 20news/kpmg-living-wage-research-2015 .pdf

11 See note 8

12 See note 10

13 T MacInnes, A Tinson, C Hughes, TB Born and H Aldridge, *Monitoring Poverty and Social Exclusion 2015*, Joseph Rowntree Foundation, 2015

14 For more information, see www.scottishlivingwage.org

Fourteen

The role of education in tackling poverty: a progress report

Andrea Bradley

The Educational Institute of Scotland (EIS), Scotland's largest teacher trade union, has been a long-standing campaigner on the issue of poverty and its detrimental impact on the lives and educational outcomes of Scotland's children. As the single greatest barrier to success within education, it is not surprising that poverty has featured as the central theme of many conferences hosted and attended by the EIS, and of several EIS publications. The stark injustice that a young person's ability to thrive, to learn, to benefit from the myriad of opportunities that education has to offer, is stunted as a consequence of socio-economic deprivation has never been acceptable to the EIS.

Education is a key force which can act in the interests of social justice and equality against those opposing forces that are currently increasing the levels of child poverty and, in so doing, blighting the life chances of one-fifth of Scotland's children. Education cannot be the sole agent of change, but it has a role to play in mitigating the effects of poverty through a careful balance of pastoral care, pupil support, curriculum and pedagogical policy making.

New policies: full of potential, short of funding

In recent years, a principal element of education policy intended to reduce the impact of poverty has been the commitment to investment in the early years of children's lives. Resources have been channelled into offering 600 hours of free childcare for all three-, four- and vulnerable two-year-olds, with entitlement soon to be doubled. This is impressive and welcome, as the importance of pre-school care and education has never been better understood. Within the under-fives service, however, it is crucial that the role of education is given adequate attention. Arguably, the quality of nursery education is being compromised by the scaling back of trained teachers in these settings, thus ignoring the wealth of research evidence that extols the impact of fully trained teachers, particularly on children from disadvantaged backgrounds.[1] While the Scottish government has committed to ensuring 'access to a teacher', local authorities, with legal impunity, have been removing teachers from nursery classrooms in order to reduce costs. Efforts to close the achievement gap must begin before formal schooling, and the pedagogical input of teaching professionals as part of an under-fives workforce is an essential ingredient in the approach outlined in the Curriculum for Excellence.

One ambition of the Curriculum for Excellence (the curriculum architecture designed to transform the character of Scottish education) is greater equity of outcome for all learners, including those who have benefited less from past curriculum models. This is to be achieved through: the adoption of more holistic, learner-centred and creative approaches; incorporating new, more inclusive assessment methodologies; recognition of wider achievement in addition to traditional attainment outcomes; and a more diverse range of learner pathways towards positive destinations beyond school. While much has been achieved since the new curriculum was officially implemented in 2010, as with early years policy, this has occurred against a backdrop of local authority budget cuts. In effect, schools have been expected to do more with less and, as a consequence, teachers' workloads have increased to unacceptable, unsustainable levels. With proper investment in education to match the size of the ambition of the Curriculum for Excellence, this could have been avoided and, at the same time, the pace of change towards greater equity of educational outcomes accelerated.

Simultaneously, the ongoing development of Getting it Right for Every Child is of significance within the policy landscape configured in recent years to tackle poverty. The overarching vision of the Getting it Right for Every Child framework is that all children and young people should thrive as confident individuals, successful learners, effective contributors and responsible citizens by having key needs met: the need to be safe, healthy, achieving, nurtured, active, respected, responsible and included (the SHANARRI indicators). Within this framework, inclusion is defined as children and young people 'having help to overcome social, educational, physical and economic inequalities',[2] pointing explicitly to the need for education to address the impact of poverty. These outcomes are used in assessing and planning to meet the needs of all children and young people.

Getting it Right for Every Child, having been implemented to varying degrees across local authorities, is now enshrined in statute within the

Children and Young People Act, the relevant section of which will come into force in August 2016. To comply, education authorities will be bound to consider the effect of socio-economic disadvantage on wellbeing. The extent to which they can act to mitigate the adverse impact of poverty on wellbeing, for example, through funding nurture groups, pupil counselling services and providing access to extra-curricular activities, will depend on available resources.

In legislative terms, another key element of education policy active in the past five years is that derived from the Additional Support for Learning Act 2009. This entitles all children and young people whose education is the responsibility of an education authority to have their needs assessed and, where an additional support need is identified, to have a support plan established and thereafter regularly reviewed. This piece of legislation has the potential to be a strong lever in tackling the effects of poverty on children's learning and achievement in light of the fact that a disproportionate number of learners with additional support needs are from deprived socio-economic backgrounds – another good piece of legislation on paper, but lacking the resources needed to realise its full ambition. For example, without investment in adequate numbers of specialist support for learning assistants and additional support needs teachers, as well as in assistive technology, the potential of the legislation to deliver greater equity of outcome is restricted.

Since January 2015, the extension of free school meals eligibility to all P1 to P3 children has been a bulwark against the rise in food poverty in Scotland, precipitated by the low-wage economy, a regime of cuts to social security and benefit sanctions, all of which have disproportionately impacted on children (and their families). Today, sadly, hunger is common in Scottish classrooms. For thousands of children living in poverty, a free school meal is the only nutritious meal of the day. However, for older children whose family's income is just above the threshold of entitlement to free school meals, there is no such policy provision.

Evidence of progress

Arguably, though, in spite of under-resourcing, some of this education policy may be beginning to bear fruit.

According to Scottish government attainment statistics published in June 2015, the percentage of school leavers in positive destinations increased to 91.7 per cent from 90.4 per cent in the previous year, marking a record high. The vast majority (97 per cent) reached literacy at SCQF level 3 or above. The figures also show that the percentage of school leavers attaining a qualification at SCQF level 6 or 7 increased from 55.8 per cent in 2011/12 to 58.8 per cent in 2013/14, while higher percentages of leavers from Scotland's most deprived communities attained one or more qualifications at SCQF level 4 or better, compared to previous years. The attainment[3] and leaver destination status[4] of learners with additional support needs is also on an upward trajectory within each of the categories examined. Clearly, then, there are some successes to be celebrated.

The same statistics, however, highlight that 79.7 per cent of the most privileged pupils passed a Higher with grade A to C, as opposed to only 39 per cent of the least affluent. Only 3 per cent of those from the wealthiest backgrounds left school with no positive destination, compared with 15 per cent of children from the most deprived. While the gap has reduced slightly from the previous year, obvious inequality remains.[5]

Challenges that lie ahead

In the coming five years, therefore, more has to be done to maximise Scottish education's ability to limit the impact of poverty.

Recently, the Scottish government, persuaded that quality of provision is as important as quantity, announced its intention to provide additional qualified teachers or degree-educated childcare workers for nurseries in the most deprived areas.[6] Though welcome, this can only be a starting point. Without universally extending the commitment to equal and minimum access to a nursery teacher, it will fall short of that required to meet the needs of the thousands of nursery-aged children living in poverty in homes whose postcodes lie outside the targeted Scottish Index of Multiple Deprivation zones.

Essential to the success of Getting it Right for Every Child will be increased investment in schools to ensure sufficient administrative support staff, teachers and professional learning relevant to the Getting it Right for Every Child agenda. Key features of the Children and Young People Act legislation – the named person service,[7] child's plan and inter-agency information sharing – place significant additional resource demands on education. If the pastoral care needs of all children and young people in Scotland are to be met in accordance with the legislation, adequate and sustained investment must be forthcoming.

Over the next five years, as the grip of austerity tightens and further so-called welfare reforms are introduced, it is imperative that the Scottish government responds with universal provision of free meals for all children of school age. Hunger and poor nutrition cannot be allowed to mar the school experiences of any pupil or student, nor can the stigma of collecting a free meal in the school canteen while classmates pay for theirs.

Simultaneously, everyone within education needs to ensure that the barriers to participation facing children from low-income families are removed. The EIS recently issued guidance to its members on how this might be done in relation to costs associated with school uniforms, equipment and resources, homework, school trips, and charity and fundraising events.[8] Consequently, relevant discussions are now underway more widely at school and local authority level. It is hoped that, within the next five years and beyond, this agenda will become increasingly central to the dialogue on education policy and practice at all levels.

Finally, an important Curriculum for Excellence design principle was avoiding the testing, targets and league table culture that characterised the previous five to 14 curriculum, and which international evidence shows has the effect of compounding educational inequality.

In January 2016 the Scottish government published the National Improvement Framework for Scottish Education, aimed at closing the attainment gap and to be incorporated within the Education (Scotland) Bill. A key component is national standardised assessment. Throughout the consultation period, the EIS urged caution against the use of standardised assessment as a data-gathering tool and also warned against the displacement of teacher professional judgement within the assessment process. While there has been some evidence that the Scottish government has heeded such concerns, the final design of the standardised assessments remains to be seen. It is hoped that what is developed will genuinely safeguard the integrity of Curriculum for Excellence philosophy, particularly as it relates to equity. What is clear now, however, is that simply measuring the attainment gap will not close it.

Conclusion

Genuine commitment to tackling poverty and ensuring more equal educational outcomes requires adequate resourcing.

The Scottish government's commitment to the Attainment Scotland

Fund, recently increased by £80 million,[9] is welcome – it must now be targeted appropriately and thereafter investment sustained.

At the very least, there must be sufficient numbers of teachers who have ongoing access to high quality continuing professional development, including input on the nature, causes and consequences of poverty. An increase in teacher numbers overall is required in order to deliver smaller class sizes arranged on the basis of mixed ability for the particular benefit of children from disadvantaged backgrounds. And adequate specialist support for learners with additional support needs, including regular and sustained support for learners at all stages whose first language is not English, is essential.

Tackling poverty requires: adequate time for pupil support staff to attend to pupils' pastoral care needs; enough time for schools to plan and deliver approaches to enhance links between school and home, crucially supporting vulnerable parents to be involved in their children's learning; allowing maximum time for teachers to engage in meaningful professional reflection and collaboration around what works in improving outcomes for children living in poverty; and the provision of classroom resources and equipment which facilitate learning that has creativity and learner collaboration at its core.

The alignment of policies within the new National Improvement Framework – the roadmap for the next phase of Scottish education's journey towards excellence and equity – needs to ensure the requisite resources to achieve the desired educational outcomes. It, and its authors, must acknowledge the fact that there is no cheap way of delivering an education system that is both excellent and equitable. Only long-term, protected investment in nurseries, schools and colleges will deliver that worthy ambition.

Notes

1 http://eppe.ioe.ac.uk/eppe/eppepdfs/rbtec1223sept0412.pdf
2 www.gov.scot/resource/doc/163531/0044420.pdf
3 http://news.scotland.gov.uk/news/more-school-leavers-in-positive-destinations-1a1d.aspx)
4 www.gov.scot/resource/0042/00426004.pdf
5 See note 3
6 http://news.scotland.gov.uk/news/developing-potential-1e71.aspx
7 www.gov.scot/topics/People/Young-People/gettingitright/named-person
8 www.eis.org.uk/images/equality/policies%20consults/eis%20poverty%20advice%20booklet%20pageweb.pdf
9 http://bbc.com/news/uk-scotland-scotland-politics-35649196

Fifteen

Poverty and the childcare challenge

Gill Scott

Childcare: how can it address poverty?

Women's equality, tackling unemployment, reducing pressures on working families, social integration, improved child development and wellbeing, and boosting the wider economy are all regularly cited as reasons for supporting high quality childcare and early years education.[1] Furthermore, they are often identified as a way of tackling child poverty, as the Institute for Public Policy Research points out:[2]

> Policymakers have sought to invest in early-years education and care in order to reduce inequalities… There is evidence that when care is provided by highly trained staff, it not only enables families to better balance work and caring responsibilities, but also delivers greater equality in children's life chances.

A major concern for those seeking to reduce poverty is that low-income families face significant barriers accessing affordable, high quality and flexible childcare. In 2014, one-quarter of all UK parents reported that more affordable childcare was the single thing that would make a positive difference to family life.[3] Lack of access to childcare has an even more significant negative impact on those trying to find a route out of poverty. Save the Children Scotland, for example, found that a high proportion of those in severe poverty had given up work, turned down a job, or not taken up education or training because of difficulties accessing childcare.[4] For today's families facing increased challenges associated with precarious, part-time work, dismal social assistance rates, limited access to training and a shortage of affordable housing, poor access to quality childcare is yet another obstacle to overcome in finding a route out of poverty.[5]

Childcare can have a measurable impact on poverty. When affordable, accessible childcare was introduced in Quebec, for example, it reduced poverty by 50 per cent in ten years, workforce participation rose, hours worked and annual earnings increased, and fewer women were on welfare.[6] In countries where there is access to direct state-funded universal free childcare, rates of poverty and inequalities are much lower than in Scotland or the rest of the UK. In Finland, for example, a vast supply of public childcare and publicly supported home care since the 1990s has been efficient in facilitating parents' participation in paid work. Finland, moreover, has the lowest income inequality in Europe, and a recent OECD report argues that, because the country uses a tapered fees structure geared to reducing inequalities, childcare has served as a significant route out of poverty and a means of reducing income inequality among Finnish families.[7]

Childcare policy as a means to tackle poverty in Scotland

Policy makers in Scotland have had little doubt that improved childcare could reduce child poverty. Throughout successive elections in the last decade, including during the independence referendum, all the major parties have embraced the idea that universal, affordable and accessible childcare is essential for families, women and the economy in a future Scotland. Debate is now about the *way* that childcare should be developed, rather than whether it should be developed at all.

During 2014/15, two independent reviews, *Scotland's Childcare Challenge* from the Commission for Childcare Reform[8] and the *Independent Review of the Scottish Early Learning and Childcare Workforce and Out of School Care Workforce*,[9] consulted with all the major service providers and users. They reported on the problems currently facing the Scottish and Westminster governments if childcare were to be transformed into quality provision that could address the needs of children, redress the impact of poverty on families and develop into a sector of employment that would retain and develop a quality workforce.

According to the Commission, there are major problems that need to be addressed in Scotland. It argues for a stronger vision than that offered by the current SNP government. The report states that funding of childcare in Scotland is 'complicated, confusing, unfair and lacking in transparency'. It also identifies that 79 per cent of councils report that there are insufficient childcare facilities or places to meet demand and that without more free or subsidised places, childcare is too costly for many. The average cost of a nursery place for a child under two is now £4.26 per hour in Britain, meaning that a parent buying 50 hours of childcare a week faces an average annual bill of around £11,000 per year. Research in 2014 showed that 27 per cent of an average family's income in Scotland is spent on childcare.[10] The childcare element of working tax credit may have reduced this burden for those on low pay, but with rising prices, a cap on the amount that can be included and little flexibility in local authority services, the ease of access is still problematic and the cost of childcare for low-income working parents is high and rising. The Commission further argues that, at present, there is no realistic or overall vision or agreed strategy at local, Scottish or UK level that could meet the needs of parents and address issues of poverty.

The Workforce Review identified problems with the quality and availability of a workforce able to deliver the type of childcare and early years education parents and politicians want. It examined skills and qualifications, recruitment and retention, as well as workforce planning across local authority, private and not-for-profit sectors. While commending the recent change in commitment to developing childcare at Scottish and UK level, the report also identifies:

- concerns about the content of qualifications for childcare workers in early learning centres and out-of-school care services: children are not being served as well as they ought;
- unlike other sectors of education, the workers themselves, as well as employers, bear the cost of training;
- a lack of integration of services;
- inequalities in working conditions, pay and opportunities for career advancement across sectors;
- a lack of strategic vision for the development of a workforce fit for purpose as childcare is expanded.

These are issues that workers' representatives also recognise. Unison's *Childcare Charter*, launched in March 2015, provides an interesting extension to the workforce debate.[11] It highlights the relative low pay of the workforce as a whole, but particularly of those in the private and not-for-profit sectors, who have poorer conditions and opportunities than those working in local authorities. For all workers, though, there is a need for flexibility alongside training and career progression, as many combine part-time working with caring responsibilities of their own.

These are major issues to address if the new 'extra hours' included in the Scottish government plans are to be delivered effectively without poor workers being put under undue pressure and poor parents continuing to struggle to access and pay for it. Between 2002 and 2012, there was a 20 per cent increase in the number of workers in the sector as a whole, and it continues to increase. Extended hours, increased demand and higher expectations of quality are likely to lead to even more pressure on childcare workers in the public, private and not-for-profit sectors, but until now there has been little discussion of increased pay or positive recruitment strategies. Local authorities are experiencing funding cuts, so are unlikely to be in a position to increase pay and improve conditions on their own. Research has found, moreover, that both the Westminster[12] and the Scottish[13] government currently underfund other childcare providers when delivering the statutory hours in partnership with a local authority. Providers must often subsidise the full cost of partnership places by charging the children of other families higher hourly rates. Many providers, however, have been unable to get partnership funding. Moreover, if partnership funding is extended and government funding remains at current levels, it is estimated that private nurseries will lose £660 a year for each child taking up extended entitlement. The result is that many private and not-for-profit providers will simply be unable to offer places to children whose parents cannot afford the higher rates the sector claims it needs to charge. These funding pressures hardly provide the basis for improved pay and conditions or better services for children.

It is not simply an issue for the Scottish government. It may have the responsibility for legislating on the supply and quality of services, but the Westminster government has a highly significant responsibility for the benefits and tax credits that affect the amount of money that parents can spend and, therefore, the 'demand' for childcare beyond the free part-time early years education provision that is a statutory right for three- and four-year-olds. Nevertheless, it is the Scottish government that has responsibility for the quality and level of provision that local authorities develop and support in the state sector, as well as in partnership with the private and not-for-profit sectors. Let us remember too that pre-school childcare and nursery learning is currently provided by a range of different institutions and individuals, among them nursery schools, private and voluntary sector daycare centres and nurseries, children's centres, childminders, and schools with nurseries. It is a messy institutional landscape in which parents cannot easily find the care they actually want and providers find it difficult to retain staff outside local authority provision.[14] So, while the Scottish government pledges to extend entitlement to free early education and childcare for three- and four-year-olds to up to 600 hours by 2016 and for vulnerable two-year-olds by 2020, there are problems that need to be addressed if it is to be effectively achieved.

Priorities for the future

Taking these issues into account, if childcare is to make a greater impact on tackling poverty in Scotland over the next five years, there are three key areas that will have to be addressed: low-income parents must have access to affordable and flexible childcare for all children aged 0–12; children must receive good quality care that meets their needs and helps them develop; and supply must be expanded in a way that moves away from dependence on a low-paid workforce. How can this be achieved?

- Fifty hours' entitlement to subsidised childcare a week for all children, with a sliding scale of fees to ensure that those on low incomes can access it, is one answer proposed by the Commission for Childcare Reform. It has to be seen as a long-term aim, but it should not be one that is abandoned. Moreover, it has been argued, for example by One Parent Families Scotland, that funding should be shifted towards 'supply side subsidy rather than subsidy to parents via working tax credits which is too complex for parents and too insecure for providers to invest.'[15]
- Better co-ordination between government at local and national level of in-work training, as well as co-ordination of services to ensure quality and affordability is delivered. This is key. When affordability becomes the main focus, quality can take a back seat. Quebec's approach has been one that has ensured far greater access to care for the majority of parents. However, researchers have also identified that when extensions to care in Quebec moved away from dependence on state and not-for-profit providers to private providers, the result was a higher ratio of children to carers and lower quality care. This is not a path that Scotland should follow.[16]
- Any expansion should recognise that a childcare workforce needs to be developed properly. Pay for childcare workers should be set, at a minimum, at the living wage; training and career progression should be available for all, whatever the sector.

Childcare cannot wait for another generation. Shifts in the wider political system have led to greater commitment to changing the childcare system by all political parties at local, Scottish and UK levels – there has been progress. However, more is needed to help families and, if we care about childcare quality, more needs to be spent. Childcare helps families and children, but it also provides the basis for a workforce and citizenship appropriate to the society in which we live.

Notes

1   D Elson, J Campbell and A McKay, *The Economic Case for Investing in High Quality Childcare and Early Years Education*, Women in Scotland's Economy Research Centre, Glasgow Caledonian University, 2013

2   D Ben-Galim, N Pearce, and S Thompson, *No More Baby Steps: a strategy for revolutionising childcare*, Institute for Public Policy Research, 2014

3   4Children, *Making Britain Great for Children and Families*, 2014, availabe at www.4children.org.uk/files/840d982a-89c2-4c76-975c-a2b301126c35/4C_30 years_manifesto_fianl_web.pdf

4   Save the Children, *Making Work Pay: the childcare trap*, 2011, availabe at www.savethechildren.org.uk/sites/default/files/docs/Making_Work_Pay_Scotland_briefing_1.pdf

5   Citizen's Advice Scotland, *Working at the Edge: childcare*, 2014

6   S St-Cerny, L Godbout and P Fortin, *Lessons From Quebec's Universal Low Fee Childcare Programme*, Institute for Public Policy Research, 2012

7   OECD, *Comparing the Effectiveness of Family Cash Benefits and Services*, OECD Publishing, 2015

8   Commission for Childcare Reform, *Meeting Scotland's Childcare Challenge: the report of the Commission for Childcare Reform*, Children in Scotland, 2015 available at www. childreninscotland.org.uk/sites/default/files/finalchildcare commissionreportjune2015.pdf

9   I Siraj and D Kingston, *An Independent Review of the Scottish Early Learning and Childcare (ELC) Workforce and the Out of School Care (OSC) Workforce*, Scottish Government, 2015

10 J Rutter and K Stocker, *The 2014 Scottish Childcare Report*, Family and Childcare Trust, 2014, available at www.familyandchildcaretrust.org

11 Unison Scotland, *Childcare Charter*, 2015, available at www.unison-scotland.org.uk/educationissues/UNISONscotlandChildcareCharter_Mar2015.pdf

12 Pre-school Learning Alliance, *Counting the Cost: an analysis of delivery costs for funded early years education and childcare*, 2014, available at www.pre-school.org.uk/document/7905

13 R Gowans, *Working at the Edge*, Citizens Advice Scotland, 2014, available at www.cas.org.uk/publications/working-edge-childcare

14 See note 2

15 OPFS, *Response to the Commission for Childcare Reform*, 2014, http://www.commissionforchildcarereform.info/wp-folder/wordpress/wp-content/uploads/cc-commission-opfs-evidence-2014_sr.doc

16 See note 6

Sixteen

The role of the health service in tackling poverty

Jackie Erdman

Introduction

Despite decades of research and policies to tackle health inequalities, the gap in mortality between the most affluent and the least affluent groups in Scotland has widened in absolute and relative terms.[1] The Scottish government has made a commitment to tackling health inequalities, but 'power inequalities, social status and connections or class inequality' remain as the root causes.[2] Meanwhile, policy makers in the UK have developed a 'parallel fantasy world'[3] where individualised lifestyle interventions, for example on smoking or diet, will somehow tackle health inequalities – and Scotland is no exception. This chapter begins by describing a tool called 'inequalities-sensitive practice', which enables health workers to tackle health inequality. Secondly, it sets out recent Scottish policy on tackling health inequalities and how health service interventions have tended towards 'lifestyle drift'.[4] Finally, it explores what could be achieved in the next five years to tackle poverty and inequality through health policy and inequalities-sensitive healthcare delivery.

Inequalities-sensitive practice

'Inequalities-sensitive practice' is a way of delivering healthcare that responds to the life circumstances that affect people's health. Evidence shows that if these issues are not taken into account by the health service, opportunities are missed to improve health and reduce health inequalities.[5] In his recent book, Michael Marmot describes a patient he treated in the early days of his medical career who was experiencing poverty, depression and domestic violence and asks: 'Why treat people and send them back to the conditions that made them sick?'[6] Sensitively enquiring about people's life circumstances and experiences as part of core health practice means that health workers can take these issues into account when devising treatment and care.

Inequalities-sensitive practice was developed in NHS Greater Glasgow and Clyde in 2009 as a response to the weaknesses of the medical model in tackling health inequality. It was rooted in approaches developed in social work and community development, termed 'anti-oppressive' or 'anti-discriminatory' practice, which argued that social workers needed to understand the socio-political context of their clients' lives to ensure they did not contribute to, or reinforce, their oppression, but rather actively sought opportunities that would change their circumstances.[7] Since 2009, inequalities-sensitive practice has been used by a range of frontline health workers, including nurses, and has been adopted as a broad term for enquiring into patients' social circumstances.

A number of programmes have developed in Scotland based on inequalities-sensitive practice, which have supported health workers to understand and respond to the life circumstances of their patients. For example, Healthier Wealthier Children focuses on identifying and responding to the needs of women and children experiencing poverty. The evaluation of this programme showed that, between October 2011 and October 2013, 5,003 referrals were made to money advice services by health visitors and midwives, which led to over £4.5 million in financial gain for families.[8] Many of the people referred through this approach did not know their entitlements and had not previously used money advice services. Healthier Wealthier Children made a significant and positive impact on family poverty.

The Gender-based Violence Programme supports health staff to routinely ask patients about their experience of abuse – a manifestation of gender inequality which persists in today's society.[9] Health staff ask key questions as part of health assessments or therapeutic interventions and support women with current or past abuse. There is now wide recognition that routine enquiry on gender-based violence is a core part of clinical practice.

These universal approaches are based on the understanding that health workers cannot treat people's symptoms without understanding other aspects of their lives. Nor can they assess people's needs based on how they look or appear, as this is likely to be a value judgement. This may miss underlying issues (for example, gender-based violence) or be based on stereotypes (for example, money worries are often hidden by people because of a fear of stigmatisation).

Discrimination and prejudice based on people's personal character-istics (for example, their ethnicity, sex, sexual orientation and age) have an impact on health, which is often directly linked to poverty. Equality legisla-tion seeks to address these issues and listed local authorities, including the NHS, are required to ensure that discrimination is eliminated.[10] Although equality law does not include poverty as a protected character-istic, some public bodies include socio-economic inequality, social class or poverty in their equality impact assessments or carry out separate poverty proofing.

These examples illustrate how inequalities-sensitive practice can become a mainstream approach to delivering health services in the con-text of people's lived experience.

Health policy in Scotland

The Scottish government has developed several key policy documents on tackling health inequalities over the last five years, including the most recent *Report on Health Inequalities*.[11] Fox has observed that Scottish health policy is distinct from that of England, with a long-standing consen-sus on the need to tackle health inequalities, a commitment to universal-ism, linking health policy to economic growth and emanating from policy makers who listen to and value medical leaders.[12]

However, a recent review of the indicators developed by the Scottish Ministerial Task Force on Health Inequalities reported that: 'Despite a lot of commitment and resource, the scale of health inequalities [...] had not reduced.'[13] This lack of progress has been attributed to a ten-dency for actions to rely on behavioural interventions, in what has been called 'lifestyle drift'.[14] In other words, actions to reduce health inequalities often revert back to tackling the behaviours that cause disease, such as smoking or unhealthy diets, rather than the root causes of unequal power, life circumstances or poverty.

More recently, Scott and others have reinforced the need to move away from behavioural interventions to tackle health inequalities.[15] Using the concept of fundamental causes, they looked at socio-economic gra-dients in disease patterns in Scotland. They found that, while some had decreased, others had appeared, suggesting that as new preventable dis-eases emerge, people deploy the resources, power and knowledge avail-able to them to reduce their risk, thus creating and re-creating the health inequalities.[16] They suggest that: 'reducing individual risk and increasing individual assets will ultimately be fruitless in reducing inequalities and may even increase them.'[17] Hatzenbuehler and others suggest that people's identity, such as their ethnicity or sexual orientation, is also a fundamental cause of health inequality due to higher exposure to other risks, such as discrimination.[18]

Therefore, to tackle health inequality going forward, the challenge for the Scottish government is to develop policy that:

- tackles the structural inequalities of power and resources which lead to health inequalities;
- acknowledges that, although diseases have changed over time, health inequalities have persisted; and
- understands the impact of discrimination on the perpetuation of health inequalities.

Policy and tools to tackle health inequality in the next five years

Actions to tackle inequalities in health policy and healthcare delivery should, therefore, be based on fairness, justice and equity. This suggests a move away from the medical model and behavioural interventions, towards redistributing health service resources, improving access to services and joining up services to meet people's needs.

In the next five years there are opportunities to tackle health inequality through the integration of health and social care. By April 2016, the Public Bodies (Joint Working) (Scotland) Act 2014 will have established local integrated health and social care partnerships. These will have the power to make local decisions on how services are delivered, including how they tackle health inequalities, and will be required to carry out an equality impact assessment of their plans. The integrated partnerships will include representatives from the voluntary sector and the community, including carers and people who use services. The Scottish government states that:[19]

> The Act enables a whole system redesign of health and social care planning and provision, around a system centred on anticipatory and preventative care [based on] GPs, social workers, district nurses, etc working together to support people in their own homes.

Reducing health inequalities is one of the Scottish government's health and wellbeing outcomes, on which integrated partnerships will be measured. Reducing the gap in health outcomes will require these partnerships to use their powers to tackle the root causes of poverty and inequality.

Frontline workers are one of the main resources available to integrated partnerships to bring about changes, and inequalities-sensitive practice is one model they can use. Allen and others identify the ways that medical practitioners can tackle inequalities in their day-to-day practice, ranging from individual measures such as 'brief interventions and social prescribing' to more radical approaches, such as using their 'expertise to advocate for change outside traditional medical areas'.[20] Health Scotland's *Health Inequalities Action Framework* presents three forms of action to reduce health inequalities: mitigating the impact of poverty; preventing inequality; and undoing inequality.[21] Craig states that the area in which health and social care services can make the most impact is in mitigating the impact of poverty, and that services should be 'sensitive to the impact of the social context around a set of symptoms including the barriers that some people might encounter on accessing services.'[22] Inequalities-sensitive practice is at the heart of this approach. It requires leadership, training for staff and partnerships with the voluntary sector. Most importantly, it should be based on a different relationship between people using services and health practitioners. The concept of inequalities-sensitive practice resonates with NHS policy on person-centredness. *The Healthcare Quality Strategy for NHS Scotland* acknowledged that quality of care required a return to a more person-centred approach.[23] To be effective, this person-centred approach needs to be rooted in an understanding of the fundamental causes of health inequality, including the impact of stigma.

Conclusion

Inequalities-sensitive practice enables health workers to deliver care that takes poverty and other forms of inequality and discrimination into account. Health and social care partnerships provide an opportunity to transform care to meet the needs of local communities. Above all, it can provide a more radical approach to social justice in the day-to-day practice of frontline workers. The tools and evidence presented here suggest that this approach could be easily adopted across Scotland.

Notes

1 C Beeston, G McCartney, J Ford, E Wimbush, S Beck, W MacDonald and A Fraser, *Health Inequalities Policy Review for the Scottish Ministerial Task Force on Health Inequalities*, NHS Health Scotland, 2014, pp22–24

2 A Scott-Samuel and K E Smith, 'Fantasy Paradigms of Health Inequalities: utopian thinking?' *Social Theory and Health*, 12, 2015, p1

3 See note 2

4 C Bambra, K E Smith, K Garthwaite, K E Joyce and D J Hunter, 'A Labour of Sisyphus? Public policy and health inequalities research from the Black and Acheson Reports to the Marmot Review', *Journal of Epidemiology and Community Health*, 65, 2011, p402

5 *Inequalities Sensitive Practice Initiative Final Evaluation Report Executive Summary*, NHS Greater Glasgow and Clyde, 2009, and M Allen, J Allen, S Hogarth and M Marmot, *Working for Health Equity: the role of health professionals*, UCL Institute of Health Equity, 2013

6 M Marmot, *The Health Gap: the challenge of an unequal world*, Bloomsbury, 2015, p6

7 N Thompson, *Anti-discriminatory Practice*, Palgrave, 2001, pp6–7

8 L Naven and J Egan, *Healthier Wealthier Children: learning from and early intervention child poverty project*, Glasgow Centre for Population Health, 2013, p7

9 Scottish Government, *Gender-based Violence Action Plan*, CEL 41, 2008, available at www.sehd.scot.nhs.uk/mels/CEL2008_41.pdf

10 *The Equality Act 2010*

11 Scottish Parliament Health and Sport Committee, *Report on Health Inequalities*, 2015

12 DM Fox, 'Health Inequality and Governance in Scotland Since 2007', *Public Health*, 127, 2013, pp504–05

13 See note 1, p3

14 See note 4, p402

15 S Scott, E Curnock, R Mitchell, M Robinson, M Taulbut, E Todd, and G McCartney, *What Would it Take to Eradicate Health Inequalities? Testing the fundamental causes theory of health inequalities in Scotland*, NHS Health Scotland, 2013

16 See note 15

17 See note 15, p6

18 ML Hatzenbuehler, JC Phelan and BG Link, 'Stigma as a Fundamental Cause of Population Health Inequalities', *American Journal of Public Health*, 103 (5), 2013, p1

19 Scottish Government, *Communications Toolkit: a guide to support the local implementation of health and social care integration*, 2015, p42, available at www.gov.scot/Resource/0047/00475356.pdf

20 M Allen, J Allen, S Hogarth and M Marmot, *Working for Health Equity: the role of health professionals*, UCL Institute of Health Equity, 2013
21 P Craig, *Health Inequalities Action Framework*, NHS Health Scotland, 2013, available at www.healthscotland.com/documents/22627.aspx
22 See note 21, p5
23 Scottish Government, *The Healthcare Quality Strategy for NHS Scotland*, NHS Scotland, 2010, available at www.gov.scot/resource/doc/311667/0098354.pdf

Seventeen
Housing and poverty

Paul Bradley

Introduction

In 2015, over 150,000 households in Scotland were on council waiting lists for a home, over 75,000 lived in overcrowded conditions and 39 per cent of all households were living in fuel poverty. In one year alone, £1.8 billion was spent on housing benefit and over 35,000 homelessness applications were made.[1] These figures show that there is very clearly a housing crisis in Scotland.

Housing and poverty are inextricably linked. While poverty makes it harder to access or sustain a home, unaffordable housing reduces disposable income, which can increase material deprivation for those on the lowest incomes. When housing costs are factored in, there are over 940,000 people living in poverty in Scotland, significantly more than the 730,000 people judged to be in poverty when housing costs are not included.[2] Poor quality housing or a lack of a permanent home can also have a harmful impact on health and the ability to access education or employment, which may have consequences for how much a person can earn – one of the main routes out of poverty.

It is unlikely that poverty and inequality in Scotland can be meaningfully tackled without a solution to the housing crisis. We need a radical shift in thinking and policy that is premised on an acceptance of the critical role of good housing in tackling poverty and improving quality of life.

Where are we now?

Housing is a devolved matter over which the Scottish Parliament has full control, and the effect of this on both the tone and direction of policy in Scotland has been clear.

Since the 1980s, over 500,000 social homes in Scotland – those owned and managed by local authorities and housing associations – have been sold under 'right to buy'.[3] This scheme gave many tenants of social housing a legal right to buy their home; those who took up the offer experienced a significant accumulation of wealth as a result of the rise in house prices. The policy clearly underpinned the growing prosperity of many households on below average incomes.

However, a lack of reinvestment in housing with the funds raised through right to buy has undoubtedly contributed to Scotland's chronic lack of social housing. This is significant, as social housing provides affordable homes for low-income households and acts as a safety net for some of the most vulnerable people in society. At a time when the UK government is extending the scheme south of the border, the Scottish government's position has fortunately diverged. Right to buy was restricted in 2002 and will end in Scotland in August 2016. Its absence will be an important step towards safeguarding the future supply of social housing.

Protecting socially renting households from the full effect of the UK government's welfare reforms has also been a priority for the Scottish government. Key social security functions and areas of taxation remain reserved to the UK government. This means that changes to housing benefit – including the controversial 'bedroom tax' – apply in Scotland as well as in the rest of the UK.[4] Introduced in 2013, the 'bedroom tax' means that a working-age household living in social housing can have its housing benefit reduced if it has a room deemed to be surplus to its needs. It is widely accepted that the policy has plunged thousands of households into hardship by forcing tenants to make up the difference in rent themselves or move to a property with fewer rooms. To counter this, the Scottish government has used its powers to cover the reduction in housing benefit through discretionary payments – an extra payment available to help people who claim housing benefit and are still struggling to pay their rent. By mitigating the impact of housing benefit changes, the Scottish government has shielded many low-income households from rent arrears, material deprivation and potential homelessness.

Perhaps of greater importance to helping those in the most abject poverty has been the Scottish government's approach to homelessness, a position that puts it well ahead of England and most other developed countries. In 2003 the then Scottish Executive vowed that, by December 2012, every unintentionally homeless household in Scotland would have the right to settled accommodation. This groundbreaking legislation meant that local authorities would have a legal duty to provide a home to those who were homeless through no fault of their own. The successful delivery of the '2012 commitment' has seen an end to the 'priority' and 'non-priority' method of determining who in the homeless system should be given a home and has fundamentally changed the legal rights of home-less people.

Where do we go from here?

Welcome as these polices are, their contribution to tackling the housing crisis is limited. Individual policy interventions focused on how we use the existing stock, such as those noted above, have been important, but with-out sufficient available homes they can only have limited impact. Building the affordable homes we need, drastically reducing housing costs and delivering more compassionate housing support for those struggling to make ends meet are three broad approaches to combatting the crisis and the prevalence of poverty throughout Scotland's communities.

It is important to remember that the fundamental housing issue in Scotland is that the demand for affordable housing – including social rented, mid-market rented, and low-cost home ownership properties – far outstrips the supply. There has been a steep decline in the level of new house building in Scotland since the early 1970s, exacerbated most recently by the global financial crisis in 2008.

A new report commissioned by Shelter Scotland, the Chartered Institute of Housing and the Scottish Federation of Housing Associations – three of Scotland's leading housing organisations – has established that at least 12,000 affordable homes need to be built each year for the next five years. This is so that we can begin to tackle the existing backlog of households on council waiting lists and the significant annual growth in household formation.[5] To ensure a safe, secure and affordable home for everyone, regardless of earning potential, the Scottish government must do more to scale up its affordable housing supply programme – which built only 4,956 affordable homes (3,823 for social rent) in 2013/14 – to deal with unmet housing need. It is also critical that a substantial percentage of the 12,000 affordable homes delivered each year are socially rented.

Beyond building the homes we need, the current system of property taxation in Scotland – the council tax – must be reformed to put an end to a tax that disproportionately affects the poorest of households. Under cur-rent council tax rules, a property's value – based on a 1991 estimate – determines to which of eight bands (A to H) it is allocated and subse-quently the amount of council tax a household must pay. The highest band – Band H – applies to all properties valued at over £212,000. However, with house prices rising significantly over the past 24 years, the current system is a significant burden on the poorest in our society, who are spending a higher proportion of the value of their property on tax compared with those who own more costly homes. A fairer, new property tax, possibly based on a percentage of capital value, should replace the current banded structure with a commitment to review property valuations on a regular basis, as recommended by the Commission on Housing and Wellbeing.

An additional area in need of reform is Scotland's private rented sector. This is home to 312,000 households, more than double the number a decade ago.[6] This increased demand is driven, in part, by a failure to provide sufficient affordable housing, as thousands of families on low incomes have turned to private landlords to meet their housing needs. What is more, the number of households in poverty in the private rented sector has increased by over 140,000 in the last decade, in contrast with the falling levels of poverty among households in other tenures.[7]

However, there is a view in Scotland that the sector is ripe for reform. This includes a need to consider levels of rent and indefinite security of tenure for those who can find themselves evicted through no fault of their own. The Scottish government's recent introduction of a Private Housing (Tenancies) Bill looks to modernise and simplify tenancies for private renters in Scotland. If passed by the Scottish Parliament, the Bill will lead to regulations required to make private renting more stable, flexible, predictable and fair. Welcome as these changes are, enforcing this and existing legislation will be critical to its success. The Scottish government must also monitor the success of the legislation and, if required, make amendments to enhance its effectiveness.

More immediate support is required for the one million people in Scotland who cannot afford adequate housing conditions.[8] Clearly, there are limitations to what the Scottish government can change in respect to housing welfare; newly devolved powers are likely to allow only for tinkering with social security. Yet, where possible, the Scottish government must make the most of the limited administrative devolution to help the thousands of households struggling with their housing costs. As soon as practically possible, the Scottish government should act to end the 'bedroom tax' permanently, it should reinstate the pre-2011 rates of local housing allowance paid to private tenants and it should ensure that the direct payment of housing costs to tenants – under the roll-out of universal credit – does not put claimants under excessive pressure when maintaining their tenancy and finances. While the Scottish Parliament is unlikely to be handed powers allowing for big structural shifts in social security, these steps will make a real difference to those that rely on housing benefit to meet their housing costs.

Homelessness remains a major problem in Scotland with 35,764 homelessness applications made by households in 2014/15 alone, a quarter of which (9,063) were families with children.[9] Despite meeting the '2012 commitment', more research is required to establish the level of service provision available for homeless people in each local authority to ensure consistency across Scotland and that statutory obligations are being met. Greater assistance is also required to help people, specifically those with multiple complex needs, to maintain and keep their homes. Different approaches are needed to increase housing options available to people to prevent the cycle of repeated homelessness. This includes groups such as prisoners, who can struggle to find a home on their release or whose families are sometimes unable to maintain the tenancy when they are in custody. Temporary accommodation is also an essential safety net for those people who find themselves homeless. Yet with over 10,000 households in temporary accommodation in 2013/14 at any one time, and one in four of those households spending over six months there, there is a clear need for a reduction in the length of time any one household must call temporary accommodation their home.[10] The bottleneck in temporary accommodation is once again a consequence of a lack of affordable, and specifically socially rented, housing across Scotland.

Conclusion

It is clear that Scotland is far from providing everyone with a suitable home they need. For all the claims that progress has been made and for all the suggested ways of strengthening our housing policy, it is striking that a housing crisis still exists. Without sufficient affordable homes available, without reducing housing costs and without delivering more compassionate housing support to those in need, low-income households will continue to be disproportionately affected by the crisis and more likely to be pushed further into poverty.

Notes

1 Commission on Housing and Wellbeing, *A Blueprint for Scotland's Future*, 2015

2 Scottish Government, *Poverty and Income Inequality in Scotland: 2013/14*, 2015

3 See note 1

4 The 'bedroom tax' is a name commonly used to refer to the 'under-occupancy charge', a reduction in housing benefit brought in under the UK government's welfare reforms

5 R Powell, R Dunning, E Ferrari and K McKee, *Affordable Housing Need in Scotland: final report*, Shelter Scotland, 2015

6 Scottish Government, *Scotland's People Annual Report: results from the 2014 Scottish Household Survey*, 2015

7 P Kenway, S Bushe, A Tinson and TB Born, *Monitoring Poverty and Social Exclusion in Scotland 2015*, Joseph Rowntree Foundation, 2015

8 See www.policyscotland.gla.ac.uk/scottish-poverty-study-calls-governments-tackle-rising-deprivation

9 Scottish Government, *Operation of the Homeless Persons Legislation in Scotland: 2014–15*, 2015

10 Scottish Government, *Quarterly Temporary Accommodation Reference Tables, September 2015*, 2015

Eighteen
Food security

Mary Anne MacLeod

Introduction

The past five years have witnessed a rapid expansion of charitable emergency food aid across the UK, and the issue has received widespread media coverage and political debate. While the provision of charitable food by voluntary and faith groups has long existed, it is the recent growth in the formalised food bank model and the extension of such services to a wide range of social security recipients and people in work which has caused particular concern. Within the context of unprecedented cuts in public spending and reforms to welfare, food banks have become the lens through which we view these changes and debate their impacts.

Defining and measuring food poverty

While headlines have focused on the dramatic growth in the number of people accessing food banks, such figures are far from representative of the extent to which UK and Scottish households are struggling to feed themselves. A significant barrier to gaining a better understanding of the problem is our lack of both an agreed definition of food insecurity and a robust, systematic means of measuring it. Food insecurity, rather than food poverty, is the term more commonly used. It refers to the inability, or uncertainty, that one will be able to access an adequate quantity or quality of food in socially acceptable ways.[1] This definition is derived from a qualitative study of women on low incomes in upstate New York, from which quantitative indicators of food insecurity were developed. These indicators are used in the routine gathering of household-level data in the USA – one of the few countries in the world to do so. The concept encompasses food insecurity as a matter of affordability and the need for a sufficient and secure income in order to have an adequate diet. Crucially, it also recognises the social role of food – the importance of being able to participate in ways of accessing food which are common to a society, and of being free from anxiety about one's future ability to do so.

In Scotland, as across the UK, such data on household food insecurity is not collected. In its absence, studies that identify levels of household expenditure on food have been used to suggest how far families may have difficulty affording food. The 2012 Living Costs and Food Survey found that, while average households spent 11.2 per cent of their income on food, those in the lowest income decile spent 16.6 per cent.[2] Recent analysis of the Scottish data from this survey identified that households living in relative poverty spent 23 per cent of their weekly income on food, which was more than twice the proportion spent by households above this income threshold, despite their spending much less in absolute terms.[3] The authors of this study recognised that the absence of a specific measure and appropriate dataset limited their ability to determine fully the nature and extent of food poverty/insecurity in Scotland.

What is clear is that the number of families struggling to afford food in Scotland is far higher than the limited data we have on levels of food bank use, which has been widely reported to be a strategy of last resort for those accessing them. While 16 per cent of the Scottish population are identified as living in relative poverty, and 10 per cent in extreme poverty after housing costs,[4] data from the Trussell Trust shows that less than 1 per cent of people in Scotland have accessed a food bank.

Policy responses

The relationship between food and poverty is complex. Adequate incomes, physical access and affordable prices are key factors, and there are significant implications for health, education, social and cultural participation. Yet government responses have consistently failed to adequately acknowledge this complexity, framing food in largely individualistic terms. Public health concerns about over-consumption of processed, energy-dense foods and the high prevalence of obesity and related conditions among those on low incomes tend to focus interventions on improving budgeting, shopping and cooking skills. Yet studies have shown that those on low incomes do not have fewer of these competencies than the rest of the population. In fact, when it comes to managing money, many have developed complex strategies for getting by on a tight budget. Indeed, policies focused on individual change have been found to have limited impact – not least because they do not engage with food poverty's structural drivers.[5]

In Scotland, our infamously poor diet and entrenched health inequalities have long been concerns of policy makers and politicians. The 1996 Scottish Diet Action Plan was significant in highlighting food poverty as a public health issue and shaping local-level responses. Acknowledging the difficulties in accessing healthy food for those in deprived areas, this called for further investment in community food initiatives, such as food co-ops. This led to the creation of Community Food and Health Scotland, which continues to support low-income communities on issues of food and health, as well as seeking to represent their interests at policy level. Support for community food and improvements to food in schools were highlighted as key successes of the Action Plan in its 10-year review.[6] Despite this progress, the most recent Scottish food and drink policy acknowledges that universal access to affordable, nutritious food is still far from realised. Furthermore, the current policy has also been widely criticised for its failure to address the issue of food insecurity or the recent expansion of food bank use directly – a strategy for which is surely essential to achieve the vision for a 'good food nation' which it presents.

The role of emergency food aid

The evidence of the reasons behind the rapid growth in demand for food banks, while still disputed by the UK government, consistently points to issues of delays and errors in the administration of social security payments, as well as the imposition of punitive benefit sanctions.[7] Under the Trussell Trust model, which is followed by many other providers, vouchers are issued by referring agencies, such as social workers and GPs, and exchanged at a food bank for a parcel containing three days' worth of non-perishable food. Recent research in Scotland identified over 160 providers of emergency food aid, including newly established food banks, as long-standing food projects and organisations which had started, or expanded, emergency food provision to meet recent growth in demand.[8]

Food banks have become an increasingly integrated part of the UK social security system. In England and Wales, one-third of local authorities report funding local food banks – in some cases, financing them with money from the recently devolved former social fund,[9] arguably depriving households of cash payments to which they were previously entitled. In 2014, the Scottish government invested £1 million into emergency food aid services – with a prerequisite that they demonstrate ways of connecting users with other forms of support beyond the provision of food. The Big Lottery Fund in Scotland's Support and Connect programme took a similar approach to funding emergency food aid activity. Such investment suggests a formalisation of charitable food aid within mainstream statutory and voluntary services beyond what was initially seen as a temporary response to a crisis situation.

Emergency food aid initiatives can be important sources of support beyond the provision of food, offering a listening ear and other advice and signposting.[10] As a local community response to need, they can be powerful examples of social solidarity. However, emergency food aid providers themselves have expressed significant concern as to the appropriateness and sustainability of their services becoming embedded into our social security systems. Providers in Scotland have reported widespread uneasiness with the increasing pressures being placed on small, voluntary-run groups, and a feeling that the state is failing in its responsibility to provide an adequate safety net.[11] UK-wide research has also highlighted the implications of food charity for the future of the British welfare state:[12]

> It is not part of the current social contract that social protection be replaced or supplemented by unaccountable, unsystematic volunteer help, and growing numbers involved in such provision are uncomfortable with the role they are being asked to play.

Evidence from North America, where charitable food aid is long established, highlights the limited impact which such provision has beyond the immediate relief of hunger. For example, in Canada only 20–30 per cent of those who are food insecure use food banks.[13] Further data have shown that where food banks are used, they do not reduce experiences of severe food insecurity. Concern as to the long-term implications of food banks in the UK has also begun to emerge. Recent research has highlighted that users commonly experience physical and mental health problems and that food bank offerings can be unsuitable for people with particular health conditions.[14] The supply-driven nature of food bank provisions means that they are not able to guarantee a consistent quality or quantity of food to meet an individual's dietary needs. In addition, the stigma associated with food bank use has been widely recognised, and calls have been made for further research in this area.[15]

Conclusion: a Scotland beyond food banks

So far there has been a degree of critical debate in Scotland surrounding the growth of food banks. The joint statement on food poverty from the leaders of Glasgow and Edinburgh City Councils and the Beyond Food Banks movement led by the Church of Scotland are important examples. Such responses take an explicitly rights-based approach to food insecurity, one which places a duty on government to enable sustainable access to nutritious food as a basic human right. Public engagement with this approach has the potential to provoke a progressive policy response from Scotland's leaders. Such a response would require a clear commitment to use further devolved powers to reduce reliance on food banks. This should include measures which reduce disruptions in income for benefit claimants, such as addressing the problems of administrative delay and errors. Welfare rights support should be prioritised to ensure people are claiming all that they are entitled to, and to increase people's access to their legal right to review. The Scottish government should seek to restore an approach to social security based on rights and starting from a position of trust in, and respect for, the claimant. This approach would recognise the state's responsibility to fulfil the human right to an adequate standard of living – including the right to food.

Beyond actions to repair the social safety net, there is also a pressing need to develop the means of measuring and recording data on household food insecurity in Scotland. Such evidence would inform the development of policies across departments of national and local government. The complex relationship between food and poverty requires holistic interventions which reach beyond a reaction to crisis, which the rise of food banks represents. Calls for legislation which would further institutionalise emergency food aid, such as the donation of surplus food by supermarkets, should be approached with extreme caution, and warnings taken from evidence from countries where such measures have been implemented. Community-led activity has an important role to play, particularly around food, which is a powerful tool in bringing communities together and reducing social isolation. However, such activities must be in the context of a comprehensive and well-resourced social security system and decent work, which are ultimately the best defence against food poverty.

Notes

1 KL Radimer, 'Measurement of Household Food Security in the USA and Other Industrialised Countries', *Public Health Nutrition*, Vol. 5, No. 6A, 2002, pp859–64

2 Department for Environment, Food and Rural Affairs, *Food Statistics Pocketbook 2014*, 2014

3 F Douglas, O Ejebu, A Garcia, F MacKenzie, S Whybrow, L McKenzie, A Ludbrook and E Dowler, *The Nature and Extent of Food Poverty/Insecurity in Scotland*, NHS Health Scotland, 2015

4 Scottish Government, *Severe Poverty in Scotland*, 2015

5 T Lang, M Caraher, R Carr-Hill and P Dixon, *Cooking Skills and Health*, Health Education Authority, 1999

6 T Lang, E Dowler and D Hunter, *Review of the Scottish Diet Action Plan*, Health Scotland, 2006

7 J Perry, T Sefton, M Williams and M Haddad, *Emergency Use Only: understanding and reducing the use of food banks in the UK*, Oxfam, 2014

8 MA MacLeod, *Making the Connections: a study of emergency food aid in Scotland*, Poverty Alliance, 2015

9 'Councils spending £3m on food poverty and food banks', BBC News Online, 3 March 2014

10 See note 8; H Lambie-Mumford, *Addressing Food Poverty in the UK: charity, rights and welfare*, Sheffield Political Economy Research Institute, 2015

11 See note 10

12 E Dowler and H Lambie-Mumford, 'How Can Households Eat in Austerity? Challenges for social policy in the UK', *Social Policy and Society*, Vol. 14, No. 3, 2015, pp417–28

13 V Tarasuk, A Mitchell and N Dachner, *Household Food Insecurity in Canada 2012*, Research to Identify Policy Options to Reduce Food Insecurity (proof), 2014

14 K A Garthwaite, P J Collins and C Bambra, 'Food for Thought: an ethnographic study of negotiating ill health and food insecurity in a UK foodbank', *Social Science and Medicine*, 132, 2015, pp38–44

15 See note 14

Nineteen

It is everyone's job to tackle poverty: a third sector perspective

Martin Sime

Introduction

People in Scottish civil society spend much time with Scotland's politicians and they may argue that this work has yielded much success. For example, voluntary organisations campaigning against poverty and inequality enjoy strong political and practical support from the Scottish government. We have a mutual interest in protecting people from the brutalities of the UK government assault on the poorest and most economically precarious citizens. We all agree that the so-called reform of social security is a euphemism for an ideological attack that has no place in a civilised society.

Scotland is a rich country. It is, however, failing many of its citizens. And yet we have a highly developed and well-endowed third sector, which is the envy of the world. With poverty set to rise, inequality persisting and hunger reappearing on the streets, our response must be more than 'business as usual' – ie, working with those who can support us, campaigning against those who do not, and plugging the gaps when the state and private enterprise fail. We need to take account of new developments, both at home and abroad. What can we learn from the extraordinary grassroots response to the plight of refugees, the food bank movement, the Arab spring, the gender rights call in India, the battle to protect data privacy, and even the ice bucket challenge? Is there another way?

Looking back

What has the third sector achieved since 2011?

We have developed our capacity to inform and influence. Since devolution we have built a cadre of policy officers and lobbyists, and established some impressive networks to maximise our political leverage in what, by international comparison, is an extremely open and welcoming parliamentary system.

We are valued by Scottish and local government as key partners in tackling disadvantage, poverty and inequality. But the business of lobbying politicians, publishing manifestos, campaigning for new laws and more public funds is never going to be enough to create the kind of society we want. We have become very good at seeing ourselves as professional lobbyists, able to get our ideas onto the table of government, get laws passed or resources acquired, to tick the issues off. Job done. End of.

We have softened the blow of welfare reform. Funds have been made available by the Scottish government to mitigate some of the adverse impacts. Evidence has been given to Parliament and its committees, some of which would make you weep. Welfare and community care funds have been rolled out via local government (although why we need 32 different versions is questionable). Working parties have been formed and strategies developed to make best use of the few additional powers that may be coming our way. Fairness, dignity and respect are back on the agenda. All of this is how it should be.

But perhaps the greatest achievements of the third sector have been inadvertent, rather than planned. Nowhere is this illustrated more clearly than with the growth of food banks. Enormously important, they work on two levels. Firstly, they help stop people in our communities from starving. Secondly, they remind the public that some of their fellow citizens are unable to feed themselves or their families, and may encourage them to think about why this has been allowed to happen. Through collections in supermarkets, those great cathedrals of consumption in the contemporary age, food banks invite people to make a small contribution towards addressing a dire collective need, as many do.

Such expressions of solidarity are priceless. People are taking the opportunity to do something, no matter how small, to assist their fellow citizens who are in dire need. In turn, this support encourages others to volunteer. A virtuous circle is formed, one which demonstrates the often latent capacity within our communities to look out for each other.

Looking forward

One of the most important challenges for the third sector, and especially poverty campaigners, is to work out what might alter hostile public attitudes to welfare benefits and how to accelerate that change. Given the next generation of cuts and their likely impact on the ground, this is an urgent question.

The big issue for our sector is: have we grown too accustomed to the idea that influencing politics is an end in itself, rather than just one way of achieving the changes we want to see? Some ten years ago, the Scottish Council of Voluntary Organisations (SCVO) launched a campaign slogan, entitled 'politicians don't change things, people do' to promote the power of community activism. There are things that the third sector can do to engage, support and mobilise people and communities – activities beyond the power of politics and government, and they matter now more than ever.

Our sector has great ideas about a citizen's income, about the expansion of self-direction and on providing more support to those who have least. We know about the positive effects of flexible childcare, the specialist support people with mental health problems need to find and keep work, and a whole host of other issues which can be addressed at the public policy level. It is what we do.

But are we devoting enough energy to winning the argument on the doorstep? Have we got the hearts and minds of the people behind us? If, for example, we ever get Scottish control over universal credit – a rational and sensible project that is dear to many hearts – will the forces of reaction raise their ugly heads and win the day?

Think back to the tone of debate during the last general election. The rhetoric about social security being unaffordable was met with little opposition, and polls suggested that Scotland was only marginally less ambivalent about the prospect of further social security cuts. There is a battle still to be won here and we should not just count on politicians to promote our visions of a fairer Scotland. Instead, we ought to carry the argument wherever we can.

Now is the time for us to draw our lines in the sand, to marshal our forces. It is time for us to fight for what we believe in. If we do not walk the talk of our values, then public support will evaporate.

We need to consider whether we have got the right balance between influencing politicians and talking with our service users, supporters, donors, staff, volunteers and trustees. We need to work harder to help people support themselves and each other. Perhaps, even more ambitiously, we need to be thinking about how we can operate in a world beyond government.

The wider strategic steps we can apply to achieving these goals are controversial. But they are necessary. National and local governments on their own cannot solve poverty and rising inequality, and they should stop pretending otherwise. Winning the argument with the public is what is important.

Civil society is not capable of matching its own rhetoric; rather, it has to play a pivotal role in driving attitudinal change. What people do for themselves and in support of their fellow citizens is the most important and sustainable duty of all citizens in public life. As discussed earlier, food banks are a powerful manifestation of a community response to a collective need – there are many others and they each deserve our unequivocal support.

Conclusion

Things can look a bit different in Scotland compared to rest of the UK. Our governance structures are more open and porous, and we share a narrative with our politicians about the need to address inequality, even if we are sometimes miles apart in how to do this. Scotland has yet to succumb fully to the notion that markets should govern everything.

The third sector must now reach beyond government. An often hand-to-mouth existence makes it easier to do the urgent thing, rather than contemplate what is important. Getting the right balance between mitigation, policy and public campaigning is not easy in a climate of fire-fighting. Despite, or perhaps because of, our sector's growing influence, many organisations are captured by the political process – which party supports which policy, what can we get government to do – rather than adopting a more holistic approach to change by involving a wider group of people.

This is a very urgent ask of devolved government, which is neither subtle nor easy to deliver. It needs to nurture and support our sector's work, even if that involves dismantling parts of the state and transferring power to people and communities. That is the only sustainable future for our public services.

The balance has shifted and will move further in our favour. This is because the third sector is able to mobilise communities and support people to do more for themselves and each other. It is a compelling demonstration of the continuing relevance of SCVO's now decade-old campaign call: politicians do not change things, people do.

Twenty
The role of local government

Annabelle Armstrong-Walter

A local authority's role as an employer, carer, corporate parent, landlord, educator, community leader and funder places it at the heart of its community. In many cases, it remains the first port of call for people in crisis, or who are vulnerable. Considered through this lens, the role played by a local authority in tackling poverty cannot be underestimated.

There is, however, much that is not in local government's control when it comes to tackling poverty, particularly when looking at major policy levers, such as taxation and social security. Furthermore, some of the 'newer' drivers of poverty, such as the rise of the private rented sector, the availability and cost of childcare, and the increase in in-work poverty, also represent areas where local government arguably has limited influence.

This chapter looks at some of the key areas in which progress has been made during the last five years, and then looks at how local government could be more effective in tackling poverty in Scotland over the next five years – examining specifically the role of local poverty and fairness commissions.

What has happened in the last five years?

In 2010 the Child Poverty Act was passed, legally binding government to a commitment to eradicate child poverty by 2020. It would be fair to say that five years later, as we push past the half-way point, progress has been underwhelming. While the Child Poverty Act places duties on English local authorities to carry out child poverty needs assessments and to co-operate with partners to address child poverty, local authorities in Scotland do not have the same direct responsibilities.

The Scottish government's Child Poverty Strategy for Scotland expressly states the role of local government in tackling poverty, but research has noted a lack of connection between the local and the national, citing neither pressure nor support from the centre in relation to devolving responsibility to tackle poverty to a local level.[1]

With decisions on appropriate local activity left to local authorities in Scotland, reviews of the local government response have been critical. In particular, research has indicated that child poverty is not consistently considered to be a political priority, with almost half of council officers reporting that either evidence is not available or that they are not aware of evidence in their local authority that demonstrates any success in tackling poverty.[2]

The rise of locally led commissions to address poverty and inequality in Scotland may well represent a turning point in local approaches. Commissions look at establishing a local picture of poverty, joining the dots of existing activities, and building momentum and commitment. A number of Scottish local authorities have formed commissions to address poverty-related issues – Renfrewshire's Tackling Poverty Commission and The Fairer Fife Commission reported in 2015,[3] and the Dundee Fairness Commission in 2016. It is important to note that this is nothing new: there has been a range of commissions established in England (predominantly focused on 'fairness') over the last five years. However, the commission approach seems to be gathering speed in Scotland as a way of rationalising and invigorating local anti-poverty practice.

What should the priorities be for the next five years?

The rise in poverty and fairness commissions in Scotland is likely to shape significantly local responses, not just in the areas hosting them, but across the local government sector in Scotland more widely.

However, with the cited lack of connection between the local and national pictures, significant questions remain around how the work of these new commissions in Scotland might join up, and their scope to have a collective, national voice. Indeed, identifying and maximising the connections between commissions appears to be a key point in the evaluation of some of the English local authorities.[4]

Commissions have already made some key recommendations for local anti-poverty practice and areas for action.

Setting priorities

It could be argued that much of the criticism of local government practice concerns a lack of profile for tackling poverty work, and a lack of an over-arching strategy. In response, all commissions seek to outline a strategic and co-ordinated vision for a local approach to tackling poverty.

They have also allowed newer research and understanding of poverty to influence their practice. For example, the *Monitoring Poverty and Social Exclusion in Scotland 2015* report flags three challenges for Scotland: the changing face of poverty to the 'young, working and renting'; the need to focus on educational inequalities; and the social disadvantage of disability.[5] While it might be widely accepted that local government lacks some of the most effective levers to tackle poverty, these three challenges sit at the heart of local government practice. Arguably, they are yet to be widely reflected within local government priorities.

Additionally, the *Shifting the Curve* report made recommendations in the areas of in-work poverty, housing affordability and the life chances of young people, as well as highlighting some cross-cutting issues. These recommendations were focused on the role of the Scottish government, but have significance for local authority practice and priorities.[6]

Working with partners

Commissions all comprise key local and national partners, in order to create 'fresher' thinking around how poverty can be tackled in partnership at a local level.

Monitoring Poverty and Social Exclusion in Scotland featured local poverty and fairness commissions as key players in the Scottish effort to tackle poverty. As well as identifying priorities for action, it flagged the challenges – citing the real challenge as the creation of bodies that contain people who take action.

It could be argued that bodies containing people who take action have already been established: community planning partnerships. In Renfrewshire's case, it is the community planning partnership which retains the strategic oversight of the Tackling Poverty Strategy and the responsibility for implementing the Renfrewshire Commission's 24 recommendations.[7]

Community planning partnerships have, however, come under fire for their response to tackling poverty, particularly the lack of anti-poverty activity reflected within the single outcome agreements.[8] It is clear that single outcome agreements themselves underestimate the work being undertaken to tackle child poverty in the area, probably due to the fact that poverty reduction is rarely the reason why local government and its partners carry out their functions. The challenge for those of us in local government is to understand the interplay between poverty and the services we provide.

Looking forward, the Community Empowerment Act will strengthen the position of community planning partnerships and, particularly, their responsibilities around reducing socio-economic inequalities. This could have a significant impact on the response of local authorities and their partners to tackling poverty. It may well be that community planning partnerships need better guidance around how poverty should be reflected within their single outcome agreements.

Managing resources

Commissions have also been useful in 'taking stock' of activities already undertaken across a local area that contribute to tackling poverty, and assessing their impact.

Budgetary challenges over the last five years have compromised the ability of local government to fully respond to the needs of communities, and research has been clear that cuts to local government at their current scale and pace are unsustainable.[9] While Scotland has avoided the depth of the cuts experienced south of the border, even Scottish local authorities are less able to invest in the early intervention and preventative services at a level that we know make a difference to our citizens who are living in poverty.

With budget challenges unlikely to relent in the next five years, local authorities will continue to face increasingly difficult decisions for meeting their shortfalls, and will have their ability to invest in early intervention further compromised. There has never been a more important time to understand and measure the impact of our activities against the outcomes we want to achieve that support tackling poverty.

Delivering localism

Commissions have looked not just at what local government and its partners should be doing to tackle poverty, but at the principles that should underpin the delivery of activities.

The principles embodied in the Christie Commission report in 2011 are now familiar territory in local government.[10] These include: focusing on early intervention and prevention; building on community assets; improving partnerships and empowering communities; and involving service users in the design of local services.

Involving people is an increasingly significant part of the Scottish policy narrative around poverty. The Poverty Truth Commission, in particular, has been at the vanguard of this approach in Scotland. With its mantra 'Nothing about us, without us, is for us', it is clear that real progress towards overcoming poverty will be made when those who experience poverty are central to the development, delivery and evaluation of solutions.

There is still much to be done to galvanise the principles of Christie with the learning from the Poverty Truth Commission on how we deliver local government services, and there remains a significant role for local government to expand the Christie principles more directly into our efforts to tackle poverty.

Maximising the opportunities of devolution

Commissions will play an important role in 'horizon scanning' the opportunities for local government, and further devolution is highlighted as one of those key opportunities.

At the time of writing, the Scotland Bill is still being developed and debated. However, a glance at the proposed devolved powers clearly shows potential for the Scottish government to provide significant levers to tackle poverty – through new taxation and social security powers. Furthermore, the potential for 'double devolution' of some powers to local government offers real opportunities – in particular, the devolution of welfare-to-work programmes and the administration of housing elements of universal credit alone will offer significant levers for local government to tackle poverty.

Conclusion

The chapter has shown some of the key areas for development in order for local government to tackle poverty more effectively and, in particular, has looked at how the momentum of poverty and fairness commissions has already shaped local government practice. Of course, the next five years will be key for those local authorities that have already embarked on this journey to show they have delivered those recommendations – and most importantly, delivered real change for our citizens as a result.

As a sector, we must put tackling poverty at the top of our agenda and invest in making the necessary strategic links within our own organisations and among our partners. Using tools such as poverty commissions has already been successful in galvanising support and profile for the poverty agenda, but this is, of course, not the only way it can be done.

The increasing emphasis on the lived experiences and voices of people living in poverty through mechanisms such as the Poverty Truth Commission has been widely applauded, but needs to be embedded into practice. At its most basic level, local government must assess how we engage with people, both in order to meet the challenge set by the Christie Commission, but also to make sure we embed these principles specifically and purposefully into our anti-poverty practice.

Moving forward, we all need to be better focused on understanding 'what has changed' for people living in poverty as a result of our activities – whether this is a commission exercise, or just being the employer, carer, corporate parent, landlord, educator, community leader and funder that we already are, every day.

Notes

1   P Kenway, S Bushe, A Tinson and TB Born, *Monitoring Poverty and Social Exclusion in Scotland 2015*, Joseph Rowntree Foundation, 2015
2   JH McKendrick and S Sinclair, *Local Action to Tackle Child Poverty in Scotland*, Save the Children, 2012
3   *Fairness Matters*, Report of the Fairer Fife Commission, 2015
4   P Bunyan and J Diamond, *Agency in Austerity: a study of fairness commissions as an approach to reducing poverty and inequality in the UK*, Edge Hill University, 2014
5   See note 1
6   Independent Adviser on Poverty and Inequality, *Shifting the Curve: a report for the First Minister*, Scottish Government, 2016, available at www.gov.scot/publications/2016/01/1984
7   *Tackling Poverty in Renfrewshire: report of Renfrewshire's Tackling Poverty Commission*, 2015
8   Campaign to End Child Poverty in Scotland, *Single Outcome Agreements 2009: an analysis by members of the Campaign to End Child Poverty in Scotland*, 2009
9   A Hastings, N Bailey, G Bramley, M Gannon and D Watkins, *The Cost of the Cuts: the impact on local government and poorer communities*, Joseph Rowntree Foundation, 2015
10 Commission on the Future Delivery of Public Services, 2011, available at www.publicservicescommission.org

Section Five
Conclusion

Twenty-one

The social harms of poverty and how to address them

Gerry Mooney

Introduction

Poverty remains one of the most socially harmful of all social problems. Writing in 2004, David Gordon notes that poverty is 'the largest source of social harm. It causes more deaths, diseases, suffering and misery than any other social phenomena'.[1] The overriding concern of this book has been to articulate what can and should be done to tackle poverty. This means raising important questions that challenge:

- the role and contribution of governments, public agencies, private companies, employers, trade unions, political parties, policy makers, third sector and campaigning organisations in addressing poverty;
- the ways in which state policies, for instance, welfare 'reforms', taxation legislation and employment policy, can lead to increases in poverty;
- the different ways in contemporary society in which poverty is often misunderstood and misrepresented as the result of the behaviours, lifestyles and cultures of those who experience poverty;
- the stigmatisation of poverty;
- the continuing exclusion of the disadvantaged and impoverished from the general conditions and ways of life that are taken to be 'the norm'.

We have explored the key policy levers, or to use the term we deploy in this book, 'tools', that can address and have an impact on levels of poverty. We have focused on different aspects of policy making, and on policy making by governments in Edinburgh and in London, by local authorities and by other public sector bodies. In doing so, we have critically assessed the extent to which policies have either helped to alleviate and tackle poverty in some way, or – and more significantly in relation to the policies of UK governments in recent years – have led to an increase in the intensity of poverty for those experiencing it, an increase in hardship and in insecurities, fuelled by a decline in the standard of living for many.

There is also another theme that cuts across the entire book and that is the extent to which poverty permeates almost every aspect of social life. However, and to highlight another significant message that this book is seeking to deliver, *policies matter*. Across the different sections and contributions, we have highlighted that policies do make a difference, and can continue to make a difference. As we have argued, some recent policy interventions have intensified levels of poverty and hardship. Other policies may have no impact, and then there are those that directly lead to a decline in poverty. In this regard, and another key thread running across this book, poverty, and its related harms and socially detrimental impacts, is entirely preventable.

The production of poverty and social harms

To say that poverty is 'produced' both reflects and opens up the beginnings of a much more informed understanding of poverty – and its causes. Taking as its cue that poverty is entirely preventable, this approach immediately challenges and contests claims that in some way poverty is a naturally recurring phenomenon that, as the story goes, *has always been with us and will always be with us*. The assumed inevitability of poverty and disadvantage has long been part of the daily common sense of society, a claim that must obviously be true as we have learned that poverty is not a recent development, nor is it confined to one or a handful of countries and societies today.

While the central focus in this book has rightly been on poverty – in many of its key forms and impacts – there is an understanding that poverty is crucially inter-related with important questions and issues relating to inequalities – again, of different kinds.

In Chapter 1 and across the book we have highlighted that inequality matters for our understanding of poverty. In a recent report, *An Economy for the 1%*, Oxfam highlights that ours is a world of growing inequality: a deepening and widening gulf between the richest 1 per cent and the rest of humanity.[2] The increasing concentration of wealth into fewer and fewer hands has been an important development in the UK too. For example, according to the annual *Sunday Times Rich List*, the collective wealth of the thousand richest people in the UK increased from £336 billion in 2010 to £519 billion in 2014.

As the authors of the Oxfam report highlight, there is no inevitability about such a development. It has not come about by accident. Once again, we must focus on the role of governments. As Chapter 1 and other sections of this book have shown, 'austerity' policies are reinforcing wider trends in inequality, leading to the vast gulf in wealth that has been depicted here. So-called 'austerity' measures are greatly reducing benefits (see Chapter 11 by Hanna McCulloch) and public services (see Chapter 20 by Anabelle Armstrong-Walter on the role of local government), but beyond this they are also dismantling the mechanisms and institutional structures which have been in place to minimise the impacts of inequality and to enhance equity. Despite the Conservative UK government in 2015 making a commitment to increase the national minimum wage for the over-25s (albeit misleadingly calling it a national living wage), there are downward pressures on wage levels, in-work and out-of-work benefits, pensions and the social wage more generally. This represents a sustained challenge on the foundations of the post-1945 welfare state and the idea enshrined in the post-1945 social contract that the state has a vital role to play in reducing inequalities, supporting the most vulnerable by providing benefits and services.

There is little doubt that the scale of cuts to benefits and services are hugely damaging to our society – but especially to those who are already living in or near poverty, whose lives are shaped by a daily struggle to make ends meet.

The distinctive Scottish context

Among the recurring myths that circulate across time and across Scottish society is a tendency to assume that 'we' in Scotland are in some way more enlightened when it comes to issues of poverty and how to address them. While such claims have been long and extensively questioned and disputed, there is some evidence of marginally more progressive attitudes in Scotland towards some aspects of social security and to the role of the state in ameliorating disadvantage. The idea of a more beneficent, socially just and progressive Scotland has, despite all the limitations of this partic-ular framing of Scottish society, real political and policy effects – and, in recent years, has helped to create a space for a more progressive discus-sion of poverty and welfare.

Furthermore, the political and policy-making landscape is also distinctive in important respects. In particular, we would draw attention to the different language that is used by the current Scottish government in relation to poverty, disadvantage, inequality and the harms these generate. Alongside this, the debate in Scotland has in recent years increasingly diverged from the one taking place in Westminster, in particular. Though this should not be taken to suggest that, in some ways, Scotland is immune to, or entirely critical of, UK government approaches – and the punitive language that often accompanies them.

The appointment by the First Minister, Nicola Sturgeon, of Naomi Eisenstadt as an independent adviser on poverty and inequality in summer 2015 signals the approach of the 2011 SNP Scottish government to take forward and initiate a wider debate around poverty. Of course, it has to be kept in mind that many of the key drivers that are leading to an increase in poverty – and which could be used to mount an effective assault on the causes of poverty – lie with the UK government. At the same time, this should not be taken to mean that the Scottish government can do little or nothing to ameliorate poverty and its impacts.

In January 2016, Naomi Eisenstadt produced her initial report to the First Minister. *Shifting the Curve* asks what actions the Scottish government and its partners, as well as other organisations, can take to seriously reduce the numbers of people in Scotland who are living in or experiencing poverty and hardship.[3] 'Policy adjustments', Eisenstadt claims, 'can bring about significant changes in poverty rates.' What are the best ways in which the Scottish government should spend the resources available to it to reduce the level of poverty in Scotland today? The report focuses on three main areas: in-work poverty; housing affordability; and the life chances of Scotland's young people.

In-work poverty

As has been highlighted in Chapter 13 by Peter Kelly, the question of 'fair work' has become much more evident in discussions of poverty, at least in the Scottish context. We are much more aware that work is not an inevitable route out of poverty. Work *can be* a means by which some people escape some forms of poverty and hardship, but this is not necessarily always the case and, indeed, there is mounting evidence that it is not.

As Kelly points out, this goes against the grain of the dominant approach to poverty that has shaped the policy of both the UK and Scottish governments over the past two to three decades. Governments of all political persuasions have adopted a 'work first' approach to tackling poverty. The claim that any work is always the best way to tackle poverty has been entrenched in much political, policy making and public thinking, whether or not it is 'fair' and adequately remunerated. This is not simply a challenge for government, however. Employers across all sectors of society, trade unions and campaigning organisations also have a role to play in advancing the case for a renewed concern with the type of work, quality of work and the extent to which work can be more and more a route from poverty for more and more people.[4]

In her report, Naomi Eisenstadt highlights that in-work poverty remains a serious problem in contemporary Scotland. In 2013/14, 50 per cent of all working-age adults in relative poverty after housing costs were in in-work poverty. Fifty-six per cent of all children in poverty were in households where this was the case. In arguing the case for the extension of the Living Wage Accreditation Scheme, the role of employers is identified as of crucial importance here. Public sector employers – for example, local authorities, who are responsible for the employment of a high proportion of Scotland's working population – could ensure that all employers in receipt of a public sector contract pay a living wage. Alongside this important measure, eradicating zero-hour contracts in the case of public sector contracts would also be a positive measure.

Among other measures highlighted in *Shifting the Curve* is the idea that the Scottish government and other public bodies should publish information on the pay ratios between the highest and lowest earners in their organisations. The long problematic area of childcare is also explored in the report, highlighting the need for good quality childcare provided by a high quality, well-educated and trained childcare workforce (see also Chapter 15 by Gill Scott). Poor quality and unaffordable childcare, along with a shortage of childcare places, is identified as a major barrier to those parents who wish to take up paid employment or extend their working hours.

Housing affordability

Housing costs and supply have become a much more significant political and policy issue in Scotland and across the UK today. This has generated what many have referred to as a 'housing crisis'. As Paul Bradley describes in Chapter 17, the cost of housing itself pushes significant numbers of people into poverty. The lack of adequate and affordable social housing provision is highlighted as a particular issue, and while the recent efforts and commitments of the Scottish government to end the 'right to buy' and to build more social housing (in stark contrast to the situation in England) are welcomed, it is argued by Eisenstadt that the challenge now is to deliver on the promise and build successful communities.

Young people's life chances

The independent adviser also calls for a focus on older children: those in their mid-teens to early adulthood. Notwithstanding a concern with NEET and positive destinations, this group has not been the focus of policy interventions or political discussion to the same degree as those in childhood and early years. In particular, the report highlights problems with mental health, depression, self-harm and a lack of self-worth as being factors that are increasing among this section of the population. The absence of work, or more importantly of meaningful work and career opportunities, is also flagged as being a serious issue for those in their mid-teens and early adulthood. That there are many and often disconnected strategies and mechanisms for increasing the take-up of employment among young people is viewed as requiring a serious overhaul. In particular, the relationship between school-based education and the skills and qualifications required by employers is seen as meriting more attention. Against this concern with the wider wellbeing of older children, the 'attainment challenge' must not sit uncomfortably, as the Scottish government aims to extend the breadth of children achieving positive outcomes in school education.

State, austerity and the social harms of exploitation

The report from the independent adviser is to be welcomed as an important contribution to the debate on poverty in Scotland and how it can be addressed. It is also important in highlighting, once again, that governments have an important role to play in addressing poverty and that the right policies can have positive outcomes in terms of reducing poverty. Across this book, but particularly in Section Four, different contributors have pointed to the positive impacts that Scottish government policies have had in relation to different dimensions and areas of poverty: each has been subject to rigorous discussion around the limitations of what has been done thus far and what more could be done.

In line with the overall goals of the *Poverty in Scotland* series, we have been concerned to ensure that policies are critically discussed. However, it is also crucial that we offer a critical analysis and exploration of the macro-level ideas and the main narratives around poverty, disadvantage, and social and welfare policies which circulate across Scottish and UK society. Some of these are also evident in Eisenstadt's report. A recurring debate in Scotland since the early days of devolution relates to the question of selective or targeted policies against universalist approaches. This continues to be something of a fault line, which is readily evident in different debates about poverty in Scotland today (discussed also in Chapters 14 and 16, with regard to education and health, respectively).

Eisenstadt has been quoted as questioning the value of universal benefit entitlements.[5] Posing the question of the extent to which there is a fair distribution of resources across society and across different age groups and such, she has claimed that spending scarce resources on those who could fund themselves is a considerable cost that could be used for more investment in education, better public services and the like. The provision of free tuition for all Scottish students has, for many years now, been a point of political controversy. Universal free tuition has been highlighted and attacked as actually diverting resources away from the provision of educational support for those who need it most. Likewise, the provision of universal benefits for the elderly, including free bus travel and winter fuel payments, has been viewed as detrimental to the need for increased resources to be spent on support and provision for younger people. Further, the freeze on council tax has also been pinpointed by critics of the SNP as primarily benefiting the most affluent in Scottish society.[6] These issues have been voiced in the Scottish press, refuelling this long-standing area of controversy. In her report, Eisenstadt claims that while universal benefits can avoid the stigma that often accompanies means testing, universal provision can also mean 'spreading a limited budget too thinly to help those who need the service most, and making little difference for those who need it less but choose to use it.'

On the other hand, a report by the Jimmy Reid Foundation in 2012 highlighted that universal provision is a hugely efficient form of provision and that, therefore, in the context of economic and fiscal constraints it makes economic sense.[7]

The developing debate around taxation in the Scottish context

The 2014 independence referendum debate and the arguments that flowed from it around additional powers for Scotland also highlighted the issue of taxation and the capacity and ability of the Scottish government to apply existing, as well as new, powers (see also Chapter 10 by David Eiser). The general issue of taxation, as we have seen, also shaped the report from the independent poverty adviser. Media headlines focused, not surprisingly, on recommendations to end the council tax freeze. Such challenges to policies central to Scottish government thinking reflect a genuine independence in Naomi Eisenstadt's approach, and open an important space for the debate needed on how Holyrood uses its powers to fund the policies needed to eradicate poverty.

However, as CPAG in Scotland has previously argued,[8] it is also important that the debate is not constrained by a focus on council tax alone, or a false sense that there is only a 'fixed budget' available to fund opportunities to invest in, using the proposed powers of the new Scotland Bill enabling 'new benefits' and the 'top up' of reserved benefits. While Eisenstadt is right to urge 'caution' in terms of developing devolved social security on account of the need to ensure that it interacts effectively with UK benefits, it is important that the Scottish government, and politicians of all parties, are ambitious in making full use of new, and existing, tax and benefit powers. They must challenge voters to support the progressive tax policies needed to fund improvements in both social security and public services. The report's recommendations – including to tackle in-work poverty; improve the quality of early years provision; build on existing benefits advice; and remove the barriers that undermine the life chances of young people – are all hugely welcome, and it is vital that ministers act on them.

Nevertheless, universal services and benefits must remain a vital part of the mix. It is better to prevent poverty than to wait for it to surface and then respond with complicated, inefficient means testing. At the same time, it is crucial that services reach those in most need. Rather than focusing only on how we target existing resources within a diminishing budget, the challenge must now be to persuade public and politicians alike of the value of investing more in our social infrastructure. That will mean building support for local and national tax systems that both tackle inequality and secure the revenue needed for the policies, including universal services and benefits, which prevent poverty – and which do not just alleviate its impact.

At the time of writing in early February 2016, the debate over taxation has taken on a new potency in the context of the developing arguments that will come to the fore once the 2016 Scottish Parliament election campaigns start in earnest. The main political contenders in the May 2016 elections have developed distinctive positions on the Scottish government's use of taxation powers. This, in turn, helps to open up wider discussions about the longer term approach to addressing poverty in the Scottish context.

This brings us back to the issue of work, here work as paid employment. One of the key absences in *Shifting the Curve* is the fact that the curve needs to be shifted much more highly if we are to really grasp the main drivers of inequality and of poverty in society today. It is in the crucially inter-related worlds of paid employment and unemployment where some of the primary mechanisms that are generating poverty are located.

The question of the role of economic growth is raised in the report. The terms 'inclusive growth' and an 'inclusive economic model' are used to highlight the fact that, without tackling poverty and achieving greater equality, it is difficult to grow the economy in ways that are sustainable and socially beneficial. However, alongside this there are a number of practical challenges that need to be made across society – including developing a radically different way of approaching the issues and questions of taxation, legal ownership frameworks and employment legislation. This will pose a direct challenge to some of the vested interests in Scotland, not least in the potential they may offer for a significant redistribution of wealth and, as such, working to limit socially harmful concentrations of wealth and income.

In the introduction to Section Four (Chapter 9), John H McKendrick speaks of the importance of knowledge as a tool to tackle poverty. This book, and many others that are also concerned to address poverty in all its forms, exclusions, marginalisations, stigmatisations and so on, as well as social and economic inequalities, contribute considerably to our knowledge and to the wider public knowledge about poverty and its underlying causes. Facilitating knowledge and understanding, moreover, is also about raising some of the more fundamental questions about our society, its organisation, the questions of who benefits and prospers, and who is marginalised and impoverished – and, importantly, *why a few benefit while many, many others lose out.*

The social harm of stigmatisation

Despite the advances in our knowledge and understanding of poverty (see Chapter 9), we find ourselves in 2016 challenging many of the same kinds of arguments and ways of misrepresenting the experiences of poverty as before. In 2016 Scotland is a prosperous country. Scotland is a wealthy country. Scotland is also a country with profound poverty. Scotland is also a country with significant inequalities.

Scotland is a society where there is vast wealth: in land, shares, property, companies, and in material goods. But Scotland is also a society in which destitution has returned, where more and more people are forced to rely on food banks on the back of a significant increase in food poverty. It is a society where some schoolchildren arrive at school hungry or undernourished and where the provision of a school meal might be their only real meal of the day. Teachers are being forced to feed children from their own pockets, and there is anecdotal evidence of pupils stealing food in order to survive.[9]

As in the past, we find ourselves in 2016 needing to be alert to the many otherings and misunderstandings about people who are experiencing and coping with poverty. In times of economic crisis, often the most socially regressive and punitive ideas, narratives and ways of thinking and acting come to the fore. So-called progressive and egalitarian Scotland – the Scotland that we would like to see – is today a Scotland in which negative and hostile attitudes to poverty and disadvantage still circulate – as they do elsewhere across the UK and beyond. These narratives are too easily reproduced by sections of the media and by some politicians, policy makers, academics, researchers and journalists. They are not hard to detect, sadly. In this, third sector organisations have an important role to play in winning the arguments with the wider public and, through this, helping to change attitudes (see Chapter 19 by Martin Sime).

'Austerity' policies focused on cutting the benefits and public services on which those on the lowest incomes rely the most are damaging society. They are damaging communities, families, individuals and social groups across the length and breadth of Scotland, as across the UK. They also damage health, wellbeing, life expectancy, educational attainment and undermine a sense of personal worth and of value to society. The current approach to austerity is creating social harm. Further, however, and against the claims that the state is being rolled back, the state is, in many ways, intervening more in the day-to-day lives of the most impoverished, destitute and deprived in our society in ways that are leading to widespread feelings of marginalisation, worthlessness and alienation. Increasing conditionality in relation to benefits now extends beyond the requirement to search for or take up employment. But our focus should not be on austerity alone. What are the other mechanisms, social relations, institutions and taken-for-granted ways of structuring and ordering society that also work to exacerbate poverty and which serve to worsen and further impoverish the lives of the most disadvantaged?[10] These too should be the focus of wider political discussions and debates. Tackling poverty – tackling poverty in a more effective way, that is – means also recovering and renewing ideas about social security and welfare.

Looking forward

We look forward with mixed feelings: an awareness of the enormity of the challenges facing us, and growing concerns about the continuing and increasing impact of macro-economic strategies, social welfare policies, economic change and the prevalence of wide-ranging and deep-seated inequalities. Yet alongside this, as has been highlighted several times here and throughout the book, we are at a rare moment. We have the opportunity to further develop the ongoing debates and discussions around the remit, role and ability of the Scottish government to make meaningful interventions to address poverty and the related issues of disadvantage, exclusion and social marginalisation.

We have also highlighted that policies can and do make an important difference to the spread, depth and intensity of poverty in our society. Policies matter. Political will also matters. There have already been signs – welcome signs – that the Scottish government has been listening to poverty campaigners, activists, carers, organisations and those experiencing poverty in reflecting long-held concerns as to how poverty is understood, approached and addressed.

In late 2015 the Scottish government laid out its 'set of principles' (see the box on the next two pages) that it says will guide and shape its approach to social security.[11] There is welcome overlap between these and the principles developed by civic organisations and coalitions, such as the Scottish Campaign on Welfare Reform, highlighted in Chapter 11. Such principles should inform the wider discussion and debate about poverty and disadvantage, as well as how we generate social welfare and social security for all those in need in Scotland.

The Scottish government's principles for social security

Principle one: Social security is an investment in the people of Scotland

- At the heart of our approach is an understanding that social security is an investment in the whole of Scotland, and an important tool for tackling poverty and inequality. Where some people in our society face additional costs in their daily lives – eg, because of ill health or disability, then it is right that society as a whole helps to meet those costs.
- Social security should help provide protection and act as a safety net in times of need. It should also aspire to provide a springboard and maximise the life chances of everyone, acting as an early intervention to give people the best possible chance. It should work with other devolved services to ensure the best outcomes, contributing to the 2020 vision for health and social care.

Principle two: Respect for the dignity of individuals is at the heart of everything we do

- At every step of our engagement with individuals, we will treat people with dignity and respect.
- Treating people with dignity and respect means using language that is carefully considered and does not stigmatise.
- Social security should be regarded by everyone in society as an integral component of a fair and prosperous country.

Principle three: Our processes and services will be evidence-based and designed with the people of Scotland

- The starting point for the design of our policies and processes is that they are based on the best evidence, and that the individuals who are affected by them should have their say and are listened to. By combining the best evidence available with the views of applicants and professionals who provide support in this area, we will be able to design more effective policies and services, and those services will be better equipped to meet the needs of those who need them.

Principle four: We will strive for continuous improvement in all our policies, processes and systems, putting the user experience first

- In the first instance, our priority will be to ensure a smooth transition from the existing UK benefits to our new Scottish arrangements, so that people have confidence that they will continue to receive the support to which they are entitled.
- Our policies, processes and systems should evolve in response to how Scotland and its people change over time. We will ensure that they remain fit for purpose, with a transparent approach to monitoring and review, built around listening to applicants and recipients.

Principle five: We will demonstrate that our services are efficient and offer value for money

- Taxpayers are entitled to expect that the investment we all make in social security should be well managed, cost effective and streamlined. We will look to align what we do with other services, where appropriate.
- We know from our consultation that the system can be complex for individuals. We will look to reduce the bureaucracy involved in claiming benefits and ensure that, at all stages, people are provided with the relevant information on how the system will work for them.
- We will continue to work closely with other Scottish public services, learning from good practice and innovation with a view to working smarter to help deliver better objectives at a time of falling budgets.

In important respects this also relates to the call for a human rights approach along the lines discussed by Pauline Nolan in Chapter 12. In this, and across many of the other contributions to Section Four, there has been important progress in some areas of Scottish government policy interventions, yet there is much more that needs to be done. This is also evidenced by the social harms of poverty and inequality that are highlighted here. Social harms are socially created. As such, they are entirely preventable and history shows us that in the context of periods when the welfare state was widely understood to play a key role in harm amelioration, when redistributive and progressive forms of taxation were implemented, and when investment in social security was increased, poverty levels fell significantly. Therefore, the various 'tools' that have been identified in Section Four, individually and in related ways, have an important role to play in taking forward anti-poverty policy in Scotland.

There is little sign that the UK government is going to retreat from its 'austerity' programme and, indeed, there are indications that cuts in welfare, public services and in social provision will become even more hard hitting. Issues such as food security (see Chapter 18 by Mary Anne MacLeod) may become a problem for more and more of the population, as well as increasing levels of economic and social insecurity. There has been a significant shift in the spread of risks across society. These appear to be falling primarily on those who are already disadvantaged.[12]

From this starting point, therefore, we offer a set of profound challenges to the readers of *Poverty in Scotland*, to the politicians, political parties, journalists, academics, researchers, campaigners, public sector employers, third-sector organisations, trade unions and activists: What is it that you are doing today and what can you do in the immediate future that advances our understanding of the main drivers of poverty, disadvantage and of inequality? What is it that you are doing that rejects harsh, punitive narratives and wholly problematic stereotypes of those experiencing poverty? And how do we collectively shift the focus of attention, the spotlight, onto those processes, systems, and ways of organising society that work to generate such widespread poverty at the same time as they enable others to accumulate such extreme wealth?

Notes

1   D Gordon, 'Poverty, Death and Disease: a social harm perspective', Paper presented at the annual meeting of the American Society of Criminology, 16 December 2013

2   D Hardoon, S Ayele and R Fuentes-Nieva, *An Economy for the 1%*, Oxfam Briefing Paper 210, Oxfam, 2016

3   Independent Adviser on Poverty and Inequality, *Shifting the Curve: a report to the First Minister*, Scottish Government, January 2016, available at www.gov.scot/publications/2016/01/1984

4   This extends to include the important world of business. Scottish Business in the Community, for instance, has played an important role in extending the living wage campaign. See www.bitc.org.uk/scotland/what-we-offer/tackling-work-poverty-make-it-your-business

5   See D Sanderson, 'SNP risk helping rich at expense of poor, warns Nicola Sturgeon's poverty advisor Naomi Eisenstadt', *The Herald*, 30 December 2015, available at www.heraldscotland.com/news/14172433.Sturgeon_s_poverty_advisor_warns_SNP_risk_helping_rich_at_expense_of_poor

6   See note 5 and M Gardham, 'Nicola Sturgeon poverty adviser calls for end to council tax freeze', *The Herald*, 20 January 2016, available at www.herald scotland.com/news/14217179.Sturgeon_poverty_adviser_calls_for_end_to_council_tax_freeze/?ref=mr&lp=13

7   http://reidfoundation.org/wp-content/uploads/2012/12/The-Case-for-Universalism.pdf

8   www.holyrood.com/articles/comment/soapbox-poverty-prevention-better-cure

9   See A Denholm, 'Poverty-hit Scottish pupils "stealing food"', *The Herald*, 31 December 2015, available at www.heraldscotland.com/news/education/1417 2438.poverty_hit_scottish_pupils_stealing_food

10 The relationship between poverty, inequality and criminal justice is the theme of the November 2015 (Vol. 3, No. 3) edition of *Scottish Justice Matters*, which contains a number of articles that will be of interest to the readers of this book. This is available at http://scottishjusticematters.com/the-journal/poverty-inequality-and-justice-november-2015

11 www.gov.scot/topics/people/fairerscotland/future-powers/future-powers

12 See D Asenova and others, *The Redistribution of Societal and Social Risk*, Joseph Rowntree Foundation, 2015, available at www.jrf.org.uk/report/redistribution-social-and-societal-risk